All That the Prophets Have Declared

All That the Prophets Have Declared

The Appropriation of Scripture in the Emergence of Christianity

Matthew R. Malcolm (Editor)

21 20 19 18 17 16 15 7 6 5 4 3 2 1

First published 2015 by Paternoster
Paternoster is an imprint of Authentic Media Limited
52 Presley Way, Crownhill, Milton Keynes, MK8 0ES.
authenticmedia.co.uk
Authentic Publishers, PO Box 185, West Ryde, Australia

British Library Cataloguing in Publication Data

A catalogue record for this book is available from the British Library

ISBN 978-1-84227-870-3
978-1-84227-871-0 (e-book)

Cover Design by Phil Houghton
Printed and bound by CPI Group (UK) Ltd., Croydon, CR0 4Y

Contents

Abbreviations

AB	Anchor Bible
ABRL	Anchor Bible Reference Library
AGJU	Arbeiten zur Geschichte des antiken Judentums und des Urchristentums
AnBib	Analecta biblica
ANTC	Abingdon New Testament Commentaries
AUS	American University Studies
BBR	*Bulletin for Biblical Research*
BDB	*A Hebrew and English Lexicon of the Old Testament* (ed. F. Brown, S.R. Driver and C.A. Briggs; Oxford, 1907)
BECNT	Baker Exegetical Commentary on the New Testament
Bib	*Biblica*
BibInt	*Biblical Interpretation*
BIS	Biblical Interpretation Series
BJRL	*Bulletin of the John Rylands University Library of Manchester*
BNTC	Black's New Testament Commentaries
BR	*Biblical Research*
CBET	Contributions to Biblical Exegesis and Theology
CBQ	*Catholic Biblical Quarterly*
CUP	Cambridge University Press
CBR	Currents in Biblical Research
ConcJ	*Concordia Journal*
DEJ	*Eerdmans Dictionary of Early Judaism* (ed. John J. Collins and Daniel C. Harlow; Grand Rapids, MI: Eerdmans, 2010)
DNTB	*Dictionary of New Testament Background: A Compendium of Contemporary Biblical Scholarship* (electronic ed.

	Stanley E. Porter and Craig A. Evans; Downers Grove, IL: InterVarsity Press, 2000)
DPL	*Dictionary of Paul and His Letters* (ed. G.F. Hawthorne and R.P. Martin; Downers Grove, IL, 1993)
EDNT	*Exegetical Dictionary of the New Testament* (ed. H. Balz and G. Schneider; Grand Rapids, MI: Eerdmans, 1990–93)
EEC	*Encyclopedia of Early Christianity* (ed. E. Ferguson, New York, 2nd edn, 1990)
EKKNT	Evangelisch-katholischer Kommentar zum Neuen Testament
EvJ	*Evangelical Journal*
EuroJTh	*European Journal of Theology*
ExpTim	*Expository Times*
GNS	*Good News Studies*
HTKNT	Herders theologischer Kommentar zum Neuen Testament
ICC	International Critical Commentary
Int	*Interpretation*
IVP	InterVarsity / Inter-Varsity Press
IVPNTC	IVP New Testament Commentary Series
JBL	*Journal of Biblical Literature*
JETS	*Journal of the Evangelical Theological Society*
JSNT	*Journal for the Study of the New Testament*
JSNTSup	Journal for the Study of the New Testament: Supplement Series
JR	*Journal of Religion*
JSHJ	*Journal for the Study of the Historical Jesus*
JSJ	*Journal for the Study of Judaism in the Persian, Hellenistic, and Roman Periods*
JSJSup	Journal for the Study of Judaism in the Persian, Hellenistic, and Roman Periods: Supplement Series
JSOT	*Journal for the Study of the Old Testament*
JSOTSup	Journal for the Study of the Old Testament: Supplement Series
JSPSup	Journal for the Study of the Pseudepigrapha: Supplement Series
LNTS	Library of New Testament Studies
LSTL	Library of Second Temple Series

LXX	Septuagint (the Greek OT)
MKEKNT	Meyers kritisch-exegetischer Kommentar über das Neue Testament
MT	Masoretic Text (of the OT)
NAC	New American Commentary
NCB	New Century Bible
NET Trans.	*The NET Bible* (Biblical Studies Press, 2006)
NIBCNT	New International Biblical Commentary on the New Testament
NICNT	New International Commentary on the New Testament
NIGTC	New International Greek Testament Commentary
NovT	*Novum Testamentum*
NovTSup	Novum Testamentum Supplements
NSBT	New Studies in Biblical Theology
NT	New Testament
NTC	New Testament Commentary
NTD	Das Neue Testament Deutsch
NTL	New Testament Library
NTS	*New Testament Studies*
NTTS	New Testament Tools and Studies
OT	Old Testament
OTP	*Old Testament Pseudepigrapha* (ed. J.H. Charlesworth; 2 vols. New York, 1983)
OUP	Oxford University Press
PNTC	Pelican New Testament Commentaries
PRSt	*Perspectives in Religious Studies*
PSTJ	*Perkins (School of Theology) Journal*
PVTG	Pseudepigrapha Veteris Testamenti Graece
RB	*Revue biblique*
ResQ	*Restoration Quarterly*
RevExp	*Review and Expositor*
RSR	*Recherches de science religieuse*
RTL	*Revue théologique de Louvain*
RTP	*Revue de théologie et de philosophie*
RTR	*Reformed Theological Review*
SBL	Society of Biblical Literature
SBLDS	Society of Biblical Literature Dissertation Series
SE	*Studia Evangelica*

SNTSMS Society for New Testament Studies Monograph Series
TDNT *Theological Dictionary of the New Testament* (ed. G. Kittel and G. Friedrich; trans. G.W. Bromiley; 10 vols; Grand Rapids, MI, 1964–76)
TENTS Texts and Editions for New Testament Study
THKNT Theologischer Handkommentar zum Neuen Testament
TNTC Tyndale New Testament Commentaries
TSAJ Texte und Studien zum antiken Judentum
TynBul *Tyndale Bulletin*
UBS United Bible Societies
UBSHS United Bible Societies Handbook Series
UP University Press
WBC Word Biblical Commentary
WMANT Wissenschaftliche Monographien zum Alten und Neuen Testament
WTJ *Westminster Theological Journal*
WUNT Wissenschaftliche Untersuchungen zum Neuen Testament
WW *Word and World*
ZECNT Zondervan Exegetical Commentary on the New Testament
ZNW *Zeitschrift für die neutestamentliche Wissenschaft und die Kunde der älteren Kirche*

Introduction

'All That the Prophets Have Declared'

Matthew R. Malcolm
Trinity Theological College, Western Australia

The circumstances in which Christianity emerged are hotly discussed in present scholarship. There are those who see a stilted evolution from the operation of an Aramaic-speaking Jewish prophet to a Gentile movement that worshipped a divine Christ.[1] There are those who emphasize a swift movement of Jewish mission into Gentile regions.[2] There are those who draw attention to the remarkable devotional practices of the earliest Christian believers.[3] Although these investigations are generally undertaken with openly historical-critical methodologies, they spark the imagination of the wider community because of their apologetic or sceptical applications: Is the Christ whom Christians worship as God really identifiable with the Jesus who operated in history? Are the New Testament accounts reliable? Is Nicene faith a distortion, an extension or a continuation of the earliest perceptions of Jesus?

The New Testament writers' use of the Old Testament is a different hotly discussed topic, which likewise sparks the imagination of those who are interested in the nature and reliability of the NT documents. In preparing this volume I contacted a number of scholars to hear their perspectives on what is at stake. Walter Kaiser Jr holds that the NT writers made demonstrably fair use of their Scriptures:

> The NT writers, when citing the OT as an authority for the point they were making, fairly exegeted the meaning of that OT text, for they

> too respected the fact that the OT was the inspired word from God on High. There may be rare occasions where they simply borrowed the words to use in another context and association of ideas, but this was rare indeed.[4]

Gerd Lüdemann, on the other hand, reaches the opposite conclusion:

> The long and short of it is that New Testament authors have systematically mistaken or distorted the meaning of OT texts in the service of polemical and doctrinal agendas. Matthew's five citations of prophecy in his nativity account are among the best-known examples of the practice, and perhaps the most comically inapposite.[5]

With such different conclusions among scholars, the matter raises further questions: How do the exegetical approaches of the early Christians compare to those of their Jewish contemporaries? Is there a general key to the way in which the NT writers use their Scriptures? What accounts for the new readings of the Scriptures that we find in the NT?

A number of scholars are keen to situate NT use of Scripture within parameters of early Judaism. Mark Nanos points out that Paul does not read Scripture 'as an outsider "appropriating" something that might not otherwise belong to him as an Israelite/Jew, since it represents God's Guidance for Israel/Jews'.[6] N.T. Wright sees a degree of continuity between the NT and other Jewish reflection on Scripture from the same time period:

> Like many other Jews of his day, Jesus saw Israel's scriptures as a huge and complex narrative in search of its (divinely promised) completion. Again like some others (e.g. Bar-Kochba a century later), he believed that it was his vocation to launch that completion and, with it, the long-awaited new age in which the world would be ordered radically differently under the rule of Israel's anointed king.[7]

However, this comment draws attention to something decisively significant about the NT writers' approach to their Scriptures: they were presenting a man who believed that his vocation was the completion of the narrative that those Scriptures had generated.

Maurice Casey comments: 'Jesus interpreted the Scriptures for his disciples including references to himself. After his Resurrection his disciples continued to interpret the Scriptures with reference to him, including his resurrection in Psalm 16 (Acts 2:31–2).'[8] It is with this insight that the two hotly discussed issues above come together: the issues of the *emergence of Christianity* and the *New Testament's use of the Old Testament* may in fact be mutually illuminative. It is the conviction of this volume that *the New Testament writers follow the lead of Jesus himself, in creatively rereading their Scriptures in the light of the Christ event.*

From one perspective, this hermeneutical innovation in the emergence of Christianity illuminates the data of the New Testament's use of the Old Testament. There is both continuity and discontinuity with methods and conclusions that came before; and a key factor is the NT conviction that Jesus rightly understood himself to be the (surprising) fulfilment of 'all that the prophets declared'.

From the other perspective, the distinctive use of the Old Testament by New Testament writers stands out as a key factor that illuminates the emergence of Christianity. Something of sufficient magnitude happened in the first century that allowed Scripture, believed to be the voice of God, to be suddenly interpreted and accepted in dramatically new (and surprisingly concordant) ways.

Of course, to put it so briefly is to oversimplify. The scholars represented in this volume offer their own distinctive perspectives, which contribute to a more nuanced picture in the book as a whole.[9] The volume proceeds in several sections. The first, 'Appropriation and Interpretation', considers the overall topic of the appropriation of OT Scripture at the time of the emergence of Christianity. The second section looks specifically at the 'Gospels and Acts'; the third at 'Pauline Letters'; the fourth at 'Non-Pauline Letters', and the fifth at 'Appropriation Today'. The 'Conclusion' revisits the contributions of each of the chapters and suggests some outcomes of the volume as a whole.

Appropriation and Interpretation

1

Two Case Studies in Earliest Christological Readings of Biblical Texts

Larry W. Hurtado
University of Edinburgh

In this chapter I focus on two key biblical (OT) texts that figured significantly in earliest christological developments. For each text I will survey evidence of how it was read previously to, and roughly contemporary with, earliest Christianity, to see how earliest Christian usage compares. As we will see, this Christian usage seems innovative, even remarkable, and also appeared surprisingly early, so I also wish to consider what prompted this novel reading of these scriptural texts.

In the main, the many studies of the use of the OT in the NT have tended to focus on what we might call the mechanics of early Christian reading/use of scriptural texts, and the theological meanings/uses derived from them as attested in early Christian writings. So, for example, scholars often have compared early Christian use of given OT texts with their use in the second-temple Jewish context, and even with later rabbinic references to them, noting similarities and differences in the way the OT texts are handled and what interpretative use was made of them. Scholars have also probed whether and how more generally early Christian use of Scripture reflects the techniques of exegesis attested in Jewish circles of the time.[1] In this chapter, however, I wish to focus on the cognitive processes involved in the earliest Christian exploration and appropriation of particular OT texts to understand and articulate christological convictions. That is, I want to ask *when, why* and *how* earliest believers came to see in certain OT texts the new (even somewhat revolutionary) meanings that they ascribed to them. What moved them to reading these texts in this radical new way, and when did this radical development commence?[2] Given the limits of this study, I will focus on the earliest evidence.

My main contention is that earliest Christian use of these two (and other) OT texts was not simply the result of the application of certain exegetical techniques/practices, but instead reflects an approach to the Scriptures that was based on a combination of key religious convictions characteristic of second-temple Jewish tradition, and radical new convictions that arose from profound religious experiences that distinguished early Christian circles.

The two scriptural texts I focus on here as case studies are Psalm 110 and Isaiah 45:22–5. As we will see, the earliest Christian interpretation of these texts is novel and noteworthy, and, I contend, cannot be accounted for except as the product of profound and distinctive christological convictions. As already indicated, I propose that the earliest and initial Christian use of these and other OT texts was likely as a key part of the process of trying to understand for themselves the meaning of events and experiences. The biblical texts were scoured in the confidence that the divine plan could be discovered in the Scriptures. Thereafter, these and other OT texts were deployed to justify to others these convictions in evangelistic and apologetic efforts. As Donald Juel urged, prior to the use of biblical texts in polemic and apologetic occasions, for the earliest believers, 'The Bible [OT] provided the data for reflection on the gospel and its implications, as well as the language of prayer and praise. Exegesis was the matrix for theologizing.'[3]

Psalm 110 (LXX 109)

Psalm 110 is rightly judged to be a key biblical text in earliest Christian circles, cited or alluded to an impressive number of times in the NT.[4] As William Loader observed about the opening verse of the psalm: 'No other passage of scripture recurs so frequently in allusion or quotation in the christological expressions of NT times as Ps. cx. 1. In this expression we stand in continuity with christological thought from the very early beginnings of its development.'[5]

In the latest (twenty-eighth) edition of the Nestle-Aland Greek New Testament, the index of OT citations and allusions lists six citations of Psalm 110:1 and another nine identifiable allusions to the verse.[6] If we also include all of the NT references to Jesus' exaltation to, or status at, God's 'right hand' we have seven more indications of the likely influence of this text.[7] In addition, the Nestle-Aland list shows three citations of Psalm 110:4, plus four allusions to it, making some twenty-nine instances of use or influence of Psalm 110 overall.[8]

Moreover, the evidence of the use/influence of Psalm 110 is found in NT writings ranging in date from Paul's epistles in the fifties (or early sixties) through to the Synoptic Gospels and Acts, Hebrews and the 'deutero-Pauline' epistles (e.g. Ephesians). This rather clearly indicates that the Christian use of Psalm 110 began early and was widespread. That Paul chose to allude to the psalm (or at least used phrasing/imagery that derives from it), apparently feeling no need to cite it explicitly, suggests that by the time he wrote to Christians in Corinth and Rome (mid/late fifties) Psalm 110 had been read and appropriated by believers for some time, its effects already familiar to Christians in various locations.[9]

Scholarly recognition of the importance of Psalm 110 in early Christianity is reflected in the several valuable studies devoted to the matter (especially, those by Gourgues, Hay, Hengel and Loader). Thanks to the intensive work done in these studies, it is possible to be brief here, drawing on them particularly in surveying the pre-Christian use of this text and the pattern of usage in earliest Christian circles.

Pre-Christian usage

It is widely thought that Psalm 110 originated as a celebration of the Judean king, and is classed as a 'royal psalm'.[10] So, the invitation given to 'my lord' by YHWH in v. 1, 'Sit at my right hand', is to be taken as originally a powerful metaphorical reference to the Judean king as having divine authorization to act uniquely as 'the viceregent [or vicegerent] of God' upon the earth.[11] In the original setting, the statement 'probably meant that the king was seated to the right of the ark, on which God was invisibly enthroned'.[12]

These royal psalms could later be read as messianic psalms by those who regarded the Messiah as a royal figure (as e.g. in *Psalms of Solomon*, and in the NT).

It is the more noteworthy, thus, that there is scant evidence that Psalm 110 was used much in second-temple Jewish tradition.[13] In particular, there is no direct evidence that it figured in Jewish messianic hopes of that time.[14] Hay cited a passage in the *Testament of Job* (33:1–3), as an allusion to Psalm 110:1 (or indication of its influence), where Job claims to have a throne 'in the upper world [τῷ ὑπερκοσμίῳ]' whose 'glory and splendour are at the right hand of [ἐκ δεξιῶν] God', the latter phrasing likely drawn from the biblical text. Along with a number of others subsequently, Hay took *Testament of Job* as coming from a Jewish provenance sometime in the first century BCE to first century CE, thus offering a possible precedent-use of Psalm 110. Indeed, on this view *Testament of Job* would give us the only clear pre-Christian use of Psalm 110. But, more recently, James Davila has judged the work as more likely stemming from Christian circles (perhaps Egyptian), 'by the early fifth century CE'.[16] So, although *Testament of Job* 33:1–3 may well reflect phrasing from Psalm 110:1, it is actually not so clear that it is evidence of pre-Christian/Jewish use of the psalm.[17]

Hay also pointed to the several places in the Similitudes of *1 Enoch* where the Elect One is enthroned by God (esp. 51:3; 55:4; 61:8; 69:29; cf. 45:1–3), noting 'no strong verbal parallelism', but nevertheless urging that 'the possibility of allusion is undeniable'.[18] This possibility cannot be discounted, but it is also difficult to move beyond the realm of mere possibility.[19] There is no use of actual phrasing from Psalm 110, and the portrayal of the royal-messianic Elect One as seated on a throne (upon the earth) that carries divine-like status is an idea echoed in various OT texts (e.g. Pss 45:6; 89:36–7), hardly requiring Psalm 110:1 to account for it.

As for the Qumran texts, these give us no clear evidence of the reading/use of Psalm 110.[20] There is the interesting but fragmentary text known as *11Q Melchizedek (11Q13)* sometimes proposed. Although this text has no clear allusion to Psalm 110 or to the Melchizedek vignette in Genesis 14:18–20, Hay urged that anyone familiar with these texts and reading *11Q Melchizedek* could not fail to think of them.[21] Perhaps. But this Qumran text is hardly direct evidence that Psalm 110:1 was drawn upon by its author, or how the psalm was interpreted more widely at the time *11Q Melchizedek* was composed. The idea of a priest–king Melchizedek could have come as readily from Genesis 14, and we have other indications of an avid interest in Genesis reflected in the Qumran scrolls.[22]

In fact, the earliest direct references to Psalm 110:1 in Jewish texts are in rabbinic writings, which date from a few centuries after the NT.[23] To be sure, these texts ascribe references to Psalm 110:1 to rabbinic figures who may date to the early second century CE (e.g. R. Ishmael). But *messianic* interpretation of the psalm is not attached to figures who can be dated earlier than the late third century CE. Nevertheless, after reviewing the rabbinic evidence many years ago, Billerbeck concluded that the messianic interpretation of Psalm 110:1 was already familiar in first-century Jewish circles.[24] Hay rightly noted that Billerbeck's view rested heavily on an inference based on the use of the psalm in the NT (esp. Mark 12:35–7/parallels); nevertheless, he echoed Billerbeck's position, urging that 'the argument of Jesus about David's son is most easily understood if a messianic interpretation prevailed'. Essentially resting on this inference, Hay then concluded, 'On balance, then, it seems fair to suppose that in the NT era a messianic interpretation of Ps 110 was current in Judaism, although we cannot know how widely it was accepted.'[25]

But the argument that the reference to Psalm 110:1 in the gospels shows that a messianic reading of the psalm must have been current in Jewish circles at the time surely ought to be recognized as the non sequitur that it obviously is.[26] All that Mark 12:35–7 requires is familiarity with a view that Messiah is son of David, and that David wrote Psalm 110. As Adela Yarbro Collins observed, if there is any prior messianic reading of the psalm presupposed in Mark 12:35–7, it is probably early Christian christological reading of it.[27] To be a bit more generous to them, the argument offered by Billerbeck and Hay can pose little more than an unconfirmed possibility.[28] In any case, there is scant basis for thinking that a messianic reading of Psalm 110 was prevalent, or any more than one of a number of interpretations of the figure addressed in v. 1. Juel's more cautious judgement is preferable, proposing, 'We may speak at best of interpretive possibilities available to Christian exegetes', and noting that Psalm 110:1 did not apparently attract a great deal of attention in ancient Jewish circles.[29]

The early Christian reading

In short, if Psalm 110 was read as a messianic text in second-temple Jewish tradition there is scant evidence of this, and in any case it was apparently not very common. So, taking account of the frequent citations and allusions to the psalm in the NT, the first thing we notice is how much more important and prominent Psalm 110 seems to have been in christological thinking and discourse from the outset. This alone is a significant distinguishing feature of earliest Christian usage of the psalm. That is, the focus and the weight placed upon Psalm 110 as an important christological text marks off earliest Christian reading of the psalm rather strongly. But there is more to say.

It is also noteworthy how early this intense usage of the psalm began. To reiterate a previous observation, the influence of Psalm 110 is already apparent in the earliest body of extant Christian texts, the undisputed letters of Paul.[30] The earliest clear allusion is in 1 Corinthians 15:25, 'ἄχρι οὗ θῇ πάντας τοὺς ἐχθροὺς ὑπὸ τοὺς πόδας αὐτοῦ'. Even though Paul's phrasing does not conform exactly to the LXX of Psalm 110:1 (the phrasing from Psalm 8:6, ὑπὸ τοὺς πόδας αὐτου, used instead of ὑποπόδιον τῶν ποδῶν σου), it is clear (and commonly accepted) that he draws on the language and imagery of Psalm 110:1 in expressing Jesus' exaltation as the divinely appointed king over all.[31] Moreover, Paul's somewhat free rephrasing of Psalm 110:1 here can be taken as an indication that it was already such a familiar christological text that allusion to it was sufficient for the original readers of 1 Corinthians, and that reference to Jesus as 'at God's right hand' was already a familiar christological trope and affirmation.[32]

Granting this, Lambrecht contended, however, that Paul in fact adapted the wording of the verse to assert a still stronger christological point. Whereas in the LXX wording of Psalm 110:1 God is the one who puts all enemies in subjection to the enthroned figure, Paul's rewording in 1 Corinthians 15:25 can be read as making Jesus the subject of the verb θῇ, and so the one who secures the subjection of 'all things', and to himself.[33] In support of this reading, Lambrecht pointed to Philippians 3:21, where Paul explicitly portrays Jesus as exercising 'his power by which he will subject all things to himself' (and which also likely alludes to Psalm 8:6).[34] Similarly, though noting that Paul's discussion in this passage is complex and that it is not always easy to decide who is referred to, Gordon Fee concluded, 'Almost certainly we must go with the grammar here and see Christ as the subject' (of the verb in v. 25).[35]

But, however one views the intended subject of the verb in 1 Corinthians 15:25, it is clear that Paul's statement here reflects a radically innovative and remarkable use of Psalm 110:1. In the original context of the psalm, the Judean king is promised rule over his earthly enemies, and his earthly throne is declared to be set and backed by God. This is strong imagery, but in the early Christian usage of the psalm reflected in this Pauline passage things are taken to a wholly new level, literally. Jesus' enthronement is clearly in heaven, comprising a quite literal and direct participation in God's own rule, exceeding any original meaning of Psalm 110, and the scope of what is included in 'all things' also goes cosmically beyond anything the author of Psalm 8 might have imagined, including here even death itself (v. 26), the resurrection-hope now anchored 'in Christ' (v. 22). This also radically surpasses even the august position of the 'Elect One' of the Similitudes of *1 Enoch*, whose glorious throne apparently will be set on the earth, where he can receive the obeisance of earthly rulers (*1 Enoch* 62:1–9). As Hengel noted, there is no notion of an equivalent 'session ad dexteram' in pre-Christian Jewish tradition.[36] We have references to heavenly ascents of humans, e.g. Moses on Mount Sinai and the unnamed figure of the Qumran 'Self-glorification Hymn' (*4Q491*[c]), who claims 'a mighty seat in the congregation of the gods, above which none of the kings of the East shall sit' (1:5).[37] But these comparisons are with other human/earthly authorities, whereas Jesus is portrayed as exalted above all things on a cosmic scale.

In his epistle to the Romans, written only a year or so later, Paul again draws upon the imagery of Psalm 110, here referring to Jesus as 'at the right hand of God', and as also interceding for believers before God in heaven (8:34).[38] Although the Greek phrasing ἐν δεξιᾷ τοῦ θεοῦ is again not exactly that of Psalm 110:1 ἐκ δεξιῶν μου, it seems clear that this reference to Jesus at God's 'right hand' reflects the influence of this psalm text.[39] This is the earliest reference to Jesus in this position in extant early Christian texts. But, as Hengel noted, here and in 1 Peter 3:22 we find almost identical expressions, ὃς καί ἐστιν ἐν δεξιᾷ τοῦ θεοῦ (Rom. 8:34), ὃς ἐστιν ἐ ν δεξιᾷ τοῦ θεοῦ (1 Pet. 3:22), and this plus the four-part structure of Paul's statement ('Christ who died, and moreover was raised, and who is at the right hand of God, and who intercedes for us') make it likely that Paul here draws on (and perhaps adapts) an earlier Christian traditional formulation in which Psalm 110:1 was already influential at the time he wrote.[40]

Indeed, if (as seems probable) this is correct, then the influence of Psalm 110 likely extended beyond its opening verse, the reference in 110:4 to the enthroned king as also 'priest forever according to the order of Melchizedek' interpreted as expressive of Jesus' heavenly intercessory role. That is, it appears that, at least in the case of Psalm 110, early believers did not simply cite v. 1 in an 'atomizing' manner, but mined perhaps the entire psalm, finding in it multiple stimuli and resources for articulating christological convictions.

To be sure, this priestly/intercessory emphasis in Psalm 110:4 is developed more fully in Hebrews, which should probably be dated perhaps a couple of decades later than Romans. But I repeat that Romans 8:34 seems to me to offer good evidence that the basic conviction and the creative reading of Psalm 110:4 (Jesus as heavenly priest–intercessor) go back to earlier years. Paul's rather matter-of-fact and compressed statement of Jesus' intercessory role is best accounted for on the inference that he expected his original readers to be acquainted with the notion. This likely means that it did not originate with Paul and circulated far wider than the churches that he founded and influenced.

Moreover, noting here that Paul designates Jesus as 'Christ' in his heavenly intercessory role, once again we see a remarkable escalation in messianic claims.[41] As Jewett observed, the word used in Romans 8:34, ἐντυγχάνει, 'belongs in "the conceptual world of the ruler's court", where accusations and requests are heard and the person closest to the throne usually has the most influential word'.[42] In the context here, Jesus' exaltation to the unique position next to God (NB: ἐν δεξιᾷ τοῦ θεοῦ) means that his intercession for believers will carry such force at the highest level that 'it is utterly preposterous to fear that anyone can impeach their status'.[43]

In some second-temple Jewish texts, Moses' intercession for Israel is highlighted (*Jubilees* 1:19-21; *4QApocryphon of Joshua*[a]*/4Q378*), apparently in reference to Moses' intercession on earth in the biblical narratives (Exod. 32:11–14; 33:12–16), and later in rabbinic texts after his death Moses sometimes intercedes for Israel in heaven.[44] Sometimes angels as well are portrayed as interceding for Israel or the righteous (e.g. *1 Enoch* 9:3; 40:6).[45] But in Jewish texts early enough to provide a precedent or analogy there is no depiction of a human figure, messiah or OT worthy with a comparable heavenly status and role to that of the exalted Jesus in Romans 8:34.[46] There is also no indication that Psalm 110:4 itself generated any previous notion of a heavenly intercessor, whether Messiah or other type of figure. Even if we regard *11Q Melchizedek* as influenced by Psalm 110, the Melchizedek in this text is more of a heavenly/angelic figure who acts as eschatological leader of the elect, and he seems not to have an intercessory role.

I noted a bit earlier that Paul's phrasing in Romans 8:34, ἐν δεξιᾷ τοῦ θεοῦ, is slightly different than the LXX of Psalm 110:1, ἐκ δεξιῶν μου, and it is now worthwhile to take a closer look at the matter.[47] Not only is ἐκ δεξιῶν the phrasing used in the LXX of this psalm text, it is also by far the more frequently preferred expression throughout the LXX to portray someone or something as 'at/to the right side' of another, including particularly depictions of persons standing/sitting on the right of a king. Only twice in the LXX do we find ἐν δεξιᾷ to describe someone either standing (1 Chron. 6:24) or sitting (1 Esdras 4:29) next to another, compared with twenty-one uses of ἐκ δεξιῶν for this, rendering several Hebrew prepositional phrases, e.g. לימיני (Ps. 110:1),[49] על־ימינך (Ps. 110:5). In other Koine Greek evidence as well, ἐκ δεξιῶν is overwhelmingly the preferred construction for describing a person on the right of another.[50]

If we look at the usage of these two expressions in the NT an interesting pattern appears. First, let us consider instances where someone is positioned at the right side/hand of another, and where no reference to, or influence of Psalm 110 is in view. In all these cases, in keeping with what appears to be the preferred expression, ἐκ δεξιῶν is used.[51] If we then look at the places where Psalm 110:1 is cited or clearly alluded to in describing Jesus as at God's right hand / side, the phrase in the LXX, ἐκ δεξιῶν, is likewise consistently used / retained.[52] But, in the numerous other places where we seem to have confessional statements simply declaring Jesus to be seated at God's right hand / side, the preferred form is ἐν δεξιᾷ.[53] In two additional instances, Acts (2:33; 5:31) has the dative form without a preposition, τῇ δεξιᾷ τοῦ θεοῦ.

So why do we have this apparent preference for ἐν δεξιᾷ in these confessional or kerygmatic expressions? They all surely show the influence of Psalm 110:1, the only biblical text that refers to a figure seated at God's 'right side / hand', and yet they all have this variant prepositional phrase, not the LXX wording. Loader allowed that ἐν δεξιᾷ may have originated 'in the Aramaic-speaking communities' where the Greek text was perhaps not consulted, Psalm 110:1 there adapted in early confessional statements; and Hengel similarly considered whether the expression in question might be 'a variant translation of the Hebrew text [of Psalm 110:1] which was independent of the LXX' and that goes 'back to the Jerusalem congregation'.[54] That these confessional statements were already traditional by the time of Paul's letters is clear, and that they reflect convictions and confessions that emerged first among earliest circles of believers is also entirely probable. But is the phrase ἐν δεξιᾷ simply the artefact of some early variant translation of Psalm 110:1, or was there some purpose involved that led early Greek-speaking believers to prefer this expression in these early confessional statements?

I propose that ἐν δεξιᾷ may have been preferred over the LXX phrase in early confessional statements because it offered a particular nuance, perhaps connoting a closer proximity and a closeness of relationship, a personal connection, not simply a positioning of someone in relation to another. Perhaps this stronger sense of closeness may not come through quite so much in ἐκ δεξιῶν.[55] Consider the two instances in the LXX where a person is referred to as ἐν δεξιᾷ of another. In 1 Esdras 4:29, the speaker refers to Apame, the king's favourite concubine, as sitting 'at the king's right hand' (καθημένην ἐν δεξιᾷ τοῦ βασιλέυς), close enough that she is able to take liberties that demonstrate her intimacy and great favour with the king.

Sometimes, she playfully takes the diadem from the king's head and puts it on herself, and even slaps the king (teasingly?) with her left hand, yet the king, besotted with her, permits it all with no offence. Did the writer here prefer ἐν δεξιᾷ to describe the position of Apame precisely because it was more suitable for characterizing her familiar and close relationship with the king?

The other instance is perhaps not so obviously further support for my proposal, but may be. In 1 Chronicles (LXX Paralipomenon I) 6:24, Asaph is referred to as the one who stood next to his brother 'on his right' (ἐν δεξιᾷ αὐτοῦ). To be sure, this statement does not depict the sort of intensely familiar relationship described in the previous text. But it is curious that this phrase is used here, whereas ἐκ δεξιῶν is elsewhere rather consistently preferred in the LXX for describing someone or something as 'on/at the right side' of someone/something else (e.g. Deut. 33:2).[56] Indeed, just a bit later in the list of names in 1 Chronicles 6, the author refers to one group in relation to another as standing 'to their left' (ἐκ ἀριστερῶν, v. 44). Did the writer prefer ἐν δεξιᾷ in v. 39, not simply to refer to Asaph's physical position in relation to his brother, but also because it seemed more appropriate in light of their fraternal relationship?

I recognize that these texts do not comprise a clinching case for my proposal, but I hope that they suffice to make it at least worth considering, perhaps even plausible. I suggest that the early (and subsequently influential) preference for ἐν δεξιᾷ τοῦ θεοῦ in confessional/kerygmatic statements was because this phrasing connoted more adequately the claim that the exalted Jesus was not only positioned next to God but also had a close relationship with God. That is, although these statements obviously reflect the influence of Psalm 110:1, specifically the image of a figure seated next to God, the ἐν δεξιᾷ phrase may have been preferred in declaring the relationship of the exalted Jesus with God because it connoted better than the ἐκ δεξιῶν of Psalm 110:1 the intimate nature of that relationship.

If this hypothesis is correct, then in these early confessional statements we see the interaction between the strong convictions of earliest believers and the scriptural text, in this case Psalm 110:1. The NT writers retain the LXX wording when citing the psalm, e.g. for apologetic purposes, and the confessional statements show also that they saw in the psalm confirmations of their christological convictions and resources for articulating them. But these confessional statements also show a creative appropriation of scriptural texts such as Psalm 110, drawing upon its imagery but preferring phrasing that more adequately expressed their profound convictions about Jesus' relationship to God.

In any case, the christological reading/appropriation of Psalm 110 is certainly a remarkable phenomenon. It demonstrates the boldness of earliest Christian convictions and the resulting creativity in their use of their Scriptures.

Isaiah 45:22–5

I turn now to consider the early Christian appropriation of Isaiah 45:22–5. Though not evidenced as much in the NT, the christological use of this text is attested as equally early as for Psalm 110, and the particular way it is read is perhaps even more remarkable; yet it has not been given nearly as much attention. The earliest and most significant christological use of the passage is, of course, in the well-known 'Christ hymn' passage, Philippians 2:6–11, in a letter that again takes us back to sometime in the fifties CE.[57] This NT passage has certainly received a massive amount of scholarly discussion, but the focus has often been on the first few verses (vv. 6–8), which present several phrases that have occupied many.[58] Particularly in the last few decades there has been a good deal of debate about whether these verses allude to Adam and whether an early 'Adam christology' is reflected in them, but this remains hotly disputed.[59] The more remarkable and the readily identifiable biblical allusion in the Philippians passage, however, is to Isaiah 45:22–5. Also, in Romans 14:11, Paul gives an explicit citation of the passage, specifically Isaiah 45:23, confirming the place of the Isaiah passage in earliest Christian thought.

Pre-Christian readings

As the case with our discussion of Psalm 110, before we consider the use of Isaiah 45:22–5 in the NT, we should inquire about any prior usage in pre-Christian Jewish circles/texts. The result, once again, is meager, even more so.[60] Although Isaiah was copied, read and mined exegetically in second-temple Jewish tradition (as reflected in the copies among the Qumran scrolls), it is hard to find any indication that 45:22–5 was particularly prominent or interpreted in any special way. This contrasts, for example, with the well-known importance of Isaiah 40:3 in Qumran (*1QS* 8; *4QS^c/4Q259*), where the biblical verse seems to have taken on special meaning as predictive of the Qumran community. Isaiah 45:22–5 was surely read, e.g. in synagogues, and studied as part of the prophetic text (e.g. in Qumran), and its affirmations about the uniqueness of the biblical deity were surely important to devout Jews of that time. But there is no evidence that the passage played any special role beyond this, or that there was any interpretation of it comparable to what we find in the NT.

Early Christian reading

That the Philippians passage incorporates phrasing from, and alludes to, Isaiah 45:22–5 is commonly recognized by commentators and other exegetes; and that v. 23 is cited/quoted in Romans 14:11 is obvious. Both Philippians and Romans are early, indeed among the earliest Christian texts extant.

So, the first thing to note is that, as the case with Psalm 110, Isaiah 45:22–5 also figured early in Christian use of the OT to articulate christological claims. Indeed, that Paul draws on Isaiah 45:22–5 allusively and without explanation in Philippians suggests again that this Isaiah passage was already a familiar part of earliest christological reflection and discourse by the time he wrote this epistle.

But this reading of the Isaiah passage is utterly novel and even astonishing. Whereas the original thrust of the passage was unquestionably to affirm the absolute uniqueness of YHWH, in Philippians 2:9–11 the passage is drawn on (and probably interpreted) to declare the universal Lordship of Jesus as the manner in which the one God will be supreme and be glorified.[61] After recounting that God (ὁ θεός) exalted Jesus and gave him 'the name above every name' in v. 9 (which I take to be 'Κύριος', and which here means that Jesus now shares in the divine name itself), the text then gives the purpose to this, which is the universal submission and acclamation of Jesus, Κύριος Ἰησοῦς Χριστός (vv. 10–11), this in turn redounding 'to the glory of God the Father' (v. 11). Some scholars have characterized this text as connoting a transference of the divine name to Jesus; but that could suggest that 'God' has handed it over to him. Instead, it seems to me that the text reflects God's sharing of the divine name with the exalted Jesus, and an accompanying inclusion of Jesus with God as rightful recipient of the universal obeisance depicted.[62] Likewise, and of great importance, the risen Jesus was included with God programmatically in the devotional pattern of early Christian circles as rightful co-recipient of their cultic devotion.[63]

It is, of course, in the reference to the universal acclamation of Jesus as Lord in vv. 10–11 that we have wording drawn identifiably from Isaiah 45:22–5. It is not an exact quotation, but instead a creative appropriation of phrasing, specifically from Isaiah 45:23, in the statement that 'every knee' is to bend/bow and 'every tongue' is to confess Jesus' supreme status. Scholars have described variously the use of the Isaiah passage here.[64] For example, in his impressive commentary on Philippians, Fee refers to 'the clear "intertextuality"' here, seeing in vv. 10–11 'a direct borrowing of language from Isa 45:23'.[65] The formal differences from the LXX of Isaiah 45:23 include word-order, and subjunctive verb-forms instead of future-indicatives: πᾶν γόνυ κάμψῃ (κάμψει πᾶν γόνυ), and πᾶσα γλῶσσα ἐξομολογήσηται (ἐξομολογήσεται πᾶσα γλῶσσα). But two more substantial differences demand further attention.

First, the universal submission represented in the Isaiah statement that 'every knee' will bow is expanded radically and cosmically to include all spheres of reality (reflecting the 'three-story universe' of the time): things (or beings) in heaven, on earth, and subterranean.[67] Fee proposed, however, that this expansion is 'in keeping' with the reference to YHWH in the larger context of Isaiah 45 (v. 18) as Creator of heaven and earth.[68] In any case, whether part of a 'pre-Pauline' hymn or Paul's own composition, this phrasing makes emphatic the multidimensional universality of the submission, including spiritual as well as physical spheres and beings.

Second, and still more remarkably, in Philippians 2:9–11 the universal submission to YHWH predicted in Isaiah 45:22–5 undergoes an astonishing 'mutation' (in comparison with pre-Christian understanding of the text), with Jesus as the direct/immediate recipient of it, and the acclamation, Κύριος Ἰησοῦς Χριστός ('Lord Jesus Christ' or 'Jesus Christ is Lord') the way that this submission is to be registered and, apparently, the manner in which Isaiah 45:22–5 is now to find its fulfilment.[69] As often noted by exegetes, Isaiah 45:18–25 is unexcelled in its forthright (even strident) declaration of the uniqueness of YHWH. But the appropriation of the phrasing from Isaiah 45:22–5 in Philippians 2:9–11 reflects a radically new reading of the passage in which two figures are seen, God and Jesus (as Lord), Jesus incorporated centrally in the obeisance that is to be given to God.[70] It seems that the wording of Isaiah 45:23–5 (LXX) in particular was taken as expressive of a duality, e.g. ἀπὸ κυρίου in v. 25 taken as referring to Jesus, and ἐν τῷ θεῷ as referring to 'God the Father', resulting in what Nagata called 'a bold reinterpretation of the traditional *kyrios*-acclamation'.[71]

Nagata posited 'a bold reinterpretation' of what he saw as a prior and less radical 'traditional *kyrios*-acclamation formula of the Christian community' (citing Rom 10:9; 1 Cor. 12:3).[72] That is, he assumed that the reading of Isaiah 45:22–5 reflected in Philippians 2:9–11 was a secondary development subsequent to some prior 'traditional' acclamation of the risen Jesus in early Christian circles that did not quite comprise the sort of christological claim reflected in the Philippians passage. Moreover, he seems to have imagined that this interpretation of Isaiah 45 arose as part of an early defence of Christian claims about Jesus against external, Jewish charges of endangering God's uniqueness.[73] But there are both logical and historical problems with his assumptions.

First, if early believers needed to defend themselves against charges that christological claims endangered God's uniqueness, then already they must have been linking Jesus with God in christological claims and in devotional practices in such a manner as to generate such charges. That is, the 'traditional *kyrios*-acclamation' of Jesus in early Jewish–Christian circles that Nagata refers to must have been viewed as problematic by fellow Jews prior to the supposed apologetic appropriation of Isaiah 45:22–5 that he assumed.

Second, the timeframe seems far too brief to posit the discrete stages required in Nagata's proposal. The timeframe was dubiously brief to allow for a *kyrios*-acclamation to become 'traditional' before the 'bold reinterpretation' of that acclamation that was supposedly effected through creatively reading the Isaiah passage.

Third, do we in fact have any evidence of such a radical reinterpretation of some less radical acclamation of Jesus as *kyrios* within the early 'post-Easter' period?[74] Do the other references to the acclamation of Jesus as *Kyrios* in the NT (Rom. 10:9; 1 Cor. 12:3) really suggest some more modest view of his status than that reflected in Philippians 2:9–11? I think not. Indeed, the earliest artefact of the acclamation of Jesus, the well-known *maranatha* (1 Cor. 16:22; and *Did*. 10:6), which must derive from early Aramaic-speaking circles of believers, surely reflects Jesus invoked as Lord of the cultic gathering.[75]

Finally, why should we imagine that Isaiah 45 was first turned to by early believers for apologetic resources against objections to their faith? It seems to me much more likely that this and other OT passages were pored over and searched by believers in the first instance to try to understand *for themselves* their religious experiences, and for resources to correlate their daring new convictions about Jesus with their Scriptures and their traditional religious commitment to the one God.[76]

In turning now to Romans 14:11, we have a direct quotation of Isaiah 45:23 that confirms the early significance of the Isaiah passage in various Christian circles, Pauline and non-Pauline.[77] Again, there are relatively minor formal differences between Paul's citation and the LXX text. The opening words, ζῶ ἐγώ, λέγει κύριος, are not a part of Isaiah 45:23, but instead a 'typical prophetic oath formula' found in various OT passages, the most proximate instance in Isaiah 49:18.[78] Also, Paul has πᾶσα γλῶσσα ἐξομολογήσηται, in contrast to the word order of Isaiah 45:23, the syntactical effect being to put the emphasis on the universality of the confession.[79] But, unlike the adaptation of Isaiah 45:23 in Philippians 2:10–11, here he preserves the future tense of both the verbs, 'shall bow' and 'shall confess'. The future tense of the verbs also happens to fit the emphasis in Romans 14:1–12 on a future accounting to be given by all.

The more substantial question, however, is how Isaiah 45:23 was likely read by Paul here. As noted in our analysis of Philippians 2:10–11, in the Isaiah passage there is an interesting combination of first-person and third-person references to the one(s) to whom universal accounting/submission is to be given: '*to me* every knee shall bow' and 'every tongue will acknowledge *God*'. Moreover, Paul's use of the introductory formula, 'As I live, says the Lord', has the effect of placing in his citation both 'the Lord' and 'God' as key terms. So, are we to see these terms simply as two designations of the one biblical deity or as designating two figures, God and Jesus? Is Jesus the κύριος in the introductory formula here in Romans 14:11? And shall we take the obeisance given 'to me' and 'to God' as reflecting the sort of duality that we see in the use of Isaiah 45:23 in the Philippians passage?

In the preceding verses of 14:1–12 Paul repeatedly refers to 'the Lord' and 'God', rather clearly having Jesus and God in mind, and interweaving these references such that the human behaviour in view is addressed with reference to both.[80] In v. 3, we have God's acceptance, and in v. 4 the ability of the *kyrios* to uphold his servants.[81] In vv. 5–8, whatever the choices on matters of days or diet, says Paul, the choices are all made 'to the Lord', with thanks given 'to God', followed by a generalizing statement that living or dying 'we are the Lord's'. Then, in v. 9, there is the statement that 'Christ died and lived again that he might be Lord [κυριεύσει] of the dead and the living.'[82] This in turn leads to Paul's warning in v. 10 that 'we shall all stand before the judgment seat of God'.

In short, the *kyrios* of 14:1–12 is rather clearly the risen/exalted Jesus, who is paired with God throughout these verses like two strands of a rope.[83] This then makes it likely that the κύριος in the introductory formula also designates Jesus.[84] So, to answer the key question posed earlier, Paul probably presents Isaiah 45:23 here as referring to a universal submission both to Jesus as Lord ('*to me* shall every knee bow') and to God ('every tongue shall acknowledge *God*').[85] Here, as in Philippians 2:9–11, Paul likely saw in the Isaiah text essentially the same duality involving obeisance and accountability to Jesus and to God.[86]

That Paul cites Isaiah 45:23 in this manner and without explanation or justification must mean that he presumed that the Roman believers (who were not his own converts) were already acquainted with this reading of this Isaiah passage as referring to God and the risen Lord Jesus. That is, he was hardly deploying here some new or idiosyncratic interpretation of the text. Instead, it is most likely that Romans 14:11 reflects a creative reading of Isaiah 45:22–5 that emerged so early and circulated so widely that Paul could presume it to be known already, even among Christian circles with whom he had no prior contact or influence.

What Produced This Creative Exegesis?

What we see in the two case studies considered here is an altogether remarkable and apparently novel reading and use of the biblical texts in question. In the case of Psalm 110:1, we have a radically escalated view of what is meant in God inviting the *kyrios* there to sit 'at my right hand'. Well beyond the original sense of the Judean king as the earthly vicegerent of God, and even beyond the grand vision of the future exalted status of the 'Elect One' of the Similitudes of *1 Enoch*, early Christians saw in Psalm 110:1 a heavenly exaltation and rule of universal and cosmic dimensions bestowed on the risen Jesus. In their view, the text spoke of Jesus as effectively *sharing God's throne*, not figuratively, but literally, and so sharing in the full dimensions of God's sovereignty. As noted earlier, this goes beyond any prior (or later) reading of Psalm 110:1 in the Jewish tradition of these earliest believers, and the status ascribed to Jesus seems to go beyond that of any other figure in ancient Jewish thought.[87]

When we consider the earliest Christian treatment of Isaiah 45:22–5, we probably see a still more astonishing phenomenon: this passage taken as presenting two figures, the 'Lord' Jesus and God, distinguishable but also linked uniquely as co-recipients of the universal obeisance depicted in the text. This surely would have raised Jewish eyebrows of the time, to put it mildly! To be sure, taking account of the flow of thought in the immediate context, the point of Philippians 2:6–11 is to depict Jesus' exemplary obedience and self-humbling to God's purposes and the spectacular divine exaltation of him that followed, Paul urging the Philippians to have a similar mindset of love and concern for one another (vv. 1–5, 12–18). But, whether adapted from an early Christian ode or freshly composed by Paul, the final verses of Philippians 2:6–11 also draw on and presuppose a reading of Isaiah 45:22–5 that emerged much earlier, as is also presupposed in Romans 14:11. In this novel reading, a passage that had likely served to assert the absolute uniqueness of the biblical deity is taken as asserting the remarkable claim that the exalted Jesus rightfully shares in the obeisance due God.

This use of the Isaiah text along with the final doxological phrase in Philippians 2:10–11 likely reflects an origin of this reading of the Isaiah passage in a context shaped by traditional Jewish religious concerns. In this kind of setting the christological claim that Jesus shares the divine rule and name was probably startling, even troubling, to believers who shared the traditional Jewish concern for God's uniqueness. Moreover, as noted earlier, the claim would also likely have been offensive to many in the larger Jewish community of the time, perhaps even taken as threatening that traditional Jewish confession.[88]

Nevertheless, given the early date and translocal distribution of the evidence, this dyadic reading of Isaiah 45:22–5, and the distinctive use of Psalm 110 must have arisen initially among circles of Jewish believers. So, how might this have happened? How did Jews who affirmed the uniqueness of the one God come to see in these biblical texts the astonishing sense reflected in the NT citations and allusions that we have considered here? That no equivalent reading of these texts can be found in Jewish circles prior to or contemporary with the early Jesus-movement surely indicates that the early Christian reading of them did not arise either accidentally or through application of exegetical principles of the time.

Before I attempt an answer, it will be helpful to take account of what may be a somewhat similarly novel reading of some other OT texts. Perhaps the closest that we get to an analogy for the dyadic reading of the biblical texts treated here is in the remarkable (albeit fragmentary) Qumran text, *11Q Melchizedek (11Q13)*. In this text a mysterious figure named Melchizedek appears to be identified as the '*Elohim*' who arises 'in the assembly of El' in Psalm 82:1 to 'carry out the vengeance of God's judgments' in the eschatological day of wrath and salvation (*11Q Melch* 2:9-13).[89] This figure also seems to be identified with the statement in Isaiah 52:7, 'your God [*Eloheyka*] reigns', and thus he will act as the agent through whom God's eschatological rule comes to earthly expression. Here, a figure is distinguished from God and yet also linked with God as the unique agent of divine purposes. Still more remarkable and directly relevant to this discussion, he is also 'read' as the *Elohim* of certain biblical passages.

Scholars widely judge that the Qumran community texts reflect a strong interest in 'mystical' experiences, revelation of eschatological secrets, communion with angels (especially in worship), and heavenly ascent.[90] These texts also reflect a strong belief that the Scriptures could be mined to reveal and confirm eschatological truths. In this religious context ('micro-climate') biblical texts were searched for eschatological meaning, and the sort of novel and remarkable interpretations of biblical passages represented in *11Q Melchizedek* (and in the *Pesharim* texts) emerged.[91] It is also thought that this mystical interest was practised in a communal setting, perhaps one in which prayer, singing of hymns/psalms, and other worship acts featured, and revelations were hoped for and expected, including revelations of the meaning of Scripture. That is, an important mode of Qumran Scripture-interpretation was what David Aune called 'charismatic exegesis'.[92]

In previous publications I have proposed that a crucial factor in the eruption of the 'high christology' reflected in the earliest NT texts was the effect of powerful religious experiences that struck recipients with the force of revelation.[93] These experiences, which included visions of the risen and exalted Jesus, generated the remarkable convictions that God had raised Jesus from death to heavenly glory, and that Jesus was now the rightful co-recipient of the devotion of believers. In early circles of Jesus-followers in which an excitement and even a certain bewilderment likely obtained, believers also searched biblical texts, initially to comprehend better what they believed was happening, and probably hoping for further revelations of divine purposes. They believed that God knew all things from the beginning, and that the events they experienced were the fulfilment of divine plans. They also believed that their Scriptures offered resources for understanding God's purposes. But they knew very well that their experiences reflected new divine acts, giving a new standpoint from which to approach their Scriptures in the hope of perceiving things anew (e.g. 1 Pet. 1:10–12).

In the Lukan scenes where the risen Jesus interprets the Scriptures to reveal his glory (Luke 24:25–7,44–7), we probably have a dramatized reflection of the phenomenon I am trying to describe. In these scenes, the Scriptures are (suddenly) opened to reveal new truths that Jesus' followers had not imagined before; this happens to them in groups, and is connected to experiences of the risen Jesus.

In sum, I propose that the remarkable and novel readings of Psalm 110:1 and Isaiah 45:22–5, and other biblical texts as well, likely emerged early, quickly, and typically in settings of group prayer and worship where the sense of the Spirit's presence and power was strong. Early believers came to their Scriptures with convictions shaped by powerful religious experiences that opened the sacred texts for them in new ways, particularly experiences of the risen and exalted Jesus, and continuing revelations from the Spirit. Gathered in corporate prayer and worship, they searched their Scriptures in the fervent expectation that new understanding and even further revelations would come in this context.[94]

2

'He Interpreted to Them the things About himself in All the Scriptures': Linguistic Perspectives on the New Testament's Use of the Old Testament

Ian G. Malcolm and Matthew R. Malcolm
Edith Cowan University and Trinity Theological College

Various problems and controversies are associated with the use of the Old Testament in the New. The conviction of this chapter is that a number of these issues can be addressed with fresh illumination when considered using certain insights from the field of linguistics. It will be useful, first, to make mention of the notable problems arising from the New Testament's use of the Old. We will then outline some linguistic approaches to the interpretation of text, before applying these insights to Luke 18 – 24. We will conclude by commenting on the relevance of these insights for the New Testament's use of the Old Testament more broadly.

Notable Problems

One notable problem concerns the question of precedence for messianic readings of Scripture in Judaism: Was there a 'Son of Man' concept in Judaism?[1] Was there an expectation that a messiah would suffer and/or rise?[2] Of what significance is it if the Evangelists' interpretation of the Scriptures finds precedent or no precedent in Jewish interpretation? Is it important for early Christianity that Jesus fulfils known Messianic expectation?[3]

A related problem concerns the extent to which the NT *'fulfilments'* of Scripture should most accurately be thought of as fair fulfilments of what the text meant 'back then', or perhaps rather *transformations* of what the text must mean for 'us now'. In other words, are we to envisage a hermeneutical direction that proceeds from OT prophecy to NT fulfilment, or one that proceeds from NT 'fulfilment' to reconfigured OT interpretation?[4]

Another problem concerns the question of whether the interpretative techniques seen in the NT, resulting sometimes in apparently haphazard or predetermined conclusions, are adopted or adapted from similar exegetical methods in second-temple Judaism, exemplified, perhaps, in the Dead Sea Scrolls or Philo. Is it a cause for concern if the NT writers use second-temple methods? Are their conclusions thereby endangered?[5] And do the NT writers evidence concern for the contexts of their citations, or do they sometimes ignore them?

The Gospel of Luke is no exception in presenting these problems to the interpreter. One may question what Luke believes was envisioned in the law and the prophets 'about the Son of Man'. What are we to make of the fact that Luke sees a need for fulfilment in the Scripture, 'he was numbered among the transgressors'? Are we to be embarrassed by the fact that what Jesus appears to find the obvious centre of the Scriptures (24:25–7) apparently eludes all prior readers? Are the Emmaus disciples really 'foolish' for having missed it?

Some Linguistic Approaches to the Interpretation of Text

Linguistics for most of the last century was primarily concerned with the formal structure of linguistic corpora. It was thought that the rule system which underlay linguistic data was best approached independently of meaning. The pervasiveness of this approach was beginning to break down by the second half of the twentieth century as *social* data – external to the linguistic system – were increasingly being asserted as a necessary element in linguistic description. Then, as the century was drawing nearer to its close, a dramatic further development occurred, as *meaning*, once excluded, came to centre stage with the development of cognitive linguistics. Cognitive linguistics can be described simply as 'an approach to language that is based on our experience of the world and the way we perceive and conceptualize it'.[6] With cognitive linguistics has come a recognition of the key role of the mind in responding to and interpreting experience, and of how we can key into this role by the way in which we analyse language.

We will see later in this chapter that Luke repeatedly draws out contrasts in the ways in which the same linguistic and non-linguistic data are interpreted by different minds. Cognitive linguists contest the idea that there is a direct mapping of elements of the external world onto language. Rather, 'they claim, a particular situation can be "construed" in different ways, and that different ways of encoding a situation constitute different conceptualizations'.[7] What is potentially of hermeneutic interest here is that cognitive approaches to linguistics may provide tools which will aid in the interpretation of texts dealing with matters of *alternative construals*.

An attempt will be made here to outline some of the key concepts in cognitive linguistics, and its offshoot cultural linguistics, and to illustrate their application in other areas of research before looking at how they might be applied to the Lukan narrative.

First, *language, culture and the human mind need to be understood together*. Cognitive and cultural linguistics assert that, far from being irrelevant to the form taken by human expression, meaning is inherent in it. Language is a product of the human mind and, as Wallace Chafe puts it, 'we can never really understand language without understanding the human mind, and vice versa.'[8] Cultural linguist Gary Palmer, who combines an anthropological with a cognitive linguistic perspective, goes further, to argue: 'it is likely that all native knowledge of language and culture belongs to cultural schemas and that the living of culture and the speaking of language consist of schemas in action.'[9] The concept of the schema, deriving ultimately from Plato and Kant,[10] relates to the mental imagery human beings depend on to enable them to make sense of their experience.[11] We are guided, for example, by event schemas to orient us to events in which we will need to participate, such as shopping or weddings or services of worship; we depend on role schemas to predict how to fulfil the expectations of roles we need to play in society; we constantly frame our discourse in line with image schemas, when we say, for example, 'he's reached a dead end' or 'we're having a busy bee'; and we expect general conformity within our group to proposition schemas such as 'Pride comes before a fall'.[12] We even use particular phonemes or phoneme combinations to convey our attitude to what we are talking about, as when we use the /sl/ in such terms as *slippery, slimy, slothful, slaphappy, slob*. We also depend on schemas when we want to communicate meaningfully with one another about what we or others have done. A story only makes sense if conforming to what our culture accepts as a story schema, which dictates what is worthy of telling, and in what way. In all these ways, and others, the schemas which are inherent in our culture and language are basic to our construal of experience, and our responses are to be understood less in terms of objective reality than of reality as interpreted in terms of those schemas.[13] This may mean that, in fact, we 'filter out' some of our experience which cannot be comprehended within our existing schemas.[14]

Second, *language and the mind are an expression of world-view*. We inherit the language we use from the culture in which we live, and along with the language comes a world-view. As Palmer puts it: 'The evidence suggests that language and world view are mutually constitutive.'[15] This is not to say that everyone who uses a particular language thinks the same way, but in many ways the language provides us with a workable 'model of reality'.[16] To some extent, using a language means accommodating to a largely shared world-view. Again, to quote Palmer: 'Cultural linguistics does not hinge on the existence of stable world views that are shared by all members of a culture or even a language community . . . But it does assume that speakers and listeners have some understanding, however rudimentary, of one another's world views.'[17]

Third, *language and conceptualization are subject to ongoing change, in response to experience*. Magdalena and Mühlhäulser[18] have observed how, in our time, the 'coinage of new terms which stand in opposition to, or parallel with existing terms' has accompanied and perhaps contributed to the reframing of mainstream perceptions about the environment. They have demonstrated that 'the new domain of greenspeaking has led to a rapid increase in lexical development and multiword formations over the last three decades' (p. 299). It might be said that the introduction of the term 'marriage equality' to refer to a desired re-conceptualization of marriage by some members of our community is another case in point. Cultural conceptualizations are, as Sharifian puts it, 'constantly being negotiated and renegotiated across generations and across time and space by members of a cultural group'.[19] In similar vein, Palmer asserts that: 'Through time and incessant patter, speakers in language communities collaborate and negotiate over the imagery of evolving world views. Old or new, unwanted ideas are filtered out. New imagery and language emerge together.'[20]

Often the kind of conceptual and linguistic change we are talking about occurs in response to events. As Sharifian puts it, 'word meanings respond to and can be shaped by concrete socio-political and cultural factors.'[21] Within cultural linguistics, the term *emergent meaning* is used to refer to 'the schematization of relatively novel and unfamiliar experiences and their framing or interpretation in terms of conventional categories'.[22] Hence, in our time, the terms '9/11', or 'the apology', or 'boat people', have emerged as evoking quite specific schemas which they did not evoke prior to the events which brought them into currency. William Labov, seeking to account for language change, has observed how, in history, events like the Norman Invasion or World War II have introduced significant change in the ways in which the English language was used. He has coined the phrase 'triggering event' to refer to 'a terminal stage in the process of tracing, backwards in time, the linked series of changes that have affected a particular dialect'.[23]

Applications of Cognitive and Cultural Linguistic Concepts

Among the significant triggering events of language change in English have been the various ventures of colonization in different parts of the world. In the case of Australia, a number of varieties of English, in particular, those of Southern England and of Ireland, were, from the late eighteenth century, uprooted from their source cultural environments and replanted in a new physical and cultural environment. A new English arose in the colony which was different in pronunciation and in idiom from those which preceded it. When English was adopted by the Aboriginal residents of Australia it underwent a more radical change in pronunciation, grammar and conceptualization, to the point that now two distinct varieties of English prevail, respectively, in the mainstream and Aboriginal communities in Australia. The insights of cognitive and cultural linguistics have been drawn on in research attempting to account for the ways in which Aboriginal and non-Aboriginal Australians, using English, often misinterpret one another. It has been demonstrated[24] that Aboriginal students and their non-Aboriginal teachers, respectively, may reconstruct what has been said to them to enable it to make sense in the context of the kind of English with which they are familiar. That is, in cultural linguistic terms, they employ culture-specific schemas in interpreting what they hear or read, a process which has been referred to as 'reschematization'.[25]

Other research has taken place with speakers of English as a second or additional language and similar processes have seen to be operating. Leng found that people who were first-language speakers of Chinese, in conversation with Australian English native speakers, drew on the schemas associated with their first language, resulting in miscommunication.[26] Similar findings were reported by Conlan with respect to Japanese native speakers.[27] Sharifian has looked in the other direction, showing what needs to be taken into account in using Persian appropriately with its native speakers.[28]

The cultural linguistic concept of emergent change has been drawn on by Sharifian in accounting for the way in which the word we understand as *jihad*, or *jahâd*, in Persian, changed its meaning after the revolution in Iran, to refer to '"striving" associated with construction and development rather than destruction and war'.[29] Malcolm and Sharifian have observed a similar process underlying the vernacularization of English by Aboriginal speakers, involving 'the modification of English lexical items, either by changing the form of individual items [like, for example, *quick way* for "quickly"] or by bringing together items which do not normally come together in the English of non-Aboriginal speakers [like, for example, *cousin brother*]'.[30]

Cognitive and Cultural Linguistics and Biblical Texts

When it comes to the application of such concepts to biblical texts, Wierzbicka, in her book *What Did Jesus Mean?* has called for linguistic resources to be brought to bear on the cultural tasks associated with exegesis, given the significance both of the relevant cultures of first-century Palestine, and the centuries of predominantly European reading of the texts.[31] In a similar vein, though from a different conceptual background, linguist Eugene Nida has argued: 'Perhaps one of the important aspects of any study of the Gospel of John is the recognition that without the historical context, much of the distinctive significance of the Gospel is lost.'[32]

Porter and Reed have recognized the significance of the story schema as 'a sort of narrative *template*', in seeking to understand the happenings, participants and themes in the Gospel of Mark[33] and Porter and Robinson, in supporting the use of linguistic insights to study the effects produced by biblical texts and the reasons for such effects, have argued: 'While many hermeneuts are inclined to think of hermeneutics as a literary method for reading texts, others – an ever-growing majority – take hermeneutics to represent a description of human understanding more generally, a way of thinking about our ontology, and the means of challenging dominant ideals of truth, reason, and knowledge that do not capture the full range of human experience.'[34]

The specific application to biblical texts of cognitive and cultural linguistic concepts and insights is in its infancy, but we would argue, and wish to demonstrate, that it can contribute to the understanding of what Bock has described as Luke's depiction of 'this seemingly new movement . . . actually rooted in old promises and in a design that God promised and now . . . executed through Jesus, the promised one of God'.[35]

Application to Luke 18 – 24

We have mentioned above that Luke presents alternative construals of Scripture from his main characters. Indeed, Luke is at pains to demonstrate a clash of interpretative models or schemas, a clash that stems from the triggering event of the coming of Jesus. This clash can be seen in the jarring ways in which Luke presents the respective interpretations given by Jesus and the disciples to scriptural or traditional data.

Scriptural or traditional data are taken up by Luke's Jesus and interpreted in the light of the *triggering event* of his own particular coming. This results in what might be called a *'coming' interpretative schema,* such that Scriptures or traditions that might otherwise be open to a variety of readings are said or shown to be decisively narrowed by the coming, not of a messiah figure in abstract, but of this particular man:

Passage	Scriptural/Traditional Data	'Coming' Interpretative Schema
18:31–4	'everything that is written by the prophets about the Son of Man'	'He will be delivered over to the Gentiles. They will mock him'
19:37–44	'the time of God's coming to you'	'Blessed is the king who comes in the name of the Lord'
22:36–51	'he was numbered with the transgressors'	'This must be fufilled in me'
24:20–7	'the one who was going to redeem Israel'	'Did not the Messiah have to suffer these things and then enter his glory?'
24:36–45	Law / prophets / psalms	'Everything must be fulfilled that is written about me in the Law / prophets / psalms'

Luke frequently demonstrates that this 'coming' interpretative schema jars in certain ways with the traditional (though no doubt variously distributed) interpretative schemas adopted by the disciples. This results in mystification and misunderstanding. Although the disciples are followers of Jesus, they do not immediately experience a comprehensive recasting of their existing interpretations or expectations. Indeed, the disciples might be seen as typical of their fellow cultural inhabitants at this point, who are likewise presented as failing to perceive the interpretative significance of the triggering event of Jesus' coming.

Passage	Scriptural/ Traditional Data	'Coming' Interpretative Schema	Schema Non-Recognition
18:31–4	'everything that is written by the prophets about the Son of Man'	'He will be delivered over to the Gentiles. They will mock him'	'The disciples did not understand'
19:37–44	'the time of God's coming to you'	'Blessed is the king who comes in the name of the Lord'	'It is hidden from your eyes'
22:36–51	'he was numbered with the transgressors'	'This must be fulfilled in me'	'Should we strike with our swords'
24:5–8	?	'The Son of Man must be delivered . . . crucified . . . rise'	'Why do you look for the living among the dead'
24:20–27	'the one who was going to redeem Israel'	'Did not the Messiah have to suffer these things and then enter his glory?'	'We had hoped he was the one who was going to redeem Israel'
24:36–45	Law/prophets/ psalms	'Everything must be fulfilled that is written about me in the Law/prophets/ psalms'	'They were startled and frightened'

However, Luke indicates that after the resurrection, the disciples' changed interpretation of Scripture and of the events they have witnessed testifies to their reschematization of these inputs. They newly recognize the impact that the triggering event of Jesus' coming must have on their understanding.

Passage	Scriptural/ Traditional data	'Coming' Interpretative Schema	Schema Non-Recognition	Reschematization
18:31–4	'everything that is written by the prophets about the Son of Man'	'He will be delivered over to the Gentiles. They will mock him'	'The disciples did not understand'	(24:27): 'the things about himself in all the scriptures

19:37–44	'the time of God's coming to you'	'Blessed is the king who comes in the name of the Lord'	'It is hidden from your eyes'	
22:31–62		'You will deny me three times'	'Lord, I am ready to go with you to death'	'Peter remembered'
22:36–51	'he was numbered with the transgres-sors'	'This must be fulfilled in me'	'Should we strike with our swords?'	'He touched the man's ear'
24:5–8	?	'The Son of Man must be delivered . . . crucified . . . rise'	'Why do you look for the living among the dead?'	'Then they remembered his words'
24:20–27	'the one who was going to redeem Israel'	'Did not the Messiah have to suffer thse things and then enter his glory?'	'We had hoped he ws the one who was going to redeem Israel'	'He explained to them what was said in the scrip-tures about himself'
24:36–45	Law/prophets/ psalms	'Everything must be fulfilled that is written about me in the Law/prophets/ psalms'	'They were startled and frightened'	'He opened their minds'

To summarize: pre-Christian Jewish interpretation of the Scriptures, exemplified in the disciples, utilizes a range of *interpretative schemas*, resulting in a range of expectations. Some of these may overlap with Jesus' own self-presentation and scriptural interpretation; but for Jesus, his own 'coming' represents a definitive *triggering event*, in the light of which the Scriptures must now be understood. He effectively calls his hearers to *reschematize*, summoning them to a particular *construal* of the Scriptures in the light of this decisive triggering event. This reschematization crystallizes for the disciples after the first Easter.

New Testament Use of the Old Testament

There are a number of ways in which this linguistic account of the disciples' reinterpretation of the Scriptures can offer benefits for the study of the New Testament's use of the Old Testament more broadly.

It alleviates the concern (which may be pro- or anti-apologetic) that Christian interpretation be seen to neatly fulfil (and perhaps supersede) expectations arising from pre-Christian Jewish readings of the Scriptures. According to Luke's presentation, the christocentric interpretation of OT Scriptures that is initiated by Jesus is a defiantly *alternative* construal of the Scriptures, in accordance with an alternative schema. Nevertheless, it is presented as a God-ordained and essential alternative, now that Jesus has come.[36] This perspective thus grants space for Jewish Scriptures, interpretations and events to have their own historical integrity and richness, while still holding to a christological climax from a Christian point of view.[37]

Following from this, the account given above frees us up from having to choose between *either* a hermeneutical direction that proceeds from OT prophecy to NT fulfilment, *or* one that proceeds from NT 'fulfilment' to reconfigured OT interpretation. The account above indicates that, according to Luke, the 'fulfilment' that Jesus brings comes via the reschematizing triggering event of his own coming. To simplify, Luke is neither claiming 'this is what it had to mean *back then*', nor 'this is what it must be *transformed* to mean', but rather, 'this is what we must *now* come to perceive it *had* to mean'.[38]

The issue, then, of whether or not Jesus and his followers made use of known Jewish interpretative techniques seems to be less decisive, and less straightforward, than it is sometimes made out to be. Our perspective is that the triggering event of the coming of Jesus prompts a rereading of the Scriptures that ultimately focuses and reconfigures the techniques themselves. For example, a conviction that texts about the temple must now be perceived to prefigure the body of Jesus takes up, but christocentrically crystallizes, a Philo-like symbolic sensitivity. This results in the Christian practice of messianic typological interpretation, a practice that thus finds both continuity and discontinuity with prior interpretative instincts.[39]

In the same way, the question of whether or not citations of Scripture in the NT have implicit concern for their broader context is not straightforward. We may find once again both continuity and discontinuity with prior contextual parameters. The triggering event of the coming of Jesus has recoloured the context of cited texts, because – and perhaps this is in fact crucial – it has begun to reconfigure 'Scripture' as 'Old Testament'.

Gospels and Acts

3

Jesus and Scripture: Scripture and the Self-Understanding of Jesus[1]

Roland Deines
University of Nottingham

Introduction: What it Means to Live with a Biblical Mindset

Before approaching the actual topic of Jesus' use of Scripture some introductory comments about what it means to live with a biblical mindset are necessary to identify what Jesus has in common with his contemporaries, and where he is distinctive. The main point to make is that Jews in the first century were accustomed to reflect on their own experiences in light of their sacred writings, that is, the Jewish Scriptures. This means historically that members of God's chosen people have understood their entire existence as individuals and as a nation to stand in relation to God. Extraordinary experiences have the potential to raise the question of whether God is addressing his people through them. Consequently, Israel has interpreted individual or national events within this interpretative context.[2]

The Psalter alone provides a wide variety of opportunities to embed oneself into a wider biblical framework by praying and meditating on these texts and in doing this fusing the actual experiences of the joy, distress, anger or thankfulness of the 'reader' with the hallowed words of David, Asaph and the other 'authors' of the Psalter. The individual laments have, for example, provided help in overcoming personal crises, and continue to do so today. Likewise the Deuteronomistic reflections on the course of history, on the interrelatedness of obedience and blessing, of disobedience and exile, can be tools for Israel to gauge her relationship with God. The history of impact of these texts clearly demonstrates that they were used and applied in exactly this way. These texts kept alive the conviction that God accompanies and guides Israel through her history and is someone to be reckoned with (see e.g. Amos 3:3–8). God does nothing, Amos proclaims, without 'revealing his secret to his servants the prophets'. The prophetic books, like other Scriptures, are the condensation or the deposit of God's revealed accompaniment of his people. Texts became Scripture because they had proven their worth in mediating between God and his people beyond their immediate time and circumstances of origin; they opened a door to God and allowed Israel to relate herself and her situation to God's master history.[3] This attitude of integrating oneself, individually and collectively, into salvation history became habitual for the Jewish people over a period of at least one millennium. Reading the world with biblical lenses can therefore be taken as the default setting for those who participate in God's covenant with Israel.

We need, however, to differentiate between those who were religiously active and lived consciously in the covenantal relationship with God and those who could not care less about anything religious. One should not assume that all Jews in the first century, just because they were Jews and members of God's chosen people, were eager to study Scripture, attend synagogue services, make regular pilgrimages to the temple in Jerusalem and structure their whole life, from morning until evening and from birth to death, according to the law of Moses and its interpretations and adaptations through the centuries. But having said this, we need to say also that it is unlikely that a Jew living in the first century in the land God has given his people would not have been confronted with Scripture on a regular basis: the calendar that determined their working and festive times was based on God's commandments; their rules of marriage and divorce were given by God through Moses; their palates were biblically tuned, in that they ate and abhorred what God allowed and forbade in Scripture; the names they and most of their neighbours bore were given to them in remembrance of biblical heroes and the choice of given names often represented an expectation on the part of the parents about the future of their children.[4] The landscape inhabited by any first-century Jew in Israel was full of biblical stories, be it the mountains of Gilboah or Mount Hermon, Samaria or Jericho, Bethlehem or Jerusalem; it would have been impossible to live in such places without awareness of the related memories (in some cases even physical remnants of the biblical past were still visible). In the first century the biblical prophets were remembered by tomb memorials erected at their assumed burial places and stories were told to visitors about these saints of old.[5]

Therefore, for Jews living in the land of Israel in the time of Jesus, the dominant culture and even the geography was biblically shaped through and through. For those with eyes to see and ears to hear the pointers to Scripture could not be missed. Regarding the people we encounter in the New Testament, we can be fairly sure that they are those who can be called 'religiously active'. And this means that the lenses they used to create meaning for their own lives, the lives of their families and communities, and for the people of Israel as a whole, were biblical lenses. We can therefore assume a certain level of applied scriptural wisdom and spirituality, which could be drawn upon every time something new, unusual, exciting, frightening or disturbing happened. The habitual question would be: What does God want to tell us through this? What is its purpose?

The extant Jewish literature from this period confirms this because, with hardly any exceptions, it is scripturally inspired and shaped. This fact is by itself quite astonishing. There is hardly a Jewish text from the times of the kings and prophets to the early Middle Ages that could be labelled as secular or devoid of a biblical thought-world and biblical imagery. As a result, every teacher and preacher could presuppose that their audience would process what they said within a scriptural framework. This does not mean that everybody – whether teacher or listener – could give precise references for the origin of every biblical phrase or every quote used. Rather, to be immersed in Scripture and allowing oneself to be guided and influenced by Scripture goes way beyond this rather technical form of knowing. I think we all know examples of Christians who have a stupendous amount of detailed biblical knowledge (knowing numerous verses and references by heart, for example) but nevertheless lack any deeper understanding of the biblical message.[6] In other words, the possession of/extent of one's biblical mindset cannot primarily be gauged by pure knowledge of biblical quotations but has to take into account the more decisive factor of the formative power of a scripturally based world-view on such a person. For Jesus and the apostles we can presuppose from all available evidence that their thought-world and available metaphorical and spiritual language was thoroughly and uniquely biblical (whereby 'biblical' is not restricted narrowly to biblical texts or biblical literacy). They lived in, with, and by Israel's master narrative. Hence I take for granted that Jesus was part of this scripturally created and inspired culture, but I contend – and this is my second assumption – that he is also to be distinguished from this culture in a very special way as the *Lord of Scripture*.

Jesus' Use of Scripture

Steve Moyise calculates that the four gospels 'record Jesus quoting about fifty different passages of scripture, along with at least twice that number of allusions and echoes'.[7] He then lists the biblical books from which the fifty passages are taken: All five books of Moses, the Psalter, Isaiah, Jeremiah, Hosea, Jonah, Micah, Zechariah, Malachi and Daniel. References to biblical characters like David, Solomon, Elijah and Elisha demonstrate further knowledge of the historical books even if they are not directly quoted. I present here another list, starting with the references given by Moyise for Matthew, but following the order of the use of Scripture in the gospel narrative. I chose Matthew as an example because it provides the longest list of all four canonical gospels, which is unsurprising if we consider that Matthew's Gospel was written with the questions and concerns in mind of those followers of Jesus who came to faith in him from within Judaism.[8] Furthermore the Gospel of Matthew also preserves traditions from Mark, and those parts which are called the double-tradition and are thought by many scholars to be drawn from the famous source 'Q'.[9]

The abbreviation 'par.' (with one 'r') or 'parr.' (with two 'r's) in the following list indicates whether the parallel is in both Mark and Luke ('parr.'), or only in one of them ('par.'). There are a number of cases where Matthew and Mark are parallel and

Luke omits material, but the majority of 'par.' are Matthew/ Luke parallels, which are thought to represent Q-material. In addition to Moyise's references, I have also included (marked by *italics*) all statements in which Jesus clearly refers to a biblical narrative (like mentioning David fleeing from Saul and eating the showbread from the temple in Nod), and I have qualified some of Moyise's references, where I see no intended allusion to a biblical source and its meaning but rather a biblical way of speaking.[10] I have not included the titles 'Son of Man,' 'Messiah,' and 'Son of David' in this list, all of which are, however, derived from the Hebrew Bible.

Jesus' and Others' Use of Scripture in the Gospel of Matthew

Matthew	Jesus	Others	Evangelist
1:1–17			Genealogy of Jesus
1:22f.			Isa 7:14 (FQ)[1:5f.]
2:5f		Micah 5:1 (high priests and scribes')	
2:15			Hosea 11:1 (FQ)
2:23			Isa 11:1 Ναζωραῖος *nezer* 'branch'
3.3 par.		Isa 40:3 (John the Baptist)	
4.4 par.	Deut 8:3 (to Satan)		
4:6 par.		Ps 91:11f. (Satan)	
4:7 par.	Deut 6:16 (to Satan)		
4:10 par.	Deut 6:13 (to Satan)		
4:14–16			Isa 8:23–9:1 (FQ)
5:17–19	**Law and Prophets**		

5:21	Exod 20:13, Deut 5:17		
5:27	Exod 20:14, Deut 5:18		
5:31	Deut 24:1		
5:33	Lev 19:12, Num 30:2		
5:38	Exod 21:24, Lev 24.20, Deut 19:18		
5:43	Lev 19:18		
6:29	*'Solomon in all his glory'*		
7:12	**Law and Prophets (Golden Rule)**		
7:15	*'false prophets'*		
8:4 parr.	*'offer the gifts Moses commanded* (to healed leper)		
8:11 parr.	*'eat with Abraham and Isaac and Jacob in the kingdom of heaven'*		
8:17			Isa 53:4 (FQ)
9:13	Hos 6:6		
10.35f.	Micah 7:6 (to disciples)[12]		
11:5 par.	Isa 35:5f., 61.1f. (to John's messengers, 10:8) [not formal, 'a short *florilegium* or *cento*' (Moyise)]		
11:10 par.	Mal 3:1 (to the crowds about John)		
11:13 par.	**All the Prophets and the Law**		
11:14	John is *'Elijah to come'*		
11:23f.	*'Sodom . . . would have remained . . .'*[13]		
12:3f.	*'have you not read what David did . . .'* [14] (to the Pharisees)		
12:5	*'have you not read in the law that on the Sabbath the priests in the temple . . .'* (to the Pharisees)		
12:7	Hos 6:6 (to the Pharisees)		

12:17–21			Isa 42:1–4 (FQ)
12:39–41 par.	Jonah 1:17 (*summary of book,* to the Pharisees)		
12:42 par.	*'The queen of the south . . . came from the ends of the earth to listen to the wisdom of Solomon'* (to the Pharisees)		
13:14f, parr.	Isa 6:9f, (to the disciples)		(FQ?)[15]
3:17	*'many prophets and righteous people longed to see what you see'* (to the disciples)		
13:35			Ps 78:2 (FQ)
15:3f. par.	Exod 20:12, 21:17, Deut 5:16 (counterargument to Pharisees)		
15:7–9 par.	Isa 29:13 (counterargument to Pharisees)		
16:4	*'the sign of Jonah'* (cf. 12:39)		
16:14 parr.		'. . . but others Elijah, . . . Jeremiah or one of the prophets' (the disciples)	
17:3	representatives of **Law an Prophets** (Moses and Elijah)		
17:17f. par.	*'Elijah is indeed coming and will restore all things; but I tell you that Elijah has already come . . .'*		
18:16	Deut 19:15 [not formal quotation]		
19:4 par.	Gen 1:27 (to Pharisees on divorce)		
19:5 par.	Gen 2:24 (to Pharisees on divorce)		
19:5 par.	Gen 5:2 (to Pharisees on divorce)		

19:7		Deut 24:1 (Pharisees on divorce)	
19:8	*'Moses allowed you to divorce your wives, but from the beginning it was not so.'*		
19:18f.	Exod 20:12–16 (to rich man)		
19:19 parr.	Lev 19:18 (to rich man)		
19:28	*'twelve tribes of Israel'*		
21:2 (FQ)			Zech 9:9
21:9 parr.		Ps 18:25f. (the following crowd)	
21:13 parr.	Isa 56:7 (to the sellers and money-changers in the Temple)		
21:16	Ps 8:3 (to the High priests and the scribes in the Temple)		
21:22	*Isa 5:1–2* (to the High priests and Pharisees)		
21:4 parr.	Ps 118:22f. (to the High priests and Pharisees)		
22:24 parr.		Deut 25:5; Gen 25:5 (Sadducees on Lev 22:32 parr. virate marriage)	
22:32 parr.	Exod 3:6 (to the Sadducee)		
22:37 parr.	Deut 6:5 (to the Pharisees)		
22:39 parr.	Lev 19:18 (to the Pharisees)		
22:40 par.	'On these two commandments hang *all the **law and the prophets'*** (cf. 22:38)		
22:43f.	Ps 110:1 (Jesus questions the Pharisees)		
23:2	*'Seat of Moses'*		

23:23	*'tithes vs. the weightier matters of the law'*		
23:29–31	*'killing of the prophets'*		
23:35 *par.*	*'all the righteous blood shed on earth, from the blood of righteous Abel to the blood of Zechariah son of Barachiah'* (2 Chron 24:20f.)		
23:38	Ps 69:26, Jer 22:5 [no formal quotation}		
23:39 par.	Ps 118:25f. (to Pharisees and Jerusalemites		
24:15 parr.	'the desolating sacrilege as was spoken of by the prophet Daniel' (Dan 9:27, 11:31)		
24:29 par.	Isa 13:10, 34:4 [no formal quotation]		
24:30 parr.	Dan 7:13 [no formal quotation]		
24:37–39 *par.*	*'the days of Noah'*		
26:24	*'The Son of Man goes as it is written of him . . .'* (???)		
26:28 *parr.*	*'blood of the covenant'* (Exod 24:8)		
26:30 *par.*	*'When they had sung the Hallel . . .'* (Pss 113–118)		
26:31 par.	Zech 13:7 (to his disciples)		
26:54	*'But how then would the Scriptures be fulfilled, which say it must happen in this way?'* (to Peter)		
26:56	*'But all this has taken place, so that the Scriptures of the prophets may be fulfilled'* (to those who arrested him)		
26:64 parr.	Ps 110:1, Dan 7:3 (to the high priest and his council)		

Matt 27:9f.			Zech 11:12f.; Jer 32:9 (FQ)
27:46 parr.	Ps 22:1 (the prayer on the cross)		

Scanning the list quickly it became apparent that besides Jesus there is only a very limited number of other people who quote Scripture: John the Baptist (3:3) is the only individual (quoting Isaiah), and there is one quote each attributed to the high priests and scribes (2:5f., quoting Micah) and the Sadducees (quoting Deuteronomy); the crowds following Jesus shout verses from Psalm 118 (21:9); and finally the disciples show some 'theological' knowledge in what they have learnt from the scribes in 17:10 (cf. 16:14). Quite astonishing is the fact that the Pharisees (unlike the Sadducees) are never presented as quoting Scripture. Instead they are regularly challenged to read and to learn what Scripture really says (9:13; 12:3–5; 19:4; 21:42; 22:43,45; 23:23; see also 3:9; 21:16). The knowledge of the Pharisees is reduced to 'what is allowed' (12:2,10; 15:6; 19:3; 22:17), and although their allegations are often related to a Torah commandment (e.g. in 19:7) the evangelist takes utter care never to present the Pharisaic allegations against Jesus or the disciples by way of them quoting Scripture against Jesus. Instead he ascribes the points they brought forward as merely belonging to the 'traditions of the elders', which are not accepted as faithful development of God's commandments (15:2–6). The only other expert in Scripture that Matthew allows for is the devil in the temptation of Jesus (4:6), a narrative that presents an interesting duel between these two heavenly beings. But overwhelmingly it is Jesus who uses Scripture, and he does so in three ways:[16]

1 Jesus as teacher: the confident and proficient use of scripture in answering questions and offering a defence

Only on *two* occasions – and this is actually rather astonishing – does Jesus begin with a scriptural verse to make a point. He does so in the antitheses (Matt. 5:21–48) and once in the only example where Jesus asks the Pharisees a question, addressing their understanding of Psalm 110:1 (Matt. 22:41–5). His saying about John the

Baptist in Matthew 11:10 (quoting Mal. 3:1) might be added here as well.

Generally, Jesus is described by Matthew to be rather proficient in the use of Scripture in arguments with Pharisees and scribes, and the references he quotes (often in his defence) reveal a wide, and in some cases detailed, knowledge. It is interesting to see that in halakic discussions (= discussion about the right understanding and application of the Jewish law) with the scribes or Pharisees, Jesus' use of Scripture is almost always a *reaction* to a request from his interlocutors (such as Matt. 9:11–13). The only case where Jesus addresses legal matters on his own initiative is in the antitheses of the Sermon on the Mount, and these are clearly not meant as an invitation to a halakic debate, even if parts of contemporary Matthean scholarship interpret them in exactly this way.[17] This is quite remarkable and important for the ongoing debate about Jesus' stance towards the Torah. When questioned he is able to give advice and apply the law, but this is not his own way of teaching and, one might add, not the issue he is concerned with predominantly as the following examples show:

- The rich young man enquiring about how to inherit eternal life is told to obey the commandments (Matt. 19:16–22 parr. Mark 10:17–22, Luke 18:18–23). Yet, to know the Ten Commandments (Jesus quotes only the 'ethical' commandments, starting with 'You shall not murder') was perhaps rather basic and it was clearly not what the man expected to hear, nor was it all that Jesus had to say about his question. The final words addressed to him carry all the weight: 'Come, follow me.'[18]

  In the case of the healed leper (Matt. 8:4), whom Jesus sent to offer sacrifices according to the command of Moses, he demonstrates his awareness of the legislation in Leviticus 13, though to what extent cannot be deduced from this verse.

The two examples given do not, however, represent the typical way that Jesus used and applied Scripture. The people who experienced both Jesus and the scribes as their teachers were quite right when they compared the two and concluded that Jesus did not teach like one of the scribes (Matt. 7:29; cf. John 7:46).

The fact that scribes, Pharisees and Sadducees engaged Jesus in scholarly disputes about matters of halakah, theological issues, and the right understanding/interpretation of Scripture shows that they regarded him as somebody worth questioning and engaging in serious debate; in these encounters they regularly address him as 'teacher' or 'Rabbi'.[19] It is not very likely that this form of address was an invention of the later church, but rather the preservation of the Aramaic 'Rabbi' (and 'Rabbuni'), in particular, presents a strong argument that these titles reflect actual usage, because they differ from those used for Jesus after his resurrection appearances. For the followers of Jesus his sonship became the key feature after his death and resurrection, and he ceased to be called 'teacher' or 'rabbi'.[20] Outside of the gospels he is nowhere designated as teacher in the NT, and the development of the gospel tradition points in the same direction:

- Mark's use of the title is not yet differentiated: Jesus refers once to himself as διδάσκαλος (14:14) and is regularly addressed as διδάσκαλος by his disciples (4:38; 9:38; 10:35; 13:1) and other people as well (5:35; 9:17; 10:17,20; 12:14,19,32); 'rabbi' is used solely as a form of address by individual disciples (9:5; 11:21 = Peter; 14:45 = Judas); 'rabbuni' is only used once, by Bartimaeus (10:51).

  Matthew reflects a more advanced use of the title. The disciples' use of 'rabbi' is acknowledged and legitimized by Jesus himself (23:8, where the titles 'rabbi' and διδάσκαλος are used interchangeably; cf. also 10:24f.; 26:18), but the salutation διδάσκαλος is used throughout the gospel only by those outside Jesus' inner circle (8:19; 9:11; 12:38; 17:24; 19:16; 22:16,24,36). The Markan usage finds no continuation here.

  Luke is less consistent and allows the title 'teacher' to be used by a wider range of people (2:46 = the teachers in the temple; 3:12 = address to John the Baptist) but also reflects features of Mark's and Matthew's usage as a self-reference by Jesus (22:11 parr. Mark 14:14; Matt. 26:18, cf. also Luke 6:40 the indirect self-reference par. Matt 10:24f.); mostly, however, it is used as a salutation by outsiders (7:40; 8:49; 9:38; 10:25; 11:45; 12:13; 18:18; 19:39; 20:21,28,39) and only rarely by the disciples (21:7). Luke employs, in addition to διδάσκαλος, also the title ἐπιστάτης but rather in the sense of 'lord' and not as teacher: Mainly the disciples refer to Jesus in this way (5:5; 8:24,45; 9:33,49) and it is used only once by the lepers calling to Jesus for help (17:13).

In John's Gospel, 'rabbi' is more prominent than in the Synoptics. The future disciples address Jesus as 'rabbi', and for the sake of the reader it is said that this translates as 'teacher' (1:38; see also 3:2 of Nicodemus, where again 'rabbi' and διδάσκαλος are used interchangeably; 11:28 Mary in her remark to Martha calls Jesus διδάσκαλος; 20:16 Mary Magdalena: 'rabbuni' = διδάσκαλε; in 3:10 Nicodemus is once addressed by Jesus as 'teacher of Israel'. The only address of Jesus using διδάσκαλε by an outsider is in 8:4, which is not part of the original gospel. Similar to Matt. 23:8, in John 13:13f. Jesus confirms the appropriateness of calling him rabbi/teacher (and lord).

It is therefore safe to conclude that for those who saw his ministry from an outsider's perspective, teaching on verses and topics taken from Scripture and with reference to Scripture was clearly a key element of Jesus' public activity. The astonishment expressed in Acts 4:13 about the apostles Peter and John's ability as public speakers despite being 'uneducated and ordinary men' (ἄνθρωποι ἀγράμματοί εἰσιν καὶ ἰδιῶται) was never brought forward in relation to Jesus. Closest in this respect comes John 7:15, the reaction of the Jews in Jerusalem, who were wondering among themselves, 'How does this man have such learning, when he has never been taught?'[21]

2 *Jesus' familiarity with biblical stories*

It would be much too narrow to focus solely on the explicitly marked quotations in the sayings of Jesus to understand the role of Scripture for Jesus' teaching. That Jesus is the kind of person who thinks and speaks biblically can be seen in the way Jesus refers to biblical stories in a more general way, and in the way he uses biblical terminology throughout his teaching. He is repeatedly described by Matthew as a person deeply shaped by a scriptural mindset, who has the word of God as daily bread. Jesus himself refers indirectly to this when he repels Satan's first attempt to make him use his powers for the sake of his own glory with the words: 'It is written, One does not live by bread alone, but by every word that comes from the mouth of God.'[22] Moreover, Jesus also presumes that his audience is familiar with such biblical narratives as the flight of David from Saul, the visit of the queen of the south to Solomon, or the story of Jonah. Jesus also presupposes (or at least discloses) a certain amount of biblically deduced knowledge when he talks about the eschatological meal with Abraham, Isaac and Jacob (Matt. 8:11), which is not actually a biblical tradition but one derived from it. This second type of speaking biblically and using biblically inspired examples is more creative than mere quotation because it includes the ability to apply the right story at the right moment, or to illuminate an occurrence with a story and thereby give it a meaning.

3 Jesus' claim of understanding the biblical 'master story' (salvation history)

The third aspect of Jesus' approach to Scripture shows that he is also oriented towards the 'big story' and the overarching themes, which assumes a cohesion between, and a common trajectory of, the individual stories and biblical quotations. 'Salvation history' is, despite the many who doubt it, still the best available conceptual term to encapsulate this unifying perspective on the pluriform biblical witnesses (see note 3 above). Jesus is presented by Matthew as the kind of teacher who could explain the overarching correlations within Scripture and how the individual elements fit together within a larger story. He is the one with the key to unlock the underlying meaning in the biblical narratives, which the others know, to be sure, but do not understand in terms of their interrelatedness. This means that one needs to understand the sending of Jesus, and therefore also Jesus' dealing with Scripture, as part of the larger history of God's involvement in the reality of this world. Jesus had more important things to discuss than halakic (legal) details derived from the Torah and of right behaviour. Jesus was, with regard to his application and interpretation of Scripture, not in the first place a teacher of morals and ethics, and not – or at least not primarily – a wisdom teacher. Nor was he an apocalyptic prophet. Rather, he dares to speak about the *overall meaning* of all these traditions. I hold this third type of scriptural knowledge to be the most important one, because it requires more than just pure knowledge of Scripture. It requires true understanding; and it requires a raised vantage point, from which one is able to gain an overview of the development of God's history with his people and, beyond this, with the whole of creation. If we want to gauge and appreciate fully the level of scriptural conversance of a specific person, it is helpful to differentiate between the knowing of some isolated quotations from Scripture (which a lot of people in the time of Jesus presumably had) and a systemic knowledge of Scripture. The latter is an understanding of Scripture that allows one to structure, to conceptualize and to use Scripture in a creative way by applying it to a current situation in such a way that it can evince God's involvement in it.

Matthew 11:7–15 as a Case Study

In the following I want to discuss in more detail the passage where Jesus talks about the role of John the Baptist (Matt. 11:7–15 par. Luke 7:24–8; 16:16), as it contains all three uses of Scripture described above. It is, in fact, a key passage in Matthew's Gospel, although commentators often overlook its hermeneutical significance. The three types of scriptural knowledge and application can be seen here as follows.

First, Jesus asks the audience about their understanding of John as a prophet, and it is clear from the context that he meant as a prophet like those mentioned in Scripture. Jesus presupposes that his audience looks at new religious experiences through biblical lenses. If they encounter something 'new', they compare it with precedents and parallels from Scripture and form their judgement based on this comparison. To simplify life by integrating new experiences in established categories is, as can be seen here, not actually a new phenomenon. We do it all the time and it is actually a necessity, because we have to make judgements based on prior knowledge and experience.[23] Jesus is shown to be aware of the people's way of reading the world through biblical lenses and it is safe to assume that Jesus had a similar approach to the world around him. Further examples of this way of gaining understanding by comparing current experiences with biblical examples are:

- Mark 8:27f. parr. Luke 9:18f.; Matthew 16:13–15: Jesus expects that the people would compare him with other 'biblical' figures in the past (or present, as in the case of John the Baptist, who modelled himself with his clothing as the Elijah to come).

  Mark 2:12 par. Luke 5:26; Matthew 9:33: Matthew relocates this verdict of the people to the end of his first miracle collection (see also Matt. 7:28f.; John 7:46 the comparison of Jesus with the scribes); Jesus' healing of the paralytic (and his other miracles) as well as elements of his preaching are regarded by his audience as going beyond anything that has happened so far 'in Israel' or has been taught by the scribes. Both points of comparison, Israel and the scribes, are based on the audience's scriptural experience and knowledge (even if one has to allow that the scribes did not only teach Scripture; yet from all we know about Jewish writing and teaching it is safe to assume that all the content of the scribes' teaching was derived in one way or another from Scripture).

The second type of scriptural proficiency can be seen in how Jesus continues to compare John with the biblical prophets. He affirms the popular understanding of John as a prophet, but then comments, 'He was more than a prophet' (καὶ περισσότερον προφήτου Matt. 11:9 = Luke 7:26). Here he is no longer merely confirming what the people think about John, but makes a further statement about John's relation to the scriptural tradition. It is only a very short and somehow unremarkable sentence, but one that carries a lot of weight. Jesus takes the role of an interpreter who is able to survey the whole list of prophets, and make judgements about a contemporary individual and his relation to the scriptural tradition. Saying that John is not just one of the prophets but more than a prophet attributes to Jesus an elevated position such that he can see things in a wider perspective than his audience. The question one might ask here is: What does he mean by 'more than a prophet'? Reading this saying in line with Matthew

13:16f. par. Luke 10:23f., where Jesus blesses his disciples because they hear and see what the prophets (and righteous ones [Matt.] / kings [Luke]) longed for, namely to see the fulfilment of what they promised in God's name, one can assume that 'more than a prophet' points to the fact that the one who inaugurates the age of fulfilment has more weight than those who 'only' announce God's future acts.

The next part of Jesus' evaluation of John adduces a quotation from Scripture in support of the Baptist being 'more than a prophet'. Jesus introduces the quotation with a disclosure of how the following scriptural verse needs to be understood: 'He is (the one) about whom it is written' (Matt. 11:10 = Luke 7:27). What follows is not a simple quote, however, but a combination of at least two verses: ἰδοὺ ἐγὼ ἀποστέλλω τὸν ἄγγελόν μου πρὸ προσώπου σου, ὃς κατασκευάσει τὴν ὁδόν σου ἔμπροσθέν σου.[24] The first part, 'Behold I send my messenger before you', is taken from Malachi 3:1 (but actually it is only the first part of the first line of this verse, 1aa), which itself is an inner-scriptural reference to Exodus 23:20 and actually a clarification of it. In Exodus 23:20 the messenger sent ahead of Israel to prepare their conquest of the land is different from God himself but so close that the two are almost conflated into one.[25] In Malachi, however, the messenger is more clearly differentiated from God. The second half of Jesus' word about John, 'he will prepare the way before you', is not actually a direct quote but a free adaptation of Isaiah 40:3 (perhaps influenced by Isa. 26:7).[26] Isaiah 40:3 was already used to characterize John's ministry at the beginning of the gospel, in Matthew 3:3 par. Luke 3:4–6 (quoting Isa. 40:3f. in full), whereby both Matthew and Luke make a clear reference to 'Isaiah, the prophet' as the origin of this saying (Matt. 3:2 par. Luke 3:4). Mark however starts his gospel with this conflation of Malachi 3:1 / Exodus 23:20 and Isaiah 40:3 by introducing the combined quote as 'written in Isaiah, the prophet'.[27]

What can we glean about Jesus and Scripture from such relatively complex evidence? No answer can be given without looking at the question *who is actually responsible* for providing the quotes from Scripture? That is, who is the expert in Scripture – Jesus, or the evangelist, or the tradition-maker between the two? The problem is clearly visible in our passage, for it does not change anything if one removes the biblical quote, which is why it is often attributed to another layer of the tradition and not to Jesus:[28] '(v. 9) What then did you go out to see? A prophet? Yes, I tell you, and more than a prophet. (v. 11) Truly I tell you, among those born of women no one has arisen greater than John the Baptist; yet the least in the kingdom of heaven is greater than he.'

A further argument against Jesus being the one who is responsible for the quote is the already mentioned fact that in Mark's Gospel the full quote is used at the beginning of his gospel, where the 'author' of the quote seems to be very clearly the evangelist and not Jesus. Matthew and Luke follow the same pattern when they describe the initial ministry of John with the second part of Mark's introductory quote (Mark 1:3 = Matt. 3:3 par. Luke 3:4), and one understands why scholars assume that later they inserted the remaining first part of the same Markan quote in their second reference to John's ministry (Mark 1:2 = Matt. 11:10 par. Luke 7:27). By doing this they even resolved the mistake of Mark in attributing the combined quotation to Isaiah, who is actually only the source of the second part. This would then mean that the evangelists (or their sources) were the true biblical experts, who are able to fit Jesus' life and teaching into a scriptural frame. Consequently, the biblical quotations in the mouth of Jesus do not tell us much if anything about Jesus' own use and understanding of Scripture.

This is the key issue in the debate about Jesus and Scripture, although 'debate' almost sounds like an exaggeration, as there is hardly any discussion of the topic. It falls somehow between Jesus research and gospel research. And this means that gospel scholars are content with describing the use of Scripture in Matthew, Mark, Luke and John, without grappling with the historical Jesus quest, while historical Jesus scholars are remarkably silent about the matter. Steve Moyise, who has done some very good recent work on this topic, confirms this observation when he writes: 'Not surprisingly, the majority of studies in this field [i.e. Jesus and Scripture][29] have been redactional studies of how the gospel writers used scripture.' Not many books on Jesus include a chapter on Jesus and Scripture and how Scripture might have shaped Jesus' ministry,[30] and they deal even less with the question of Jesus' education. Rick T. France made a point about this over forty years ago in the introduction to his *Jesus and the Old Testa-*

ment, which is still true today despite the changes brought about in the study of Jesus and his Jewishness by the third questers: 'The reason is not far to seek. The prevalent attitude to the words of Jesus recorded in the Gospels is one of scepticism as to their dominical origin. The quotations of the OT attributed to him are tacitly, and sometimes explicitly, regarded as reflecting the scriptural interpretation not of Jesus himself, but of the churches in which the Gospels emerged.'[31] A good example that even evangelical scholars adopt this pattern is the massive commentary of Greg Beale and Don Carson.[32] In this impressive volume, to which mainly conservative evangelical scholars contributed, there is no chapter dedicated to the use of Scripture by Jesus. That the extensive use of Scripture in the NT and especially in the gospels needs to be understood as a consequence of Jesus' particular use of Scripture seems to be so obvious that it is not worth mentioning at all. The authors of the individual sections in this commentary clearly presuppose that the majority of quotations attributed to Jesus in the gospels were actually said and used by him.[33] But in the introduction to the sections on the individual gospels, the fact that Jesus explained Scripture to make his mission understandable is not mentioned even once.[34] That this is not a casual omission seems clear from Beale's most recent book, *Handbook on the New Testament Use of the Old*.[35] It contains a rather short chapter on 'Hermeneutical and Theological Presuppositions of the New Testament Writers' (pp. 95–102). Here he mentions five points, and all five are valid and important. But he says nothing about what Jesus did and said to lay the foundation for this new way of reading Scripture. It clearly seems that there is some more work to do on this topic.

What is rarely explored with regard to the scriptural quotations in the gospels, which are *now* within the editorial parts and form the commentary of the evangelist, is the possibility that the evangelists or their sources actually *learned something from Jesus' own handling of Scripture.* We may have in the gospels not so much the result of the creative exegesis of unknown source compilers but a reflection of the influence of Jesus as teacher of Scripture. Looking back at the example just discussed, it is regularly assumed that the evangelist Mark is responsible for the quotation at the beginning of his gospel, which is then split up by Matthew and Luke into two. The other at least theoretical possibility is that Jesus (as in Matt. 11:10 par. Luke 7:27) used the saying of Malachi for John, and perhaps used also Isaiah 40:3 (and 26:7) to explain the role of the baptizer in relation to his own mission. The evangelist or his sources could then have turned Jesus' scriptural explanation of his mission from a transcript (what Jesus actually said) to a metascript that allows a conceptualization of Jesus' teaching within a wider frame. 'The beginning of the gospel of Jesus Christ' – as Mark opens his gospel, is then not primarily an objective genitive (the beginning of the gospel *about* Jesus) but a subjective one:[36] This is how Jesus starts the gospel message: 'As it is written in Isaiah the prophet: "Behold I send my messenger before you"' and by doing this introduces *himself* as the one about whom the unidentified 'voice in the wilderness' has spoken, which the prophet Isaiah has heard. By combining this saying with Malachi 3:1, Jesus could then be seen as revealing his divine sending in a veiled way. This would mean differentiating between four voices in these opening verses: v. 1 is the evangelist's opening comment (first voice) and this introduces vv. 2 and 3 as a saying of Jesus (second voice). This saying presents a citation from Isaiah (third voice), who quotes an unspecified 'voice' (fourth voice, speaking in the first person) addressing an undefined 'you' whose arrival will be prepared for by a messenger. Jesus, if we allow him tentatively to be the speaker of vv. 2 and 3, applies these words about God's coming to his own mission by subtly changing the wording, which turns the announcement of God's coming into a direct divine address regarding his own sending.[37] The 'I' who sends, and the 'you' who is sent and introduced by the 'voice in the wilderness', are then presented as the promise of the divine Father ('I') to his 'beloved son' ('you'; see Mark 1:11). The father promises the son that he will send ahead of him a messenger, who will prepare the way. The voice *from heaven* (φωνὴ ἐγένετο ἐκ τῶν οὐρανῶν) after the baptism of Jesus and the voice in the *wilderness* (φωνὴ βοῶντος ἐν τῇ ἐρήμῳ), that is John the Baptist, both prepare the way for the mission of Jesus. The evangelist would then begin his narrative only in 1:4.

I concede that such a reading of the opening of Mark's Gospel sounds strange initially. But is this strangeness not partly due to the fact that we distinguish Jesus' use of Scripture from that of the evangelists? And have we really explored sufficiently the possibility that the evangelists (or the persons whose knowledge of Jesus is brought together in the gospels) actually learnt something from Jesus? Otherwise on the assumption that Jesus' teaching was scripturally something of a low-calorie variety, one needs to explain *where* the subsequent number of scriptural references does come from and *why* they were seen as necessary in the first place. If Jesus was able to fulfil his mission without appealing to Scripture (which is inherently difficult to imagine), why do the earliest confessional statements insist that everything happened 'according to Scriptures' (cf. the twice-used κατὰ τὰς γραφάς in 1 Cor. 15:3f.)? And if the 'class' to which Jesus belonged and among which he found his followers was overwhelmingly illiterate, where does the scribal knowledge and sophistication come from that is displayed throughout the gospel tradition?[38] Why do the Galilean 'peasants'[39] who were used to listening to short and pithy sayings (so Burton L. Mack and others) suddenly turn to a more sophisticated scriptural argumentation? Who convinced them that to follow Jesus meant also to learn and study Scripture? Should we assume that the anonymous tradents behind the Q source were able to convert illiterate peasants into eager listeners of Scripture? Or was it the anonymous compilers of the sources that were used by the (anonymous) evangelists? Already C.H. Dodd enquired intriguingly after 'the forgotten geniuses', who must be assumed to lurk 'in the shadows of those first twenty years of Church history about which we are so scantily informed', if we want to explain how the scripturally unconnected message of Jesus resurfaced all of a sudden as fulfilment of Scripture. Instead of looking for such anonymous individuals, Dodd reminds his readers of the one genius the sources themselves present:

> But the New Testament itself avers that it was Jesus Christ Himself who first directed the minds of His followers to certain parts of the scriptures as those in which they might find illumination upon the meaning of His mission and destiny. That He formally set before them a comprehensive scheme of biblical interpretation, after the manner of Lk. xxiv.25-27, 44-45, we may well hesitate to believe; but I can see no reasonable ground for rejecting the statements of the Gospels that (for example) He pointed to Psalm cx as a better guide to the truth

> about His mission and destiny than the popular beliefs about the Son of David, or that He made that connection of the 'Lord' at God's right hand with the Son of Man in Daniel which proved so momentous for Christian thought; or that He associated with the Son of Man language which had been used of the Servant of the Lord, and employed it to hint at the meaning, and the issue, of His own approaching death. To account for the beginning of this most original and fruitful process of rethinking the Old Testament we found need to postulate a creative mind. The Gospels offer us one. Are we compelled to reject the offer?[40]

Jesus as Lord of Scripture

Dodd's conclusion, made in the form of a question, has been left unanswered. His book appeared when redaction history was on the rise and the focus shifted from Jesus to the evangelists and their contribution to our knowledge about Jesus. The third quest, with its renewed interest in the historical Jesus notwithstanding, displays a remarkable lack of interest in the question of Jesus and Scripture, and the more recent discussion about the literacy (or rather illiteracy) of Jesus further discourages any attempts to search for Jesus' own engagement with Scripture.[41] The provocatively suggestive question of Dodd, however, is still hanging in the air. Shall we really continue 'to reject the offer' of the evidence available in the gospels? Greg Beale in his already mentioned *Handbook* names as one of the presuppositions of the NT writers that 'History is unified by a wise and sovereign plan so that the earlier parts are designated to correspond and point to the later parts.' In support of this he references Matthew 5:17; 11:13; 13:16f.[42] But the adduced verses are all (admittedly disputed) sayings of Jesus, which preserve, according to my understanding, first and foremost the systemic approach taken by Jesus.[43] Hence Jesus is *remembered* in his handling of Scripture as making sweeping summarizing statements about its ultimate meaning, which can be grouped in two ways: matter-of-fact sayings, and, even more presumptive, self-referential sayings. To the first category I would assign the following.

Group 1: Matter-of-fact sayings

Matthew 7:12 'In everything do to others as you would have them do to you; for this is the law and the prophets.'

Matthew 11:13f. 'For all the prophets and the law prophesied until John came; and if you are willing to accept it, he is Elijah who is to come.' Even stronger is the parallel to this saying in Luke 16:16: 'The law and the prophets were in effect until John came; since then the good news of the kingdom of God is proclaimed.'

Matthew 13:16f. 'But blessed are your eyes, for they see, and your ears, for they hear. Truly I tell you, many prophets and righteous people longed to see what you see, but did not see it, and to hear what you hear, but did not hear it.'

Matthew 19:7–9: The Pharisees asked Jesus, 'Why then did Moses command us to give a certificate of dismissal and to divorce her?' And Jesus answered: 'It was because you were so hard-hearted that Moses allowed you to divorce your wives, but from the beginning it was not so. And I say to you, whoever divorces his wife, except for unchastity, and marries another commits adultery.' Jesus claims to know the motivations of Moses and what was intended 'from the beginning', that is when God first created man and woman.

Matthew 22:34–40, when Jesus is asked by a scribe about 'which commandment in the law is the greatest?', he is not content with quoting the two that he thinks are the greatest, but he adds (v. 40): 'On these two commandments hang all the law and the prophets.'

Matthew 23:23f. 'Woe to you, scribes and Pharisees, hypocrites! For you tithe the mint, dill, and cummin, and have neglected the weightier matters of the law: justice and mercy and faith. It is these you ought to have practiced without neglecting the others.'

The value of this list, in my eyes, is not diminished by the fact that there are parallels to such sayings in the Jewish tradition. If one carefully compares these parallels (which cannot be done here), it becomes evident that they contain some of the same elements, but very rarely – if at all – the boldness with which Jesus makes such statements. This is confirmed by the second group, which brings the 'ego' of Jesus into even stronger focus.

Group 2: Self-referential sayings

In Matthew 13:14–17 (par. Luke 10:23f.) Jesus declares a word from the prophet Isaiah as fulfilled in his teaching in parables, and he blesses the disciples because they are able to see and to hear what the righteous and prophets of old longed to see and to hear. This means nothing less than that he presents himself as the fulfilment of their eschatological hopes. His interrogation about the meaning of Psalm 110:1 can be mentioned here as well. In Jesus' interpretation, David heard God talking to Jesus and offering him the place at his right-hand side (Mark 12:35–7 parr. Matt 22:41–6; Luke 20:41–4). But it is not just that Jesus presumes to know how the prophets and saints from old understood Scripture as pointing towards him. No, he goes even further and claims that he himself is behind the prophetic voices that were heard throughout Israel's history:

> Matt 23:37 'Jerusalem, Jerusalem, the city that kills the prophets and stones those who are sent to it! How often have I desired to gather your children together as a hen gathers her brood under her wings, and you were not willing!'

Jesus, being in Jerusalem, expects to suffer the same fate as the biblical prophets and the other messengers sent to her. But Jesus is not just one more in the line of those 'sent', but he claims to be also the 'I' that is behind those before him. 'I desired' points towards God, as Jerusalem is his city (see Matt. 5:35), but it is Jesus who takes God's role and voice! God sent the prophets, and Jesus claims for himself what God did.[44] The same intimacy and shared knowledge between the Father and the Son is also expressed in the saying Matthew 11:25–7 par. Luke 10:21f., the most 'Johannine' verses in Matthew (see also Matt. 10:32f.). And that is not all: Jesus not only knows the true sense of Scripture, and is the voice behind Scripture, but he is also the ultimate fulfilment of Scripture (5:17):

'Do not think that I have come to abolish the law or the prophets; I have come not to abolish but to fulfil.'

And from now on – one is even tempted to say not surprisingly – it is his words and how people relate to them that determine eschatological fate (7:24–7). The Sermon on the Mount finishes with the parable of the two houses: the one built on rock, the other on sand. The house that stands is built by the one 'who hears these *words of mine* and acts on them'.[45]

It is interesting to evaluate the teaching of Jesus from this perspective offered by his use of Scripture. He preaches about God, the spirit of God, but also about himself, then about Israel and the nations, times past, present and future in relation to God's plan, and, as key to all of this, the kingdom of God as coming, being near, as a hope or as a threat; how to enter, how to stay in it and what to yearn for. Throughout this teaching a perspective is taken of the one who knows: Jesus in his handling of Scripture, as well as in most parts of his teaching, teaches from a divine perspective.

A text from John's Gospel, which concludes a long debate about Abraham, brings the whole discussion to a head. If one reads the passage John 8:48–58 in the light of the synoptic material presented here, the gap between John and the Synoptics looks less insurmountable than is assumed:

> The Jews answered him, 'Are we not right in saying that you are a Samaritan and have a demon?' Jesus answered, 'I do not have a demon; but I honor my Father, and you dishonor me. Yet I do not seek my own glory; there is one who seeks it and he is the judge. Very truly, I tell you, whoever keeps my word will never see death.' The Jews said to him, 'Now we know that you have a demon. Abraham died, and so did the prophets; yet you say, 'Whoever keeps my word will never taste death.' Are you greater than our father Abraham, who died? The prophets also died. Who do you claim to be?' Jesus answered, 'If I glorify myself, my glory is nothing. It is my Father who glorifies me, he of whom you say, 'He is our God,' though you do not know him. But I know him; if I would say that I do not know him, I would be a liar like you. But I do know him and I keep his word. Your ancestor Abraham rejoiced that he would see my day; he saw it and was glad.' Then the Jews said to him, 'You are not yet fifty years old, and have

you seen Abraham?' Jesus said to them, 'Very truly, I tell you, before Abraham was, I am.'

In all the above references, Jesus is Lord over Scripture. He knows what are the greatest commandments in the law, he knows about the motivations of Moses when he allowed divorce for the Israelites, and he also knows that God intended it differently from the beginning. He can say about himself that he came to fulfil the Torah and prophets, and he knows that the Golden Rule comprises both of them fully; he knows that with the coming of John the Baptist, whom he can identify with the promised Elijah from the book of Malachi, the kingdom of God starts, and somehow that this also ends the time of the law and prophets. In the transfiguration story he even has a consultation with Moses and Elijah as the representatives of the law and prophets, and he is 'on good terms' with the prophets of old. If we allow for a moment the full weight of these claims, we can understand why some of his Jewish hearers were totally outraged by them. How can he, not even fifty years old, claim to know what Abraham had thought and felt about him? And we might feel compelled to ask what stands at the beginning of this extraordinary sovereignty in the handling of Scripture.

Where Did All This Knowledge Come From? The Education and Training of Jesus

The family

The most natural place to start a search for evidence of Jesus' education, especially his learning in the Scriptures, would be with his family. This is, most probably, where the first encounter with scriptural content would have taken place. The Torah obliges parents to tell their children about what God has done for his people and to teach them the commandments (Deut. 6:7,20–5). We should not assume that all Jewish families did this just because they were Jewish, although the Jewish historian Josephus wanted his readers to believe that every child could recite the most important things from the Torah without any difficulty.[46] Josephus' family background was the priestly aristocracy in Jerusalem – so we can assume that he was more privileged in this respect and spent his youth among other ambitious young priests and aristocrats who could afford formal teaching. But Jesus? The son of a carpenter from Nazareth in Galilee? Luke 2:40–51, the story of the twelve-year-old Jesus in the temple in the midst of teachers is all we have in the NT that gives us any kind of hint about the formal education of Jesus. All the rest has to be deduced from what we know about the 'adult' Jesus. And here the most important element is the depiction of Jesus in the gospels as someone who is able to read, and who is familiar with the biblical and religious traditions of his people.[47] With regard to Jesus' literacy, a hot debate has gathered momentum in the last years, mainly focusing on the question of whether Jesus could read (and write), which is obviously an important prerequisite for gaining a deeper scriptural knowledge. But here, as always within Jesus research, the situation is a bit like that in a supermarket, where more or less everything is on offer: a low-calorie yogurt next to a full-fat one. One can follow scholars like Rainer Riesner, Alan Millard or Paul Foster, to name just a few, who allow the possibility that Jesus had a relatively high level of literacy; or you can go to the other extreme, where Jesus, mainly because he is taken to be a member of the so-called peasant class, is thought to be illiterate because peasants had neither the time nor the money to spend on the education of their children. And there is of course a position somewhere between these extremes that attributes to Jesus the limited literacy of a craftsman, who might be able to make some notes and jottings and could read enough for maintaining his business, but is fairly limited the moment he is outside of his area of expertise.[48] I think such generalizations are highly unhelpful because they do not allow for individual developments within a single family, for example. What is true for a majority is not necessarily true for the individual, and history is often made exactly by those who do not follow the 'normal' pattern. Jesus became a historic figure because he was the exception and not like you and me.[49] But that does not mean, of course, that he was an outsider or an exception in every respect. Hence, when we return to the question of the formative influence of his family, the first thing one can deduce from his custom as an adult of regularly attending the synagogue on Shabbat is the likelihood that he became accustomed to this practice in his family. So we have a family (for his siblings see John 7:2–10), who regularly attended the synagogue and also went regularly to the pilgrimage festivals in Jerusalem, which was, from all we know, a widespread attitude in Galilee and Judea. In other words, we can presume a religiously active family.

If one takes a maximalist view,[50] and also allows for some 'creative history', there is even more to say about the religious profile of Jesus' family. Take the names of his brothers: *James*, that is Jacob, the father of the twelve sons, who is also called Israel; *Jude*, that is the tribal ancestor of the Davidic line; *Simon* who is another son of Jacob, the one who avenged the rape of his sister Dina, or the Hasmonean Simon, a famous fighter, perhaps even more famous in the time of Jesus than his biblical namesake; and then *Joses* or Joseph, the fourth brother of Jesus, which is another biblical name that represents a special calling: Joseph prepared a place in Egypt for the clan of Jacob to survive and to become a people. These are rather telling names, and from their use for Jesus' brothers it is possible to deduce among Jesus immediate family an Israel-centred perspective and perhaps a certain militant zealous messianism. This may then reveal much about the family of Jesus. And what about the related priestly family of John the Baptist? The messianic hymns in Luke's Gospel (two of them attributed to members of this extended family) might reflect the spiritual milieu and the kind of songs and prayers that were used in the private or inner-group worship of these families.[51]

There is even more to say, and although I am not sure how far we can press this, it shows at least how the family of Jesus could be imagined by others very early on. We have two letters in the NT that are attributed to two of Jesus' brothers, James and Jude. Both letters display a good knowledge of Greek and at the same time a certain tone absent in other NT writings: Both letters employ strongly Enochic-type apocalyptic language. Jude is the only NT text which quotes from *1 Enoch*, and James 5:1–6, the damnation of the rich who feasted in the last times, has its closest parallel within Jewish literature not in the NT but again in the Enochic literature.[52] If Richard Bauckham is right and the two brothers of Jesus are actually the authors of these two letters,[53] what does this tell us about the educational background of Jesus' family? Suddenly these Galilean peasants shine in a totally different light: knowledge of Greek; a certain apocalyptic-eschatological theology; more sectarian than mainstream. Actually, in church history there are many analogies to such a phenomenon: families with very specific educational traditions, expressed in a sophisticated literacy and deep knowledge in a certain religious field or a certain 'holy' book, but otherwise not widely read, not literate in a wider sense, but just farmers, or craftsmen or minor traders. Their wisdom and knowledge is for the small group, but within these groups such knowledge is dearly treasured and acclaimed. This is how I imagine the family clan in which Jesus was born. It is quite likely, from the scant evidence we have, that this was indeed a family that traced its pedigree to the Davidic dynasty and waited actively for the Messiah who was promised to the very house of David. In this light, one can take it for granted that a messianic reading and interpretation of Jewish Scriptures was part of the family tradition, and that the family perhaps also had particular exegetical traditions relating to the Messiah. I follow those who assume that behind the designation 'Jesus the Nazarene' is actually a reference to the *nezer*, the sprout who is promised to the Davidic dynasty in Isaiah 11:1: 'A shoot shall come out from the stump of Jesse, and a branch (a *nezer* in Hebrew) shall grow out of his roots.'[54] Jesus' hometown Nazareth might even have been founded by a Davidic family branch who lived in the expectation of the coming of the nezer. This would explain quite naturally why Nathanael ridiculed the message that his friend had found 'him about whom Moses in the law and also the prophets wrote, Jesus son of Joseph from Nazareth.' Nathanael replies, 'Can anything good come out of Nazareth?' (John 1:45f.). If Nazareth was known as the hometown of a crazy messianic sect called the Nazoreans (see also Acts 24:5), then Nathanael's reaction makes sense.[55]

To finish this rather speculative part, which is nevertheless meant to be taken seriously, I propose that Jesus was born into a family with a long-standing messianic tradition and expectation. Joseph is designated as 'a son of David' in Matthew 1:20, and Mary was clearly an extraordinary spiritual woman as well. They were therefore not chosen by chance as parents of Jesus. He was born into a family well prepared for what was going to be fulfilled. The birth of Jesus itself was such that the parents and the wider family had great expectations with regard to the newborn child. In other words, even if we cannot know what precisely happened with the pregnancy of Mary, it is at least feasible that the family had a sense that this child was special. The conflicts between Jesus and his family, when he turned away from the apocalyptic-judgemental theology of John the Baptist (which, I think, is evident also in the letters of his brothers), can easily be explained by their own great expectations being disappointed, in particular when Jesus began to provoke the Pharisees, who were clearly the Jewish religious branch closest to the Jesus family. So, where does all this scriptural knowledge come from? First answer: it is part of a wider family tradition, based on the expectation of the *nezer* promised by Isaiah, and accordingly called *the Nazoraioi*. It is, therefore, possible and indeed likely, that the Nazoreans already existed as a group before Jesus.

John the Baptist

A probable second source of Jesus' scriptural understanding appears to have been John the Baptist, who was a powerful teacher and preacher in his own right. He attracted a large audience, according to Mark 1:5, mainly from Judea and Jerusalem, though we know from the Gospel of John that Galileans were numbered among his followers as well (Andreas, Peter, Nathanael; for followers of John in Ephesus see Acts 19:1–5). Josephus in his short summary of John's ministry also highlights his effect on the people, which raised the suspicions of Herod Antipas.[56] His message is preserved only in a few verses (Mark 1:4; Matt. 3:2 [the only reference in which John is connected with the announcement of the kingdom]; Matt. 3:7–10 par. Luke 3:7–9; Luke 3:10–14 [addressed to the crowds, the tax-collectors, the soldiers]). The limited amount of teaching material preserved should not lead to the assumption that this was all John had to say. What we have is perhaps not even the tip of the iceberg (the same is true for Jesus). John had also a group of disciples (Mark 2:18; 6:29; Matt. 11:2 par. Luke 7:18f.), which means he was not only a public preacher but also a teacher, who taught his disciples how to pray (Luke 11:1) or to fast (Mark 2:18 parr.). From the biblical imagery visible in John's language ('Abraham's children', as well as his clothing like that of Elijah) one can further deduce that the Jewish Scriptures were the 'textbook' for his teaching. Luke is the only one who mentions his priestly origin and background, which adds further detail of his training and formative teaching about God, Israel, the temple and other topics. Though it is debated whether Jesus was ever a disciple of John, he is clearly influenced by him in many ways, and even if he 'reinterpreted this inheritance' considerably, the point can be made that with John we can identify another significant influence on the formation of Jesus.[57]

Divine knowledge?

Finally, I want at least to raise the question of whether we should consider the pre-existence of the Son of God as a source of Jesus' scriptural authority and self-understanding. We have already seen the texts that show Jesus in contact with biblical figures: Abraham, Moses, Elijah, the prophets. For Paul and John's Gospel, Jesus is the mediator of creation, and he was present yet hidden in the history of Israel (1 Cor. 10:3). If one takes such texts seriously then Jesus is the voice behind the prophets, and this makes the pre-existent Son of God not primarily a reader of Scripture but its author! Of course, such a statement requires a lot of qualification, and cannot simply be used as an argument within a historical discussion, even in the most open-minded of all conceivable settings where one can presuppose that all share a high view of Scripture and agree on the christological teachings of the early church. The available texts just do not allow any justifiable conceptualization of how the divine and human nature in Jesus came together in one person. What the earthly Jesus knew about his divine prehistory is beyond the grasp of the historian and theologian alike, but the inaccessibility of this innermost level of Jesus' self-perception does not mean that he could not possibly have accessed a divine perception that transcended space and time. Though this remains a difficult issue, I have found some helpful discussion about this question of the interface between exegesis, historical Jesus research and systematic reflection of Christology in some of the more sympathetic books and papers that appeared in reaction to Pope Benedict XVI's books on Jesus. Let me therefore just provide here a reminder that in a theologically rigorous discussion of

Jesus' self-understanding and the source of his scriptural proficiency the implications of his pre-existence need to considered.[58]

Conclusion

This chapter leaves open a number of questions and has offered some highly speculative avenues for approaching them. I have taken this opportunity to open the theological conundrums that need to be addressed when it comes to the question of Jesus and Scripture. My aim was to put the issue on the table and so contribute to overcoming the strange omission within modern Jesus scholarship of discussion about the influence of Jewish Scriptures on Jesus and his authoritative handling of them. To sum up my main point: Jesus is – from the earliest available testimonies – depicted as one who lived by Scripture; saw himself guided by Scripture; fulfilled Scripture through his ministry; and knows the Scripture's true meaning and motivations. Those who followed him and believed him to be God's Son and messianic Saviour, sent from the Father and the heavenly realm into the world 'to save his people from their sins' (Matt. 1:21), continued Jesus' use of Scripture. They examined the Scripture after Jesus had given them a new understanding of it (Luke 24:25–7,32,45–8), enabling them to understand his own mission as fulfilment of Scripture more fully retrospectively (John 2:22; 20:9; Rom. 1:1b–4; 1 Cor. 15:3–5). The fusion of his followers' experience of his earthly life with a scriptural horizon resulted in a double transformation: Jesus emerged fully as the biblical Christ and Lord of Scripture, and Scripture became a testimony to him. The difficulty in the gospels in differentiating between Jesus' own use of Scripture and the work of the evangelists or their sources is the result of this fusion. It was Jesus' 'distinctive use of Scripture' (J.A.T. Robinson) for which he was remembered.

4

Acts 4:23–31 and a Biblical Theology of Prayer

Donald S. West
Trinity Theological College, Western Australia

A century or more of historical-critical scholarship has been valuable at the level of uncovering the form and function of prayer but less successful at helping Christians and churches to appropriate the biblical prayer material for their own use. Biblical scholarship inclines to specialization whereas prayer is an integrative task that is at its heart relational. Prayer confesses the God whose character and purposes are revealed in the Scriptures which reach their climax in his Son. To speak about 'prayer in the OT' or 'prayer in the NT' brackets out the very nature of biblical prayer. The task of helping Christians to pray in a biblically informed way is a big task, perhaps too big, but our forebears were able to digest Scripture and bring theological and pastoral reflection to bear upon it as they prayed and wrote prayers for others and I would like to think it can still (and must) be done.[1]

The first step in developing a practical theology of prayer based on Scripture is to break down the artificial wall between the Old and New Testaments and establish their literary, historical and theological connections. The prayer materials of the OT and NT are similar in their forms and terminology but differ in their goal and basis. A full-scale consideration of the relationship between the prayer materials of the OT and NT and their practical implications is clearly beyond a brief chapter such as this, but we can begin with an exploration of how NT writers appropriate key OT prayer texts when writing about prayer. A noted example of this is

Acts 4:23–31 which is presented as the first post-Pentecost prayer of the Jerusalem church and as the longest prayer in the book of Acts. The prayer quotes Psalm 2 which is a crucial text from the OT book of prayer (the Psalter) and used or alluded to frequently in the NT in light of the Christ-event. Given Luke's well-known interest in the theme of prayer[2] it is arguable that Acts 4:23–31 is being presented as a prayer paradigm for readers.[3]

In this chapter I will explore Acts 4:23–31 as a prayer paradigm, particularly focusing on its appropriation of the OT. The first section will analyze the function and form of the prayer in Acts 4:23–31, particularly noting its conformity to the OT thanksgiving pattern. The second section will turn to Psalm 2, the OT text quoted in Acts 4:23–31, to consider its literary and theological contribution to the prayer of Acts 4. In the final section I will draw some principles from the study for Christian prayer in general and for developing a biblical theology of prayer.

The Function and Form of Acts 4:23–31

The prayer of Acts 4:23–31 concludes the dramatic story that begins with the healing of a lame man by Peter and John at the temple gate in Jerusalem in Jesus' name and ends with their release from prison (Acts 3:1 – 4:22). The prayer is the church's response to the release of the apostles and continues the theme of the uniqueness of Jesus' name for salvation (cf. 4:12,30). The structure of the unit comprises a narrative introduction (v. 23), a prayer to the 'Sovereign Lord' by the gathered Jerusalem church (vv. 24–30), and a conclusion showing that the prayer had been heard by God (v. 31).

The prayer of vv. 24–30 is offered in response to a report of the apostles of what the religious leaders 'said' to them throughout the ordeal of their arrest, trial and release (v. 23).[4] The prayer first praises God as the supreme master (Gk *Despota*), the Creator of all realms (vv. 24–5a; cf. 1 Kgs 19:15; Isa. 37:16; Neh. 9:6; Ps. 146:6) and the one who spoke through David by his Spirit (Acts 4:25b). The request which follows in vv. 23–30 builds on specific words quoted in Psalm 2:1–2 already used by Luke in the trials of Jesus ('your holy servant . . . whom you anointed') and of the apostles in Acts 3:1 – 4:22 (see Table 4.1). By repeating these terms Luke thus draws an *interlocking narrative* in readers' minds between David's words/prophecy in Ps 2 and his reports of the experiences of Jesus, the experiences of the apostles – and via the prayer the experiences of the Jerusalem church and the readers of Acts (who are now part of this story). Undergirding this multilayered narrative is God's 'hand' (v. 29) which brought all creation into being (v. 24), worked salvation through his 'holy servant' in spite of official opposition (vv. 27–8) and will now empower his servants in the ongoing proclamation of his word while he works 'signs and wonders through Jesus' name' (vv. 29–30).[5]

Term (in Greek)	Psalm 2	Acts 3:1 – 4:22	Acts 4:23–31
'kings [of the earth]' (*hoi basileis*)	v. 1	Acts 4:27; cf. Luke 23:12[6]	v. 23
'rulers' (*hoi archontes*)	v. 1	Acts 3:17; 4:5; cf. 13:27	v. 26
'gathered' (*sunēchthēsan*)	v. 2	Acts 4:5	v. 27
'your holy servant jesus' (*ton hagion paida sou Iēsoun*)	vv. 7,12(?)[7]	Acts 3:13,26	vv. 27, 30
God's 'plan' (*hē boulē*)	v. 7 (?)	Acts 2:23; 3:18; 5:58; 13:36; 20:27; luke 10:22; 22:42	v. 28
'threats' (*apeilas*)	v. 3 (?)	4:17	v. 29

Table 4.1 Common Terms in Psalm 2, Acts 3 – 4:22 and Acts 4:23–31

As many scholars have noted, the content of the church's prayer in Acts 4:24–30 is shaped in the form of a *thanksgiving prayer*, a form found throughout the OT (especially in the Psalter) and in second-temple texts.[8] The form of a thanksgiving song is usually attributed to Herman Gunkel who suggests three basic elements:

1. Confession or praise of the Lord;
2. A narrative of salvation; and
3. The public singing of a thanksgiving song.

Subsequent scholarship has not veered far from this analysis. A comparison of the classic thanksgiving form and Acts 4:24–30 shows remarkable similarities in all three elements (see Table 4.2).

Elements of a Thanksgiving Song	Acts 4:24–30
1. *Confession* of love (or praise) for YHWH who has heard the petitioner's request (Ps. 116:1) and/or a call to listeners to give thanks to YHWH (e.g. Ps. 107:1–3)	1. Vv. 24–6 the church's prayer begins with a *confession of praise* to God who is acknowledged as supreme in creation (v. 24 using the words of Ps. 146:6)[11] and in 'salvation' (vv. 25–6 quoting Ps, 2:1–2)[12]
2. Three-part *narraavie of salvation* in which the story of rescue is recounted (or reported), namely: a. The dire circumstances in which the psalmist called on YHWH; b. The fact that YHWH heard the cry of the psalmist; and c. The fact that it was YHWH alone who rescued them (e.g. Ps. 116:2–4)	2. A narrative of the apostles' salvation: a. The circumstances of their arraignment and trial detailed in Acts 3:1 – 4:22 are summarized in v. 23 (cf. vv. 27–8); b. Their release presumes a prior petition to the 'Sovereign Lord'; to which an answer has been given. This presumption of a prior prayer is justified given that elsewhere in Acts Luke tells readers about the fervent prayer life of the Jerusalem church (1:14,24–5; 2:42,47; 3:1). Indeed, in Acts 12:1–17 Luke provides a parallel example of the church's fervent prayer when Peter was again imprisoned (see esp. vv. 5, 12); and c. It was God alone who did this as emphasized by the frequent mention of 'you', the Sovereign Lord
3. Thanksgiving song is *sung in the presence of the congregation* (e.g. Ps. 116:5–14) who thereby participate in the victorious rescue	3. The whole congregation is caught up in the rescue that has taken place and 'sings' this song (vv. 24–8)
Other features are added to this basic pattern from time to time including a final prayer of petition (Pss 40:12[13?]; 118:25; 138:8c) and a call to live wisely (e.g. Ps. 34:8–14)	In vv. 29–30 a final petition is offered for boldness in preaching the word as God continues to extend his hand in the performance of signs and wonders in the name of Jesus. The hearing of this prayer is confirmed via cosmic signs (cf. John 12:28–9)

Table 4.2 Gunkel's Thanksgiving Pattern and the Prayer of Acts 4:24–30

The significance of Luke's placement of a prayer of thanksgiving at this point in Acts is rarely noted by scholars. An exception is a 1991 study by Linda Maloney of the reporting or 'telling' of God's wondrous acts in and for community in the book of Acts (esp. 4:23–31; 11:1–18; 12:11–17; 14:26–7; 15:1–35; 21:18–20), a feature which she rightly relates to the thanksgiving pattern of the OT which she relates to the unfurling of the 'works of God' within or for the church communities. Maloney sees Acts 4:24–30 'as a kind of model response [of the community to the works of God], which can then be imaginatively supplied in the later pericopes',[13] and taken up by the later church.[14] When it comes to the reason for the quotation of Psalm 2:1–2, Maloney concludes that it is due to a 'Messianic interpretation . . . current in the Christian communities with which Luke himself was familiar'.[15] This conclusion sounds reasonable but it has the effect of blocking out additional purposes Luke may have had in his report of the church citing Psalm 2. It is clear that a thanksgiving prayer was the most appropriate way for the church to respond both circumstantially and within salvation history, but did Luke and the early Christian communities that he portrays use the prayer book of the Scriptures only for its prophetic-apologetic value? There is no question that the fulfilment of the Scriptures by and through Jesus is at the forefront of Luke's mind.[16] But, given Luke's interest in prayer and the position of this prayer in his second volume it is worth asking whether Psalm 2 is being taken up for its significance as a prayer.

The Significance of Psalm 2 in the Prayer of Acts 4:23–31

In the previous section, I highlighted the way by which (in Luke's hands) the church drew a salvation-historical narrative from David's words in Psalm 2 for the experiences of Jesus and the apostles and then for the Jerusalem church and Luke's readers. In this section I will argue that Psalm 2 was chosen not only for its precise, prophetic content but also because of its form and theological significance as a prayer.

It is generally recognized that NT authors, including Luke, assume the context of an OT citation and not just the citation itself.[17] In the case of the prayer of Acts 4:24–30, we may assume that the *whole psalm* is to be read into the narrative. This observation allows us to step back from the details of christological fulfilment to consider the vessel of reception: Psalm 2 as a psalm in the book of prayer. As is well known, Gunkel classified Psalm 2 among the so-called royal psalms, a category based not on form but on content.[18] Royal psalms deal with the theme of the king's rule or his victory over enemies, usually adapting the existing prayer forms of complaint, thanksgiving or hymn.[19] In the majority of royal psalms the chosen form is relatively easy to discern, but for Psalm 2 it is not. It may be because it does not present itself as a *prayer*. Although this may be a problem for us it was not for believers in the second-temple period who received Psalm 2 as a prayer by using it in liturgical contexts along with other psalms in the Psalter (cf. *11QPs^{a-c}*). Its use by the church in Jerusalem as a whole song about the Messiah and in a prayer is not strange.

Now if Psalm 2 is taken up in corporate prayer in Acts 2, it is worth asking *how*, that is, *in what form*, it was appropriated, since prayer must have form if it is to have function. The answer to this question is I think found in the nature of Psalm 2, which, like the majority of psalms, presents itself as a story or narrative. Note the movement through its well-marked sections from problem to resolution: futile earthly opposition against YHWH and his anointed one (vv. 1–3) → divine wrath exercised from heaven and the appointment of 'my king upon Zion, my holy mountain' (vv. 4–6) → the declaration by the king of his intimate relationship with God and God's promised inheritance to him (vv. 7–9) → the king's warning to the nations to submit and not rebel so that they (and anyone) might find blessing 'in' YHWH (vv. 10–12).[20] Table 4.3 provides a detailed comparison of Psalm 2 and Gunkel's thanksgiving criteria.

Although the comparison is not as neat as that with Acts 4 above, I think it is clear that Psalm 2 is best placed in the category of a song of thanksgiving. Its story plays out at a cosmic level and so it is rightly placed at the front of the Psalter as one of its two foundation stones. It leads the royal psalms as a group[23] and, with Psalm 1, it leads the Psalter as a whole.[24] In this context Psalm 2 declares to readers and prayers of the Psalter that the king's rule remains firm even in the midst of opposition because YWHW has chosen David and his 'house' and promised to protect David and to establish his rule. The 'story' of Psalm 2 has an 'eternal' nature

Thanksgiving Form in Psalter (Gunkel)	Psalm 2
1. *Confession* of love (or praise) for YHWH	1. God is not directly addressed in Psalm 2 so praise is absent; however the psalm does lay the foundation for such praise which is recommended in v. 12b
2. Three-part *narrative of salvation*: a. The circumstances in which the psalmist calls out to YHWH;	2. The narrative of salvation is less structured in Psalm 2 because it begins 'in the middle of things'[2.1] Nevertheless, the elements of such a narrative are present; a. Psalm 2 has the three key characters of a lament and hence a thanksgiving (God, petitioner, enemies), the David figure and YHWH are threatned by enemies (vv. 1–3; we even hear their taunts, cf. Pss 3:2b; 22:8); b. no petition is offered but the certainty of being heard is expressed in v. 8, which is based on the promise of vv. 4–6 to take us to the divine throne and presume that c. YHWH alone could do this for the king
3. Thanksgiving song is sung in the presence of the congregation	3. In vv. 7–9 the thanksgiving pattern is unmistakable. Note especially v. 7 where the king says that he will 'tell' (ESV; NRSV) or 'proclaim' (TNIV; NIV 2011) the decree of YHWH (v. 7). The verb used here (*spr*) often marks the opening of a narrative of salvation in thanksgiing songs.[22] In v. 8 the king is assured that his prayers will be heard by the Lord, another feature of thanksgivings (e.g. Ps. 34:6)
Other features (petition; call to live wisely)	The king exhorts the enemies to be wise or mindful in v. 10 and not rebellious

Table 4.3 Gunkel's Thanksgiving Criteria as Reflected in Psalm 2

about it, it is always true (cf. 2 Sam. 7:11b–16; Ps. 89:3–4,19–37; 132:11–12,17). This, of course, explains the shock voiced in Psalm 89:38–45, that God has covered 'David' in a mantle of shame: was the plotting of the peoples and nations 'in vain' after all (Ps. 2:1)? Luke's answer from the beginning of his two-volume work is that

Psalm 2 always looked beyond the failure of Israelite kingship to Jesus, the 'anointed one', whom God raised from the dead. Psalm 2 thus places the specific ways by which the king and his people (and now Christ and his church) would be treated by his accusers within a divinely governed narrative of salvation. In short, throughout salvation history God reverses human expectations by bringing down the strong and raising up the weak; the resurrection of Jesus now guarantees this and affirms the song of Psalm 2.[25]

In Luke's hands, we see in Acts 4:23–31 how the Jerusalem church picks up the wonder of God's exaltation of Jesus from the grave and celebrates the victory of God's 'holy servant' in and through the release of the apostles. They celebrate not at a distance but as people who participate in Christ's victory through the apostles' release and who now dedicate themselves to the mission of the Sovereign Lord to the nations. We recall that community participation was a hallmark of the song of thanksgiving in the OT; the same is true of thanksgiving in the NT. On this point we may consider Paul's opening paragraphs in 2 Corinthians 1 where the twin poles of distress and comfort bind Paul and his readers in Christ. He then reports an ordeal from which he and others had been rescued by God, an ordeal in which he 'felt the sentence of death'. This deliverance reaffirmed for Paul God's true nature as he who raises the dead. The Corinthian church can and should participate with Paul in his distress ('death') and comfort ('resurrection') through prayer and thanksgiving (2 Cor. 1:3–11).

When the Jerusalem church lifted up their voices to the Sovereign Lord who rescued the apostles, they did so knowing that he is the kind of God he has shown himself ultimately to be in his 'anointed one', spoken of by David in Psalm 2 and now proclaimed by them. They lock into the narrative of the cosmic victory of the king promised in Psalm 2. This story continues to be told as they, by God's power, speak his word with boldness and witness miracles performed in Jesus' name. In a way, the Jerusalem church is showing other churches how to pray in the light of the coming of the Messiah.

What Acts 4 Teaches About Prayer

I began this chapter with comments on the mixed contribution of recent biblical scholarship to the practice of Christian prayer.

I suggested that more theological integration of the prayer materials of OT and NT was needed. In order to show how this might be done, I examined the prayer of the church in Acts 4:23–31 which is itself grounded in Psalm 2, a text from the OT book of prayer. In the examination we noted that the thanksgiving pattern was the 'natural' response to the release of the apostles but that, in the light of the citation of Psalm 2, the church also saw itself as participants in the outworking of God's salvation plan. In this section I want to focus on two aspects by way of conclusion: (1) what Acts 4:23–31 has to teach us about prayer; and (2) what Acts 4:23–31 teaches us about doing biblical theology with regards to prayer.

The main message of Acts 4:23–31 about prayer is that it is integrally related to God's saving purposes which climax in the death and resurrection of Jesus Christ. Prayer is grounded in what God has promised in his word and fulfilled in his Son. Two practical conclusions may be drawn from this: (1) Christians must be thoroughly informed of God's saving purposes revealed in both the OT and the NT; we should know the 'narrative'; (2) however, knowing the narrative is not enough on its own: we must own it and see ourselves as part of it because we are Christ's people. Unless we see ourselves as participants in the unfolding of God's plan of salvation we will not really grasp the essential forms of biblical prayer: thanksgiving and petition. However, with a deep and daily awareness of the big picture of God's saving purposes and grace we will pray in tune with the narrative and join in God's saving work with joyful energy. I take this to be prayer according to God's will.

With regards to the practice of biblical theology we should note how deeply soaked Acts 4:23–31 is in the message and content of Psalm 2. Psalm 2 is not only embraced for the specific christological fulfilments it pictures but for the cosmic story of God's dealing with the nations through the appointment of his 'son'. The narrative of salvation history that is encapsulated in Psalm 2 – as read through the revelation of God's 'anointed one' – provided the Jerusalem church with a framework for the form, content and purpose of its prayer. This means that we must reconsider how NT prayer material appropriates OT texts, themes and forms, mindful that this is not done lightly.

Becoming Prophets: Acts 10:34–35 and Peter's Appropriation of Prophecies About Jesus

Benjamin L. Sutton
Ridley College, Melbourne

Introduction

The importance of remembering the past for the study of Christian origins is inherent in the attempt to understand the New Testament's repeated use of Israel's Scriptures. However, the intricacies of 'memory in culture' require at least an attempted explanation of the means and methods of remembering (conscious or subconscious). It is therefore necessary to provide a brief sketch of 'memory in culture' before looking at the memory functions of one particular group – first-century Christians. In the following sections there will be specific attention given to defining 'cultural memory' and 'social memory' before looking at the role of the memory paradigm for the Acts of the Apostles and the appropriation of Scripture.

Three Levels of Memory

There are three levels of memory which interact in any given group or society: cultural memory, communicative memory, and individual memory. The term cultural memory (*kulturelle Gedächtnis*) came about as Jan and Aleida Assmann articulated the differences between communication in proximate generations and memories which extend further into the past. Assmann explains that communication between individuals who share aspects of a singular society or group is what constitutes *communicative memory*. The limits of communicative memory are marked by the oldest members' memory of personally experienced events (three generations or eighty to one hundred years is typically the range of communicative memory). On the other hand, *cultural memory* is constituted by traditions which can span one to one thousand generations. Assmann notes, 'In this way, cultural memory can be considered to be a special form of communicative memory. It has a different temporal structure. If we think of the typical three-generation cycle of communicative memory as a synchronic memory-space, then cultural memory, with its traditions reaching far back into the past, forms a diachronic axis.'[1] The pertinent result of Assmann's assessment is the intersection between cultural memory and communicative memory. In other words, he is interested in how even the far distant past can still exercise a controlling force on the present identity of a group.

One example of this controlling force is what Yael Zerubavel calls a 'master commemorative narrative',[2] which is employed by a community/society (in the present) to explain its origins and unique identity. Zerubavel notes:

> Each commemoration reconstructs a specific segment of the past and is therefore fragmentary in nature. Yet these commemorations together contribute to the formation of a *master commemorative narrative* that structures collective memory. With this concept I refer to a broader view of history, a basic 'story line' that is culturally constructed and provides the group members with a general notion of their shared past . . . Since collective memory highlights the group's distinct identity, the master commemorative narrative focuses on the event that marks the group's emergence as an independent social entity.[3]

Due to the fragmentation of an extensive cultural memory there is added value to a *consolidated* master commemorative narrative (MCN). An MCN thus organizes the available cultural memory, making it easier to guide a community's pursuit of a unified identity.

The *individual* level is the beginning of memory in a biological or organic sense. It is the individual or group of individuals who experience any given event. Each experience that an individual encounters, however socially formed, is 'theirs'. Thus, an individual refers to the 'past' in order to *communicate and identify* with the group which shares the same experience of the 'past'.[4] As Olick, Vinitzky-Seroussi and Levy note, 'Memory – relating past and present – is thus the central faculty of being in time, through which we define individual and collective selves.'[5] Neuroscientist Merlin Donald has written extensively on the mind and its memory capabilities. He notes that as the amount of information increases, monads (a 'biologically encapsulated mind', ie. an individual)[6] are unable to retain a majority of it. Instead it is recorded (via XYZ medium) and placed into 'external symbolic storage' or ESS.[7] Donald goes on, 'The major locus of stored knowledge is *out there*, not within the bounds of biological memory. Biological memories carry around the code, rather than a great deal of specific information.'[8]

Donald is describing on the individual level what cultural memory observes about the 'crisis of memory' within social groups – when there becomes a need to make permanent the important memories of those witnesses who are dying. The code(s) to which he refers are the various frames or schemata which allow a 'monad' access to information. With regard to that externalized information, the need to preserve any given record or foundational narrative is based on the fact that an increasing amount of information (multiple generations of tradition, etc.) cannot be contained in an individual alone.[9]

Social Memory

The brief introduction to the three levels of memory can be further simplified: the cultural memory refers to the distant past (preserved in various memory artifacts), the communicative memory describes the three- to four-generation 'present' of each specific group, and the individual memory comprises the present experiences of an individual within a group. With that in mind we can move on to social memory which concerns the dynamic *relationship* between the three levels of memory just outlined. Chris Keith notes that:

> By focusing upon the *social* formation of memory in the present, whether that means autobiographical memory that is socially formed or cultural memory that is autobiographically appropriated, the primary task of social memory theory is to conceptualize and explain the various manners in which cultures (and individuals as culture-members) appropriate the past in light of, in terms of, and on behalf of the present.[10]

This relationship leads to three preliminary discussions which each have bearing on the appropriation of Scripture: refraction, the impact of significant events, and identity formation.

Refraction and significant events

All memory is interpreted. This has been variously described as distortion (Schacter, et al.) or refraction (Le Donne, et al.). A primary reason for using 'distortion' is to alert our sensibilities to the fact that memory or remembering is not as easy as simple recall.[11] Le Donne notes, 'Matters of emphasis, perspective, and interpretation are the very basis for memory's existence. It is simply impossible to know every detail about any given object; put another way, it is impossible to see an object from every vantage point. In the same way it is impossible to recollect an object without emphasizing certain details.'[12] Le Donne opts for the term 'refraction' since it is less jarring for people who assume (unreflectively) that 'distortion' denotes false memory, fabrication, or egregious manipulation of memory. Underlying refraction is the fact that all memory is selective, but not necessarily fabricated.[13]

Le Donne highlights the refraction type 'narrativization'. In his system, narrativization is one of several ways a person can make sense of the past in light of a present circumstance. Narrativization is a refraction process of remembering a past event by telling one's own story through an existing story (framework). 'The narrativization process forces both the storyteller and the audience into stereotypical patterns . . . Narrativization not only shapes our memories as we retrieve them in storytelling, but also provides a grid by which we interpret our environment and our role therein.'[14] The mind follows past stories and uses them in order to make sense of the new story which needs to be told at present. '*The climactic moments of our lives are measured against, and interpreted by, the climactic moments of great stories, and indeed, of history itself.*'[15] As an individual experiences a significant event, often times in order for that memory to be preserved it is 'refracted' by a scene from their MCN.

The interpretation and reinforcement of a present memory are a part of Le Donne's 'mnemonic cycle', which represents an instance of refraction (Fig. 1).[16]

Figure 1[17]

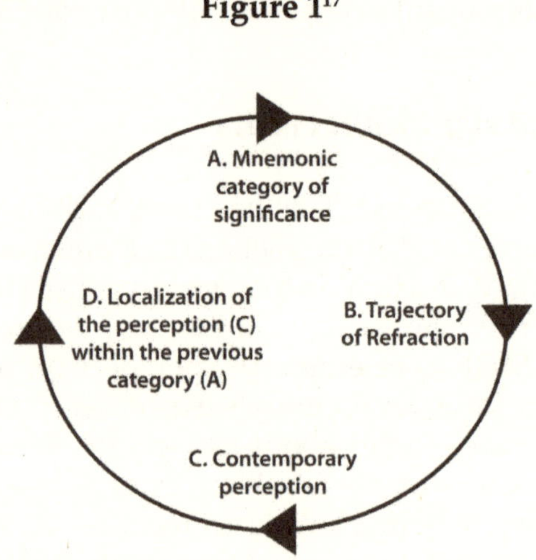

The dynamic process of social memory can be seen by incorporating Le Donne's model of memory refraction into the three levels of memory discussed above (cultural memory, communicative memory, and the individual memory)(Fig. 2).

The contents of this model provide a snapshot of the process of social memory. Point 'A' is a mnemonic category of significance or cultural frame/schemata based on the MCN/cultural memory of a specific society. Point 'B' represents the 'refraction trajectory' or the influence of the initial frame. In Figure 2 it is significant that the 'shaping' influences both the communicative and the individual levels because the individual is interactive with *both* the 'present' and the 'distant past'. Point 'C' represents the individual as they experience new events (the string of sequential moments called

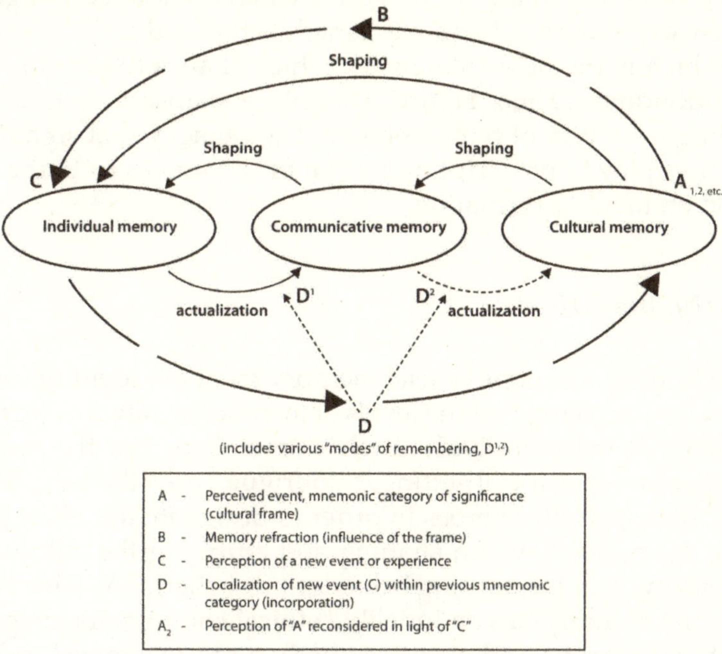

'life'). Point 'D' is the 'localization' of the new experience ('C') within the previous mnemonic category. In other words, localization is understanding or explaining the new experience in light of their existing mnemonic frame. Depending on the type of experience, it will either confirm (legitimize), expand, or even emend the initial frame 'A'. This process of localization is represented by two levels of 'actualization' by various 'modes of remembering'.

Significantly for social memory, actualization occurs at two levels reflected in 'D^1' and 'D^2'. The difference is that 'D^1' may be significant for the individual to participate in their groups' communicative memory, but unless it is significant for future generations, it will fade after that generation. Alternatively in 'D^2', if it is a significant memory because of its connection to the cultural memory/MCN, then that memory shifts to a more permanent mode of remembering. The events' significance to the group identity (MCN) plus its permanence cause it to become part of the cultural memory.[18] The label 'modes of remembering' reflects the various media that can contain and/or express the memory.

Finally, when the initial framework 'A' is reconsidered in light of the new experience 'C' and explained/actualized in 'D', it forms 'A^2', which is the new framework which shapes the community and individuals. Thus, Figure 2 is only a snapshot or slice of a spiraling trajectory of remembrance. The capacity that significant memories play in proscription for the future moves us to the next section on identity formation.

Identity formation

Rafael Rodriguez applies social memory theory to identity formation by first agreeing that the levels of memory are always working together – it is the individual who remembers, but the remembering occurs in a social setting.[19] Rodriguez uses the term 'reputation' of (especially) heroes in order to designate the effect these strong memories have on shaping and affirming the values of a community, thus influencing behavior (i.e. belief).[20] As Kirk notes, 'the social memory has an indelible ethical coloring; its images of archetypal persons and events embody a group's moral order.'[21] This confirms the above observations, from Le Donne on narrativization, that narrative is highly formative insofar as the archetypal characters are those most frequently involved in the stories told.

For Rodriguez, tradition and performance are necessarily connected. With regard to our model of social memory (Fig. 2), tradition is analogous to the MCN or cultural memory and performance is analogous to 'actualization' since it is the instance of communicating or enacting that tradition in the community. To use Rodriguez's terms, 'performance actualizes tradition'.[22] The actualization of tradition is both the foundation and result of memory – hence the cycle of Figure 2. As Merlin Donald noted earlier, the abundance of tradition forces its existence to an increasingly external medium. Therefore, it can be referred to and accessed by members of a group. But performance is necessary for the tradition to be interpreted and applied in the present.[23] The inference from this is the power of such reputations and traditions to *prescribe* action for the future. In this way, reputation in a narrative 'performance' is a *mode* of remembering the past which empowers the cultural memory to continue shaping the group.

Two Levels of Analyzing Acts 10:34–43

In light of the observations above, there are two pertinent ways to analyze Peter's speech in Acts 10:34–43. First, Peter's speech can be analyzed from Luke's presentation of Peter's perspective as it relates to the paradigm shift of Gentile inclusion. Second, Peter's speech can be analyzed from Luke's perspective as a historian recording the development of Christianity in a more permanent medium. Both means of analysis provide important insights to our understanding of the appropriation of Scripture.

Peter's perspective in Acts 10:34–43

Our analysis of Peter's speech before Cornelius will follow the lettered components in the model of social memory provided (Fig. 2). What will be shown below is the trajectory of Peter going through three cycles of memory refraction throughout this speech. The first cycle (A^1–D^1) reorients Peter's Jewish past concerning the clean/unclean distinction. The second cycle (A^2–D^2) clarifies Peter's new framework in the present by recalling the teachings of Jesus and the prophets. The final cycle (A^3–D^3) moves Peter into the future as a catalyst to God's restoration of Israel and the world.

For the first cycle, we must look at the situation in which Luke places Peter, since the speech is essentially Peter's response to a series of prior events. Growing up as a Jew provided Peter with an identity informed by Israel's 'master commemorative narrative'. Wright notes that the first-century Jewish life comprised four primary symbols: 'Temple, Land, Torah, and racial identity'.[24] Related to the last symbol and significant for this passage, Peter would have understood Gentiles as ceremonially unclean.[25] Markus Bockmuehl even suggests that it is possible Peter relocated from Bethsaida to Capernaum in order to remove himself from the unclean fishing village since the former was inhabited primarily by unclean individuals and practices.[26] Working backward for a moment, Acts 10:28a confirms Peter's pre-vision commitment to the dietary separation between Jews and Gentiles.[27] This forms A^1 on our mnemonic trajectory as it reflects Peter's starting point. The influence of this initial position B^1 is evinced by Peter's reluctance to accept the vision and command of God (10:14).

This perception is challenged by a new experience (C^1) of Peter seeing a vision in which God tells him directly that his former categories of clean/unclean must be transformed. Upon the arrival of Cornelius' messengers, Peter immediately has the opportunity to wrestle with the implications of the vision.

As Peter processes this new experience (C^1) in light of his existing mnemonic frame (A^1) there is a conflict (10:28a) which forces him to reconsider. The conflict is brought on by the two overarching elements of Israel's MCN, which Mike Bird notes are, 'the universalism of monotheism and the particularity of Israel's election'.[28] Israel's election is a primary influence for Israel's rigid purity. As Bird notes, 'election necessitated the avoidance of idolatry, intermarriage with foreigners, and the maintenance of national purity.'[29] The immediate result of the vision is Peter's confession to Cornelius that God doesn't consider any man common or unclean in 10:28b. This reflects Peter's localization (D^1) of his new experience (C^1 = vision from God) into his previous framework (A^1). At first, this simply means that Peter's initial framework now includes an altered mnemonic framework where Gentiles are no longer unclean (A^2).[30] Luke has presented us with at least three facts: Peter's initial framework, a striking new experience (vision from God), and a confession evincing a new framework for understanding Gentiles. That effectively moves us from A^1 to A^2 according to the mnemonic cycle of Figure 2, which brings us to Peter's speech before Cornelius and the second mnemonic trajectory.

Peter's most immediate reaction of resistance to Gentile contact is the result of his much more ingrained Jewish life. He has responded to God's prompting to change this position on a Gentile being clean/unclean, but Peter must still wrestle with the primary points of monotheism and election: even if Gentiles are no longer to be considered unclean or common, what is their place within God's plan?

At this point Peter must again re-evaluate his previously accepted cultural memory (A^1) in light of his more immediate communicative memory – Jesus. The influence of Peter's new mnemonic frame that Gentiles are clean (A^2 and B^2) pushes him to recall the teachings of Jesus to consider how they might explain his vision from God. In this case C^2 (Jesus) is chronologically 'past' but it is part of Peter's own experience and is part of the communicative memory surrounding Jesus. Thus, compared with Peter's Jewish upbringing (A^1) it pertains to Peter's 'present'.

Any thorough recall of Jesus' ministry would have taken some considerable reflection. However, Luke's narrative runs much faster and we receive Peter's localization of that reflection in 10:34–6. Here, Peter concludes his fresh understanding with the bold statement that God's good news for the sons of Israel is now for everyone, since Jesus the Messiah – who brings peace – is Lord of all, with no partiality. This is a considerable jump from A^2 where Gentiles are no longer common or unclean, now it is possible for them to be part of the people of God.

Up to this point, it is understandable that Peter has continued his mission to proclaim Jesus as Messiah to the Jews of Judea and the Samaritans, since Jesus himself is quite clear that he is sent as a prophet to call Israel to God. So what exactly would Peter have recalled from Jesus' ministry that pushed him to make such a declaration? There are several aspects of C^2 which need to be unpacked. First, we noted earlier that one part of Israel's election is their purity from idolatry, etc., but another part of their election is Israel's witness of YHWH to the nations. Regardless of the numerous views of Israel's ultimate relation to Gentiles in the eschaton (conquering or rescuing)[31] there is no doubt that the fate of Gentiles rests with the restoration of Israel.[32] When it comes to Jesus it is apparent that his view of Israel included their responsibility to *bless* the nations. This is supported by the Jewish texts which refer to the temple as the location where Gentiles will come to worship God,[33] combined with Jesus' critique of the temple as not being a house of prayer for the nations (Mark 11:17//Luke 19:46//Matt. 21:13//John 2:16). Bird argues that, 'in view of Israel's corporate failure to realize this universal vocation, [Jesus] regarded the restored Israel that he was forming around himself as taking up this role'.[34] In support of this is Jesus' prophetic action of collecting twelve apostles.[35] The significance of 'twelve' is connected with Israel's messianic hopes of eschatological restoration.[36]

Second, Jesus repeatedly identifies and demonstrates prophetic characteristics. In connection with the restoration of Israel, Luke

4:16–21 records Jesus' identification of himself with the prophet of Isaiah 61:1–3 who brings good news – a passage in which several lines are intimately linked to Isaiah 52:7–9 ('good news of peace'). These confirm Jesus' understanding of a new eschatological period, of which he is the inaugurating prophet.[37] In addition to relocating God's command from the vision into his existing Jewish framework, Peter has also located the ministry of Jesus within that same Jewish framework (by calling him the Messiah and recognizing his being sent to the sons of Israel). This is D^2, which leads to Peter declaring: *Jesus is Lord of all.*

If Acts 10:36 is the summary of Peter's reflections on his own time with Jesus, then the summary of Jesus' ministry, death and resurrection in 10:37–41 comprise the new extended framework from which all subsequent events are viewed – this is the beginning of the third mnemonic cycle, A^3–B^3. Peter is recognizing his audience of Gentiles who may need an extended explanation of Jesus' significance. This 'gospel' report is Peter extending the mission of Jesus beyond the sons of Israel. With Peter called to be one of the twelve, his recollection of Jesus' teaching would reasonably have included the reminder of his participation in God's mission of restoration. He has now realized that he is a prophetic vehicle that will inform the Gentiles of God's universal message of salvation. But a part of this message also includes Peter's new understanding (from A^2 to D^2) that the prophets spoke of this – 10:43. The most concentrated and influential material on the restoration of Israel and Gentile inclusion is Isaiah 40 – 55.[38] In these texts we find the roots of Jesus' restoration vision including the people and the temple – two themes we've already seen connected to Jesus, which Peter would have witnessed. Furthermore, Peter's inclusion of John the Baptist in his legacy of Jesus points to an understanding of prophetic lineage.

Thus, when the Holy Spirit interrupts Peter proclaiming this message and comes on the Gentiles (C^3=10:44), Peter is able to see the connection with his new mnemonic frame: Israel's restoration leading to Gentile inclusion. This event hearkens back to the events at Pentecost, thus confirming the validity of the previous frameworks – *the Holy Spirit coming on the Gentiles is the proof of the ongoing restoration of Israel begun in Jesus and continued at Pentecost.*[39] Peter's response (D^3) is to continue his re-envisioned prophetic role and baptize the household of Cornelius since they have experienced the same Spirit-coming as the Jewish believers have (10:47–8).

In summary, the first cycle moved us from Peter's past framework of Jew/Gentile separation to Gentiles not being unclean. Then in the second cycle the dietary purity of Gentiles became Gentile inclusion in God's people through Peter's 'present' memories of Jesus – including Jesus' appropriation of the prophets to explain the inauguration of Israel's restoration. Finally, the third cycle demonstrated Peter's new understanding of his role for the future, where he continues the restoration of Israel through proclaiming Jesus' gospel to all people.

Luke and Peter's paradigm shift

The significance of Peter's new understanding of salvation for the Gentiles is taken further by Luke. As Luke has been recording the ministry of Peter, it has repeatedly paralleled Jesus' prophetic ministry. This includes re-establishment of the twelve disciples, miracles, and bold prophetic statements that the present is fulfilling God's promise to restore Israel.[40] In order to achieve lasting formation of all Christians Luke is pushing the memories of Peter into the category of cultural memory. By writing Acts, Luke is contributing a more permanent medium or 'mode of remembering' = D^2. At this level Peter is held up as a hero and the model of Christian proclamation to be followed by all Christians who are participating in God's plan.

Conclusion

We have seen how studying memory has significant explanatory power in understanding the development, preservation and formation of a group's identity. Jesus boldly proclaimed that as Messiah he was bringing the good news of peace to Israel, and now Peter has realized that the significance of Jesus' mission to restore Israel extends to Gentiles. Luke then elevates Peter as the example for all Christians to follow as they spread the good news of Jesus to all people. This future perspective is in continuity with the master commemorative narrative of Judaism as it has been refracted by the ministries of Jesus and Peter.

Pauline Letters

6

Scripture and Identity in Galatians

Mark A. Seifrid
The Southern Baptist Theological Seminary

Paul and Christian Identity

Christian identity, both corporate and individual, was constituted by Scripture from the beginning. In considering the way in which the Scriptures determine Christian identity for Paul, we are examining only one example of Christian faith at its inception. Yet Paul's letters represent perhaps the most prominent example of the way in which the identity of the earliest Christians was formed by Scripture. The new understanding of Scripture that came to Paul in the gospel remade his identity and reset the entire course of his life. In a similar way the identity that he seeks to impart to his churches stands in conflict with the various ways in which they were otherwise tempted to understand themselves. His appeals to Scripture serve as weapons in his battles over Christian self-definition.

It will be necessary in this brief chapter to limit our attention to Paul's letter to the Galatian churches. In so doing, we must not forget that there are aspects of Paul's use of Scripture that do not come into view in Galatians, especially those that appear in Romans and the Corinthian correspondence. Nevertheless, it is remarkably fruitful to consider Galatians from the perspective of the formation of identity, since Paul's argument, from beginning to end, has to do with this very matter. Indeed, as the letter to the Galatian churches makes clear, for Paul the question of 'who we are' determines 'what we do', and not the other way around.

In engaging the question of ethnicity, and thus presenting his apostolic understanding of Christian identity in Galatians, Paul appeals to the Jewish Scriptures in order to establish the common humanity of Jew and Gentile; a common humanity, as we shall see, is found in an exchange of persons and identities. In the crucified and risen Christ, the Jew and Gentile are made one, yet not in such a way that their ethnic identities are denied or destroyed. Christian identity for Paul, as it is given in the Scriptures, is eschatological, transcending our earthly identities, and yet not removing them.[1] Neither his closing blessing of 'the Israel of God' (Gal. 6:16), nor his reference elsewhere to the 'church of God' as a tertium quid, change his eschatological perspective in the least.[2] His conception of Christian identity is profoundly theo-logical: for Paul, our true identity is found in God's recognition of us and in our recognition of God in response. This mutual recognition of the sinner and the God who saves takes place in the crucified and risen Christ.[3] It is not a matter of visible boundary markers, but a matter of unseen hope. That, in a nutshell, is the thesis I want to explain and defend in what follows.

Paul and Ethnicity

As the interpretation of Paul over the last forty years has become acutely aware, the identity of the earliest Christians cannot be separated from the question of their ethnicity. Indeed, it is this very question of ethnicity that Paul engages in Galatians. According to one currently prominent theory, ethnic identity is to be defined by internal and external ascription, and not, as we might suppose, by birth or location.[4] Thus understood, ethnic identity is constructed and changeable, and not primordial, essential and fixed. Ethnic and racial boundaries may be traversed.[5] That is not to say that ancestry or a connection with a land does not play an important role in the constitution of ethnic identity. But birth and origin are not in themselves determinative. Jews living in the Diaspora generally remained Jews nevertheless.[6] Conversely, those who had been born Jews could come to be regarded by others as no longer being Jews on the basis of their conduct, no matter where they resided.[7] The fictional Jewish figure of which Paul makes use in his diatribe in Romans 2:17–24 is by no means simply one who was born a Jew. The figure appears instead to reflect the conflict between a positive, internal construction of Jewish identity and a critical construction of outsiders. Conversely, Gentiles who allowed themselves to be circumcised and baptized could become Israelites – admittedly with qualifications in certain circumstances – and thus could be regarded as having entered into a fictive kinship with Abraham, as appears to be the view of Paul's opponents in Galatia.[8] The very name 'the Gentiles' (or 'the nations', τὰ ἔθνη is an external ascription, an element of a construct that distinguishes the Jewish people from all others. It is not without significance that Paul employs this term in his letters: he understands the distinction between Jew and Gentile as continuing within the present world, even though it has been overcome in Christ. Something similar may be said of the term 'Greek' Ἑλλην, which serves to distinguish a cultural and linguistic group from Jews, and more fundamentally from 'the barbarians' οἱ βάρβαροι. This latter term is itself, of course, an external ascription. In short, there is ample evidence within Paul's letters that ethnicity is implicitly conceived not merely in terms of birth, but in terms of culture and conduct.

In reading Paul's statements about his own Jewish identity, it quickly becomes apparent that he conceives it in the terms of internal and external ascription that have come to be recognized in social anthropology. That is true even in Romans 11:1–6, where he appeals without qualification to his birth and origin as an indication that God 'has not abandoned his people' (Rom. 11:1). The evidence of his claim is not merely his existence, but his fidelity to God, which, for Paul, finds its expression in his faith in Jesus. Just as there remained in Elijah's day 'seven thousand, who did not bend their knee to Baal', so God has preserved a 'remnant' in Paul's time (Rom. 11:5–6). Birth and origin did not preserve the many upon whom judgement came.[9]

A similar dynamic appears in Philippians 3:1–6, in which Paul contrasts the new identity of believers with his former identity within Judaism. His opening claim that 'we are the circumcision' (Phil. 3:2) is set over against his depreciating description of circumcision as 'the mutilation' (Phil. 3:1). Much as in Galatians, the eschatological reality that has now arrived in Christ displaces the most significant boundary marker of Jewish identity. It is this boundary marker to which Paul assigns first importance in his listing of his privileges: he was an 'eighth-day circumcised'. He names it before he recalls his descent (ἐκ γένους Ἰσραήλ, φυλῆς Βενιαμίν). He follows these benefits with a description of his upbringing and his zeal. Birth and lineage count, but they are set within the context of language and culture.[10] In a sense, Paul's 'Jewishness' was given at birth. But it was actualized, and thus constituted in practice.

One gains much the same impression when one turns to Paul's account of his calling in Galatians 1:14–15. In a manner that corresponds to his larger argument in Galatians, Paul presents Jewish identity emphatically in terms of conduct. While he refers to the contemporaries of his 'race' (γένος), he makes the point that he outstripped them 'in Judaism', as he was a more exceeding zealot for his ancestral traditions. With his usage of the infrequent ethnic term Ἰουδαϊσμός[11] and his description of his zeal, Paul again presents Jewish identity in terms of practice and conduct, his implicit reference to his descent notwithstanding.

The same is the case in regard to Paul's subsequent report of his confrontation of Cephas at Antioch. The sharp irony of his opening address should not be overlooked: 'If you, who exist as a Jew (Ἰουδαῖος ὑπάρχων), live as a Gentile and not as a Jew, how is it that you compel the Gentiles to Judaize?' (Gal. 2:14). We cannot here take up the details of Paul's argument.[12] It is important only to note that he speaks of Cephas' Jewish identity not has a matter of 'being' but as a matter of 'being there', i.e. as a matter of concrete existence, which implicitly includes upbringing and culture. Paul takes up this thought in the following verse: 'We (are) Jews by nature (φύσει)' (Gal. 2:15). Φύσις or 'nature' does not merely have to do with origin or birth, but also with the character or inherent 'nature' of a person (or thing), which may well include culture and practice. Paul thus speaks elsewhere of a Gentile as 'the uncircumcision by nature' (ἡ ἐκ φύσεως ἀκροβυστία).[13] This identification of a person in terms of their bodily state, striking as it is, is based on cultural location, and not on birth. Not even Jews are born circumcised. Likewise, elsewhere, taking up a Stoic *topos*, Paul asks the Corinthians if nature itself (ἡ φύσις αὐτός) does not teach them that long hair is a dishonour to men, but an honour to women (1 Cor. 11:14–15). Once again cultural practice is included within 'nature'. It is altogether likely that the same understanding of 'nature' is operative in Paul's ad hominem characterization of Jews in Galatians 2:15. The counterpart in the second half of the verse most likely has conduct in view: 'we are by nature Jews, and not *sinners from among the Gentiles.*' In seeking their justification in Christ, Jews themselves 'are found to be sinners', abandoning the law and its works (Gal. 2:16–17). Paul's earlier description of 'those from James' as 'the circumcision' (Gal. 2:12) – which in all likelihood refers to them simply as observant Jews, and not as a particular party within the earliest church[15] – points in the same direction: Jewish identity is defined by culture and practice. The same may be said for Paul's language in Galatians 2:16, which immediately follows his reference to 'nature'. It is probable that the phrase 'of the works of the Law' is to be taken as an adjectival modifier, and not as an adverb.[16] Paul speaks of 'a person of the works of the Law' (ἄνθρωπος ἐξ ἔργων νόμου). According to Paul, a Jew is such a person 'by nature'. Ethnic identity includes birth, but also cultural practices that serve as boundary markers.

God and Christian Identity (Gal. 3:1–5)

Paul's scriptural argument appears in the body of Galatians (Gal. 3:1 – 4:31), framed by the christological and autobiographical arguments of the opening and closing (Gal. 1:1 – 2:21; 5:1 – 6:18). As we have noted, it is oriented entirely to the question of Christian identity, which Paul addresses by his eschatological redefinition of ethnic identity. The advocates of Judaizing who have made their way to Galatia offer one definition of identity; Paul offers another, very different one. Theirs is an ethnic identity defined by the maintenance of a boundary. By virtue of visible practices, communities and individuals within them recognize themselves as Jewish, and outsiders do so as well.

Paul himself once regarded himself and others in this way. But the gospel reconfigured all his assumptions. In contrast to his opponents and to the Galatians, and much to our surprise, Paul turns out to be a 'birther', or more precisely a 'new birther'. With respect to the gospel, he takes a 'primordialist' stance. His definition of believing identity is not based on boundary markers.[18] He insists that identity is established by an ontological, familial relation that is found in a new creation.[19] He offers a new identity in Christ, beyond the distinction between Jew and Gentile, an eschatological tertium quid, that encompasses both of them, without dissolving either of them.

Our thematic concern directs us to Paul's scriptural argument in the body of Galatians.[20] It is of fundamental significance that Paul begins this argument with the question of God's identity. In his opening appeal, he pointedly asks his readers, 'Is the One who supplies you with the Spirit and performs mighty deeds among you of the works of the Law or of the message of faith?' (Gal. 3:5: ἐξ ἔργων νόμου ἢ ἐξ ἀκοῆς πίστεως;).[21] Paul sets before the Galatians the question as to whether God's identity is found in the law and its works, or whether it lies in the promises fulfilled in Christ, and thus in faith. Prior to the question of our identity, and yet inseparable from it, is the question of God's identity. It is clear for the apostle who God is: God is 'of faith'. Only those who are 'of faith' share in this God (Gal. 3:5,7,9). Much as he does in Romans, in Galatians Paul goes on to insist on the oneness of God as integral and essential to salvation itself (Gal. 3:20). In Galatians he develops that argument christologically, particularly in 3:15 – 4:20. The 'faith' of which he speaks is 'the faith of Christ'[22] crucified and risen (cf. Gal. 2:20-21). Christian identity is found in him.

Faith, Works and Christian Identity (Gal. 3:6–14)

The second, following movement of Paul's scriptural argument (Gal. 3:6–14) begins with human identity as it is determined by faith and, as we have noted, not just any faith, but a *fides specialis*, the faith that proceeds from God's promise to Abraham. Paul's argument is assertive in form, guided by the word concerning Abraham that appears in Genesis 15:6: 'He believed God, and it was reckoned to him as righteousness.' According to Paul, this word determines Abraham's identity, as is clear from his immediate assertion, 'know, then, that those of faith, these are the sons [children] of Abraham' (Gal. 3:7). Visible boundary markers are trumped by faith. Divine recognition and acceptance determine Abraham's identity and that of his children (cf. Gal. 4:9). Paul's second appeal to Scripture proceeds from this assertion. The promise that 'in Abraham' blessing will be pronounced upon all the Gentiles means that those of faith are blessed with the believing Abraham. In this way, the Scriptures anticipate the apostle and proclaim the gospel to Abraham in advance (Gal. 3:8–9).[23] The divine, justifying word to Abraham determines who Abraham is, and makes the believing Abraham into a figure of hope and source of blessing for the Gentiles.

Paul immediately contrasts Abraham and 'those of faith' (Gal. 3:7) with 'those of the works of the Law' (Gal. 3:10). It should be clear that neither the Galatian believers nor the advocates of Judaizing who had arrived in Galatia conceived of ethnicity in fixed terms of race and descent. The message that one should live as a Jew was an invitation to the Galatian believers to complete what they had begun with their faith in the Messiah. They should become fully and manifestly Jewish.[24] The Galatians, it should be remembered, received the invitation rather happily.[25] It is their hearts and minds that Paul seeks to win. When he speaks of those 'compelling' Gentiles to Judaize, he is expressing a theological judgement, not describing legitimate authority, let alone human force.[26]

Consequently, it is also clear that Paul's expression, 'those of the works of the law' (Gal. 3:10), refers to Jews, yet obviously not in terms of birth and descent. Indeed, the Jewish Christian agitators in Galatia have rolled out the welcome mat to the Gentiles. They, too, may and should become Jewish, and thus persons, 'of the works of the Law'. The identification must be understood in this open-ended way, since Paul already has raised the issue with the Galatians as to whether God is 'of the works of the Law' (Gal. 3:5). Ethnic identity appears here as a constructed identity, marked by the maintenance of boundaries – boundaries that could be traversed.

Citing Scripture, Paul asserts that those who find their identity in 'the works of the Law' fall under a curse. If the Galatians Judaize, they shall fall under this curse, the force of which is accentuated in the septuagintal text of Deuteronomy 27:26 that Paul follows: 'cursed is *everyone* who does not remain in *all things* written in the book of the Law to do them' (Gal. 3:10).

As many recent interpreters have noted, Paul omits the minor premise of his argument, that those 'of the works of the Law' do not perform all that the law demands. How are we to understand this apparent lapse in the syllogism? It is not likely that Paul presupposes a common understanding that Israel remains in exile on account of its failure to perform the demands of the law.[27] The Gentiles in Galatia surely did not perceive Jewish identity in this way, or else they would not have been so strongly inclined to Judaize. They sought to join an exemplary piety, not a failed people lost in their sins. Nor is it likely that the Judaizers who came to Galatia arrived with the message, 'Join us in exile!' Paul's subsequent assertion that 'the present Jerusalem' is enslaved came to his first readers not as a confirmation of their assumptions, but as a shock (Gal. 4:25). From another, more fundamental perspective, the appeal to the corporate state of Israel as remaining in the exile on account of its sins is not persuasive. Paul does not address Israel as a corporate reality in Galatians 3:10, but speaks in an individualizing manner of 'those who are of the works of the Law'. Indeed, one might have protested against the assumption of a continuing exile that while it might be true of many within Israel, it is *not* the case for those of 'us' who have repented of our sins and practise 'the works of the Law'. That is, in fact, the stance taken by early Jewish sectarian groups.

In this regard, although we cannot pursue the matter at length, the argument that ethnic identity is socially constructed bears further relevance. The idea that Israel continued to live in 'exile', which appears in early Jewish sources, and extends well beyond them, is socially constructed.[28] It was not the only paradigm by which first-century Jews understood themselves. At the very least, alongside the pattern of sin–exile–return, there was also the pattern of destruction and preservation of a remnant, which was especially favoured by sectarian groups.[29] Paul himself employs the paradigm of a remnant extensively in Romans 9 – 11. Moreover, Habakkuk 2:4, to which he appeals in Galatians 3:11, presupposes the pattern of 'destruction and preservation', and clearly informs his argument.[30]

Rather than serving as a recollection of a continuing exile, Paul's unexpressed presupposition that no one does all that the law requires may be regarded as an invitation to his readers to confess that this is true of them. Indeed, it finally requires individual confession, by virtue of sweeping, universal claim, that is intended to penetrate and deconstruct an identity based on 'works of the Law'. Paul's implicit invitation to that confession may be found in vv. 13–14, where he shifts his usage to the first-person plural: 'Christ redeemed us from the curse of the Law, so that the blessing of Abraham might come about in Christ Jesus, so that we might receive the promise of the Spirit through faith.'

The critical question at this point, and the subject of current debate is the identity of the 'we'. Whom did Christ redeem from the curse of the law? The answer quite clearly has to be found in the antecedent identification of v. 10, 'those of the works of the Law', that is to say Jews as they are defined by this boundary marker. Paul's announcement that Christ redeemed 'us' from the law's curse is a confession made on behalf of all who are 'of the works of the Law'. Paul is included in the 'us'.[31] He, along with all others, is under the curse of the law, not because of Israel's past rebellion, but because here and now neither he nor they do what the law requires. It is obvious that for Paul the 'works of the Law' are not sufficient. The 'works of the Law' do not fulfil what the law requires, as is obvious from his announcement of the Deuteronomic curse upon all who do not do all that the law requires (Gal. 3:10). Paul's point is not one of quantity – as if one were supposed to aim at mere outward performance – but one of quality. The law requires much more than the outward 'works'. According to Paul, it requires a performance of the Spirit, who overcomes 'the works of the flesh' and effects the fruit of 'love, joy, peace' and so on, qualities that are characteristic of an entirely new person. Paul's fundamental difference with the advocates of Judaizing is anthropological: he understands the human being as a radical sinner. If law-keeping counts as the boundary marker of ethnic identity, Paul and his fellow Jews effectively have become Gentiles. That is Paul's point in the paradigmatic self-confession that he reports in his confrontation with Cephas at Antioch.[32] In being justified in Christ, Paul confesses that 'we [Jews] ourselves are found to be sinners' (Gal. 2:17). This use of the first-person plural functions as Paul's self-confession, to which he invites Cephas and all the rest. His further shift to the first-person singular in vv. 18–21 individualizes that invitation. The same dynamic is at work in Paul's first-person plural usage in Galatians 3:13–14.

Paul's implicit confession in Galatians 3:13 thus paves the way for the twofold purpose clause in v. 14. The redeeming exchange took place 'so that Abraham's blessing might take place in Christ Jesus *for the Gentiles*, so that we might receive the promise of the Spirit through faith'. In Christ, the Abrahamic blessing of the Gentiles has come to pass. The second purpose clause, which, by virtue of its reference to the Spirit and faith (Gal. 3:5,9) is surely to be regarded as a parallel to the first, restates its content: Abraham's blessing is nothing other than the promised Spirit. The 'we' who are Jews thus appear effectively as Gentiles, on account of their transgressions.[33] Paul's position is opposite to that which his opponents supposed: it was not becoming a Jew, but becoming a Gentile that was necessary to salvation. Of course, Paul does not have in mind a change of ethnic identity, but the deconstruction of Jewish identity in the recognition of oneself as a sinner.

This attribution of Gentile status to Jews corresponds to Paul's subsequent appeal to the Galatians to become as he is, for he had become as they are (Gal. 4:12; cf. 1 Cor. 9:19–23). It also matches his rhetoric in Galatians 4:1–11, according to which slavery to 'the elements of the world' under the law is equivalent to the former enslavement of the pagan Galatians to 'things that are not gods'. In Judaizing, the Galatians want to return to that state (Gal. 4:8–11). Here, then, in Paul's appeal to Scripture, Galatians 3:6–14 is the counterpart to his christological confession of his identity in Galatians 2:15–21. In both instances Jews become Gentiles in order to be made something entirely new, and to find their identity in the crucified and risen Christ, in whom 'there is no longer Jew or Greek' (Gal. 3:28).

We must not overlook that Paul rounds out the first movement of his argument by introducing Christ in vv. 13–14. What is of interest to us at the moment is the exchange of identity that Paul expresses in this summary of his message: 'Christ redeemed us from the curse of the Law, having become a curse for us.'[34] It is of critical importance to see that Paul does not speak here of Christ bearing a curse. He speaks instead of Christ *becoming* a curse for us. 'Substitution' here entails an exchange of persons. Redemption took place in Christ taking on 'our' identity in the cross, so that we thereby might take on his identity. The one and only 'seed of Abraham', to whom belong the promises of blessing, became a curse 'for us'. Christ became a 'sinner' under the curse of the law, so that we might become the 'seed' who is the object of blessing of the promise. The exchange of identity that takes place in faith corresponds to the exchange of blessing and curse that has taken place in Christ. Indeed, faith is present only 'in Christ' who is not only its object, but also its source.[35] Consequently, in Christ and in faith, Jews take their place alongside Gentiles as redeemed sinners. Paul has said this explicitly in self-confession in Galatians 2:17. He now invites the Galatian believers to this identity through his appeal to Scripture.

It is worth pausing to reflect on Paul's identification of Christ as Abraham's promised seed in v. 16.[36] His appeal to the singular form is no mere grammatical trick. Within the Genesis narrative itself, the singular form σπέρμα (זֶרַע) obviously serves as a collective singular, in which numerous descendants are identified with their single progenitor. In his following argument, Paul himself makes use of the collective sense of the term, as he describes those who belong to Christ as 'Abraham's seed' (Gal. 3:29), and children of promise, according to the pattern of Isaac (Gal. 4:28). Christ is thus simultaneously an individual and incorporative figure, in whom believers are included as 'children of promise'.

In both Romans and Galatians, Paul identifies Christ by means of the figure of Isaac, who nevertheless remains a mere shadow in Paul's discourse,[37] and whose significance lies *in his birth* and not in his deeds.[38] This figural interpretation of Christ in the form of Isaac provides an essential clue to the manner in which Paul presents Christ in Galatians. It is not the story of Jesus' obedience or faithfulness toward God that lies behind his appeal to Christ. The 'faith of Christ' is not the faithfulness of Christ, but the faith that comes from him.[39] It is the story of Jesus' cross and resurrection and the dramatic exchange that has taken place in it to which Paul points in his reference to Christ as Abraham's seed, and the heir of blessing.

Christ and Christian Identity

As we have noted, within the body of the letter, Paul first speaks of Christ as the Crucified, who became a curse for us in order to redeem us (Gal. 3:13). When he speaks of Christ elsewhere in the letter, he consistently speaks of that redemptive event, especially in its ontological significance. Christ gave himself for our sins, that he might redeem us from the present, evil age (Gal. 1:4). Paul has been crucified with Christ (Gal. 2:19). The life that Paul now lives is that of the risen Christ who lives in him (Gal. 2:20). In the risen Christ, earthly differences of Jew or Greek, slave or free, male and female have been transcended (Gal. 3:28). Paul has been crucified to 'the world', namely the fallen order of all things, including human beings. And the world has been crucified to him (Gal. 6:14). Paul's perspective appears most pointedly in his closing words: in Christ nothing counts, other than a new creation (Gal. 6:15).[40]

As is apparent in Paul's reference to the cross in Galatians 3:13, Paul presents Christ's saving work in Galatians not as an act of obedience directed toward God, but an act of love and giving directed toward human beings. Christ gave himself for our sins '*in order to deliver us* from the present, evil age' (Gal. 1:4). As Paul subsequently confesses, '[Christ] loved me, and gave himself up for me' (Gal. 2:20). *Christ has set us free,* and that for no other end than freedom itself (Gal. 5:1).

Of course, for Paul, Christ gave himself, 'according to the will of our God and Father' (Gal. 1:4). It is God who sent forth his Son to be born of a woman and under the law, in order to redeem those under the law (Gal. 4:6). According to Paul, God is at work in what Christ has done: believers have been made heirs *through God* (Gal. 4:7). But nowhere in the letter does Paul describe Christ's work as an act of obedience performed toward God. He speaks instead of God savingly acting through Christ. God has called the Galatians 'by the grace of Christ' (Gal. 1:6).[41] We might say that Paul does not present Christ in Galatians as the true human being faithfully doing his best before God, but as the true God, faithfully doing God's best for fallen human beings.[42] That does not mean that Jesus' earthly life was of no significance for Paul. It means only that in speaking of salvation, Paul's focus is fixed on Christ's cross and resurrection.[43]

The Law and Christian Identity (Gal. 3:15 – 4:7)

As is already apparent, Paul's presentation of Christ in Galatians is essential to his attempt to reform the Galatians' understanding of Christian identity. In a paradoxical manner, the law serves the promise to Abraham, and not the other way around – as the Galatians supposed. The law 'was added' to promise not as its fulfilment, but as a prevention to its fulfilment apart from Christ, 'the promised seed'. In the time of waiting until the promised seed arrived, the law was given in order to produce transgressions (Gal. 3:19; τῶν παραβάσεων χάριν), widening the gap between God and humanity. That gap is already manifest in the law's having been ordained 'through angels by a mediator'.[44] The law provoked transgressions effecting a curse on all human beings, and making that curse public and manifest. The distance between the God who promises blessing and the human being caught in transgression thereby becomes absolute.

Paul accentuates that distance by his appeal to the Shema: 'God is one'. Just as he does in Romans, he interprets this fundamental Jewish confession as essential to salvation.[45] Paul's point here appears to be that since God is one, salvation or, as he describes it in his following statements, 'life and righteousness', are present only where there is a meeting and union between God and human beings.[46] In this regard, we may point to the instatement as 'sons of God' as the realization of this salvific union (Gal. 4:4–7). It is a union that has come about through Christ, God's Son whom God sent forth and who came to be 'of a woman, [and] under the Law' (Gal. 4:4). It is not a union of mystical merging, but one of communication, within which God sends the Spirit into our hearts, and we respond with the cry of faith and hope, 'Abba, that is, Father' (Gal. 4:6). It is likewise a union in which we, with Paul, confess that we are sinners and that Christ, God's Son, has loved us and delivered himself up – to a curse and death – for us (Gal. 2:20). It is thereby also a union in which we not only come to God, but also come to be one with one another in Christ, whether Jew or Greek, slave or free, and as both male and female (Gal. 3:28). The ground is level at the foot of the cross, and only there. The giving of the law thus served to prevent the promise from being realized in any way other than in Christ and by faith. As Paul says, 'the Scripture imprisoned all things under sin, in order that the promise, which is of the faith of Jesus Christ might be given to those who believe' (Gal. 3:29).[47]

The law thus paradoxically served to bring imprisonment for the purpose of freedom, a curse for the purpose of blessing, disobedience for the only true obedience, which is found in faith and in Christ. In his discussion of the law in Gal 3:15 – 4:7, Paul continues to present his argument in terms of Christian identity. 'We were under guard under the Law, imprisoned for the faith that was to be revealed' (Gal. 3:23). Within the larger purpose of God, the subjection to sin effected by the law was to end with the arrival of the eschaton in Christ. Paul consequently is able to speak of the law as a παιδαγωγός, a tutor and guardian of children in a Greco-Roman household. Now it is not the Scriptures that 'figure out' Christ, but Christ who figures out the law. Only because of Christ has the law become a παιδαγωγός, rather that remaining a jailer. We need not explore here the debates concerning the significance of the παιδαγωγός. It suffices to note that Paul presents the παιδαγωγός as serving to constrain and rule, not to educate. Paul goes on to liken the minor status of the heirs of a household as equivalent to that of a slave (Gal. 4:1–6). In so doing, he does not at all suggest that human beings recognize their condition. Indeed, his argument presupposes just the opposite. He expresses surprise that the Galatians prefer slavery, which they already had experienced as pagans, to the freedom that has come to them (Gal. 4:8–11). He likewise provides no indication that he himself suffered from guilt prior to his encounter with Christ: he was advancing within Judaism, outstripping his contemporaries (Gal. 1:14–15). As we have noted, the same is true in a corporate sense of Israel: Paul's equation of the 'present Jerusalem' with Hagar, the slave, was not a commonplace for his readers, but an assault on their assumptions.

The law, then, serves the promise, by preventing the realization of its blessing apart from Christ. He alone is the 'seed of Abraham' to whom the promises have been given (Gal. 3:16). We may remind ourselves that Paul does not present Christ in Galatians as the model human being, but as the Crucified and Risen One, who stands apart from all other human beings, as the one sent forth by God to be born of a woman, to come under the law, in order to redeem those under the law (Gal. 4:5–6). Sharing in the promise, and thus in life, righteousness, the kingdom of God and the new creation depends entirely on being 'of Christ', i.e. belonging to and participating in him as the Crucified and Risen One (Gal. 3:29). That is to say, it depends entirely not on acquiring, but on being *given* a new identity in faith and baptism. It depends on being clothed with Christ. The clothing makes the person. Indeed, it makes them new. Paul's argument from Scripture concerning Christian identity thus corresponds to his christological self-narration in Galatians 2:19–20: 'I have been crucified with Christ. I live, yet no longer I, but Christ lives in me.' Paul goes on to describe his apostolic labours as birth pangs that continue until Christ is formed in the Galatians (Gal. 4:19). He is giving birth to Christ in them. Paul thus subsequently asserts that to be justified in the law is to be severed from Christ (Gal. 5:3).

While Paul does not conceive of participation in Christ in terms of a merging of persons or an ineffable experience, he certainly regards our relationship with Christ as decidedly ontological in nature, and not only ontological, but eschatological. In him there is 'neither Jew nor Greek, neither slave nor free, neither male and female, but you are all one in Christ Jesus'. The final pairing, 'male and female', which obviously recalls Genesis 1:27, anticipates Paul's closing statement in Galatians 6:15: in Christ there is a new creation. Moreover, just as sharing in Christ does not entail a merging of persons, the presence of Christ obviously does not mean that earthly distinctions have been set aside. Eschatological life has entered the present unseen in the form of the gospel and faith. It thereby shatters the pretense of any piety based on boundary markers that may be outwardly observed.

Once Again, God and Christian Identity (Gal. 4:8–11)

As we have seen, the fundamental role that Paul gives not only to identity, but also to an ontology of relation within the structure of promise, Christ, and faith in Galatians, bears a distinctly theological dimension. At the end of the second movement of his argument, Paul returns to his opening question concerning the identity of God: 'And, now, knowing God, or rather being known by God, how is it that you turn again to the weak and poor elements, to which you desire to be enslaved again?' (Gal. 4:9). As Paul's diorthotic remark makes clear, 'knowing' entails the recognition and acceptance of the other.[48] Being recognized by God is prior and fundamental to our recognizing God. Having effected our adoption to sonship, God has sent forth the Spirit of the Son into our hearts (Gal. 4:6), as an act of recognition that creates our recognition of him in the cry, 'Abba, Father!' Christian identity for Paul is to be found within this relationship of mutual recognition by God and of God, and not by self-recognition or recognition by others. This mutual recognition is an eschatological reality that presently remains hidden behind human weakness and suffering. For Paul, it cannot be located in 'works of the Law', i.e. in outward and visible deeds that serve as boundary markers. Things are not as they outwardly appear. Paul thus at the very start reminds the Galatians of the way in which Jesus Christ was visibly presented to them as crucified, and what they themselves suffered at the beginning of their faith (Gal. 3:1–4). These opening statements anticipate Paul's personal appeal to the Galatians in 4:12–20. There he reminds them that it was a 'weakness of the flesh' that brought him to evangelize them, and that they did not reject this trial, but received him as an angel of God, as Christ Jesus (Gal. 4:12–14). The good news arrived in an unappealing package: angelic power (and more) was present in one who bore the form of the Crucified.[49] To preach circumcision, or to seek to have Gentile believers circumcised becomes a means of avoiding persecution on account of the cross (Gal. 5:11; 6:12–13). The cross brings a stigma, or rather the stigmata of Jesus, which Paul bears in his body (Gal. 6:17). According to Paul, this persecution comes, in part at least, from Jews themselves (Gal. 4:28–9; cf. Gen. 21:9).[50] The quest for recognition before oneself and before others thus presents a fundamental temptation. Recognition by God means rejection by the world, and vice versa. For Paul, this external disgrace is inherent to Christian identity. It is opposed to the piety that the Galatians sought.

What Paul strives for, then, with the Galatians is the reformation of their identity through the reformation of the place that they find recognition. Just as Paul once was progressing in Judaism beyond his contemporaries (Gal. 1:14), but found himself as the object of God's work of displaying Christ in him (Gal. 1:16), and thus found himself a sinner along with all the pagans (Gal. 2:16), so he calls the Galatians to find their righteousness in Christ, and therefore not to seek to find it in the law, 'the works of the Law', circumcision, and becoming Jewish. That would mean a slavery to the mere elements of the world (Gal. 4:7–11). It would also mean a vying for recognition among one another that already has led to infighting among the Galatians, a 'biting and devouring' of one another (Gal. 5:15), and a failure to help and restore those caught in transgression (Gal. 6:1–2).

Ethnic Identity and Christian Identity (Gal. 4:21–31)

In the conclusion of his argument (Gal. 4:21–31), Paul returns to the law, no longer as a body of demands, but as the Scripture which provides the context of those demands, and which itself speaks here and now in witness to Christ: 'Tell me, you who desire to be under the Law, do you listen to the Law?' (Gal. 4:21). In the light of the imprisonment worked by the law (Gal. 3:22), Paul provides his account of the Judaism to which his Gentile churches were so strongly attracted. Just as Christ establishes a people, the law establishes a people and has its own story. Paul finds that story in the narrative of Sarah and Hagar.[51] His reading of this story, which he openly names as an allegory, corresponds to the theology of promise that he has presented, and is built upon the distinction between present earthly recognition by human beings and eschatological recognition by God. Abraham had two sons. He had them by two different women, one a slave and one free. The two women are two different covenants. One of these covenants, playing the role of woman, gives birth to slavery. The other covenant remains unnamed, as Paul draws his readers into the allegory. They surely would recognize it from the words of institution in the Pauline tradition as the new covenant (Jer. 31:31–4; 1 Cor. 11:23–6). And they would recognize it as giving birth to freedom, a new birth. These two covenants are given from two different mountains, one of which is alien, outside the land, and enslaved. The other is 'in the land', and free.

Paul thus establishes a distinction that his readers did not expect, between the old covenant and the new (cf. 2 Cor. 3:14), and thereby inverts all the identities that they had assumed. The law, the Sinai covenant, Paul reminds his readers, was issued from Arabia, a remote and alien place. He shockingly identifies it with the 'present Jerusalem', to which the Galatians looked for affirmation. The metaphor of motherhood continues throughout Paul's argument. The 'present Jerusalem' – this alien place – is enslaved along with all her children (Gal. 4:25). The 'Jerusalem above' is free, she is our mother (Gal. 4:26).

Paul continues this inversion of expectations in an appeal to Isaiah 54:1 (Gal. 4:27), 'Rejoice, O barren one, who did not give birth . . . the children of the desolate one are more than those of the one who has a husband.' The present, earthly Jerusalem is the woman 'who has a husband'. 'She' thus corresponds to Babylon, the place of exile. Within the Isaianic imagery to which Paul alludes in his citation, 'having a husband' signifies having visible and manifest blessing as a sign of the presence of a god.[52] The present Jerusalem is happily settled in the land, and enjoys a measure of prosperity and apparent piety as well, at least in Paul's view – and that of the Galatians, whom he seeks to persuade.

Paul contrasts this 'present Jerusalem', not with the Jerusalem that is to come, but with 'the Jerusalem above'. As has become clear in this letter, eschatological realities exist already for Paul. That is true 'geographically'.[53] Paul thus confesses that the free, eschatological Jerusalem is 'our' mother here and now. This 'Jerusalem above' remains unseen. She is barren and desolate. Nevertheless, her children, who are born 'according to the Spirit' (Gal. 4:29), will outnumber those of the present Jerusalem with her visible, earthly glory. According to Paul's scriptural imagery, the children of the 'Jerusalem above' remain in exile, distant from their eschatological home, waiting for its arrival. As Paul will later remind the Galatian churches, 'we by the Spirit, out of faith, await the hope of righteousness' (Gal. 5:4).

The son of the slave woman was born 'according to the flesh' (Gal. 4:28). The earthly, visible glory of the 'present Jerusalem' thus corresponds to all human calculations and efforts, including 'works of the Law', those visible and outward deeds, which, according to Paul, are done 'by the flesh' (Gal. 3:3). The son of the free woman was born 'according to promise', that is by the word and work of God alone (Gal. 4:28).[54] Isaac, displaced by Christ in

Galatians 3:16, now appears on the scene and presents the eschatological identity of believers in Christ, and not the earthly identity of Jews – even if he was the first to be circumcised on the eighth day (Gal. 4:28).[55] Visible ethnic and religious identity, established by boundary markers is replaced by an eschatological identity that remains unseen, a matter of faith and hope.[56]

The present, visible, earthly Jerusalem thus serves as a figure, pattern or type of the unseen, eschatological, heavenly Jerusalem from whom believers were born, and to whom they belong. It is certainly not 'the church',[57] but the new creation itself, pictured as a place of community.[58] But Paul again leaves it to his readers to make this connection. Just as Jews have become 'Gentiles' through transgression of the law, Gentiles have become 'eschatological Jews' not only by virtue of Abraham, their father, but also through this heavenly mother.[59]

Conclusion: Identity Redefined in Galatians

Paul's message to the Galatian churches is that our identity is found in God's word of promise fulfilled in Christ and in the human response to that word in faith. He thereby deconstructs the identity based on 'works of the Law' to which the Galatians were attracted, shattering its superficial assumptions concerning the human being. According to Paul, we are radical sinners who require death and a new birth in order to come to ourselves. Christian identity is not established by our works. It is given to us in Christ. In Christ and in faith human beings have been brought into union with God, a union of mutual recognition and communication. This union is not the result of a natural inclination or a mystical quest on the part of the human being. It is the result of the dramatic overcoming of sin and the curse of the law by the unconditioned love of Christ and the will of the Father. This union with God through Christ also brings us into union with one another, above and beyond all earthly differences, without any of those differences being yet set aside. Boundary markers remain, but their significance is now limited to the earthly roles that God has assigned to us: 'Our community with one another consists solely in what Christ has done to both of us.'[60]

Paul understands the Scriptures to bear witness to this work of God in Christ in figures that make that work visible.[61] The Scriptures and Christ stand in the relationship of promise and fulfilment, earthly anticipation and eschatological reality. The earthly anticipation is by no means negated in this relation, but rather affirmed: Christ is given to us through the Scriptures alone.[62] In Galatians, where Paul treats the law in terms of its demands, it is not Christ who is figured out by the law, but the law that is figured out by Christ. In his presence it is shown to be a mere παιδαγωγός directed toward the coming of Christ and faith. The law in its demands has been transcended by the new creation that has entered the world in the crucified and risen Christ. Our being and worth is a gift, given prior to and apart from anything of our doing. In place of the ethnic and religious identity that the Galatians seek to construct for themselves in the visible works of the law, Paul calls them to find their identity in Christ and in faith. They will thus share together with Paul in the scandal of the cross. But as Abraham's seed, they will also share – already here and now – in Abraham's blessing.

7

The 'Seed', the 'Many' and the 'One' in Galatians 3:16: Paul's Reading of Genesis 17 and its Significance for Gentiles

Lionel Windsor
Moore Theological College, Sydney, Australia

The Puzzle of Galatians 3:16

In Galatians 3:16, Paul engages in a piece of scriptural interpretation which has turned out to be a puzzle for modern readers. The verse appears in a passage in which Paul is contrasting God's promises to Abraham with the obligations of the law of Moses (Gal. 3:15–18). Verse 16 reads: 'Now it is to Abraham that the promises were spoken – and to his seed. It does not say, "and to the seeds" (kai tois spermasin), as referring to many (*epi pollōn*), but as referring to one (*hōs eph' henos*): "and to your seed" (*kai tō spermati sou*) – who is Christ.' Paul is here commenting on the details of the promises of land to Abraham in Genesis, particularly on those promises connected with the phrase 'and to your seed' in Genesis 17:8.[1] He is applying these promises to the eschatological gift of the Spirit to believers (Gal 3:14; cf. 5:5; 6:15).

Galatians 3:16 raises a number of questions for us:

1. What is the nature of Paul's contrast between the plural 'seeds' and the singular 'seed'?
2. How is Paul using his source text? Is he exploiting it arbitrarily in service of his own agenda, or exegeting it fairly with due regard to its context?

3. What is the significance of 'Christ' – i.e. why does Paul at this point identify Christ with the singular seed of Abraham?
4. What is the purpose of Galatians 3:16 in Paul's overall argument?

There are two broad sets of answers to these questions in the scholarship: a majority interpretation, and a significant minority interpretation. However, both the majority and the minority interpretations present us with problems.

The Majority Interpretation: Israelites Versus Christ/ Christians

The nature of the contrast: The majority of interpreters argue, in various ways, that Paul is making a contrast here between the many physical descendants of Abraham – Israelites – and the single descendant of Abraham who is the only true heir to the promises – Christ.[2]

Paul's use of his source text: Paul is highlighting the fact that the term 'seed' in his source text is grammatically singular in order to show that the true seed of Abraham must be understood as a single individual, whom he identifies as Christ.

The significance of 'Christ': Paul is here claiming that Christ is an individual who has become the only true heir to the promises to Abraham. Furthermore, as v. 29 argues, Christ is ultimately a representative of all believers by way of corporate solidarity.

The purpose in Paul's overall argument: This verse forms one important step in Paul's argument that those characterized by faith in Christ, not those characterized by Torah, are the true seed of Abraham and heirs to the promises. This helps Paul to dissuade the Galatians from being circumcised and adopting the law of Moses (cf. Gal. 5:3–6, 6:13–15).

Problems with the majority interpretation

The key problems for proponents of the majority interpretation arise from their explanations of Paul's use of his source text.

Genesis 17:8 reads: 'And I will give to you and to your seed (LXX *kai tō spermati sou*) after you the land in which you sojourn, all the land of Canaan, for an everlasting possession; and I will be their (LXX *autois*) God.' The first problem arises from Paul's supposed insistence that the singular 'seed' must denote a single individual. In the Scriptures, the 'seed' of Abraham in the singular is commonly a collective term referring to all of Abraham's descendants through Isaac.[3] Indeed, here in Genesis 17:8, 'seed' is clearly a collective term – as demonstrated by the anaphoric third-person *plural* pronoun in the later part of the verse: 'I will be *their* God'.[4] However, according to the majority interpretation, Paul is claiming – against the clear sense of Genesis 17:8 – that the singular use of the term 'seed' denotes an individual descendant as opposed to a collective posterity. Indeed, just a few verses later, Paul himself uses the singular 'seed' in a collective sense (Gal. 3:29; cf. Rom. 4:13–18; 9:6–8). Why, then, does Paul's argument in Galatians 3:16 supposedly proceed as if the possibility of a collective meaning does not exist?

Some interpreters regard Paul simply as ignoring the meaning of the original passage in order to score an ad hominem point against his opponents.[5] Others seek to explain Paul's exegesis of Genesis 17 by referring to various aspects of its wider context. Daube, for example, points to Genesis 21:12, referring to a rabbinic interpretation in which Isaac is identified as the specific seed of Abraham.[6] DeRouchie and Meyer argue that Paul is taking his cue from Genesis 3:15 and 22:17–18, in which the 'seed' may be understood as a specific descendant.[7] A number of others point out that Paul's argument is consistent with a broad scriptural theme: the distillation of the Abrahamic 'seed' to a single individual king, a Son of David who is the Messiah/Christ (cf. 2 Sam. 7:12–14, Ps. 89:3–4, cf. Ps. 17.4).[8]

This last observation that the Messiah was frequently seen as the ultimate representative seed of Abraham is promising. Nevertheless, the observation by itself does not explain Paul's specific argument about the meaning of his source text. Galatians 3:16 has all the hallmarks of a careful piece of exegesis proceeding from a particular citation, not simply a general statement about the fulfilment of the Scriptures in Christ. Paul takes care explicitly to locate his citation within the Abrahamic narrative, he demarcates the citation with verbs of speech,[9] he discusses the details of a specific word, and he even presents a hypothetical alternative in order to emphasize further the meaning of that word. Any interpretation of Galatians 3:16 must demonstrate how – and why – Paul is using this particular source text. The majority interpretation, which resorts to contextual factors apart from the source text, ultimately fails to do so.

A second problem with the majority interpretation is that it fails to explain adequately why Paul would choose this particular source text in the first place – since in the very next verse after the cited text, Abraham and his 'seed' are commanded to be circumcised (Gen. 17:9)! Paul's opponents would surely have referred to and exploited this command.[10] Why would Paul, who is trying to argue that the true seed of Abraham is *not* obliged to be circumcised, deliberately choose to cite from a passage which states that Abraham's seed is obliged to be circumcised?

A Minority Interpretation: A Plurality of Families Versus a United Family

The nature of the contrast: Another minority line of interpretation – argued most extensively by N.T. Wright[11] – understands the contrast between plurality and singularity not as a contrast between the collective Israel and the individual Christ, but rather as a contrast between *two different collective possibilities* for Abraham's posterity. The first possibility is the plurality of 'families' (Jews and Gentiles) which would result if the people of God were demarcated by circumcision and Torah. The second possibility is the single, united family which will result if the people of God are demarcated by faith in Christ.

Paul's use of his source text: Wright's interpretation neatly eliminates the grammatical conundrum associated with Paul's insistence on the singular 'seed', since in this interpretation Paul is consistently using the term 'seed' as a collective. The contrast is not between a collective 'seed' and an individual 'seed', but between a plurality of divided collective 'seeds' and a *united* collective 'seed'.

The significance of 'Christ': For Wright's understanding to work, however, 'Christ' must be seen primarily as a corporate figure standing in for the united 'people of God' (cf. Gal. 3:28).

The purpose in Paul's overall argument: The purpose of Paul's reference to Christ is to demonstrate that Jews and Gentiles are already united in 'Christ' – i.e. the people of God – and therefore: 'they do not need to "judaize" in order to belong to the true people of God.'[12]

Problems with the minority interpretation

However, Wright's interpretation is also subject to a number of serious criticisms.

First, Wright does not deal adequately with the Abraham narrative itself. According to Wright, Paul is arguing that 'the promises of Genesis 15, 17 and 18 always envisaged a single worldwide family [which] . . . would be characterized by faith, not by circumcision or Torah'.[13] However, this claim is not supported by the Genesis text itself. Genesis does *not* envisage a 'single family'; it explicitly envisages a 'plurality of families'[14] with Abraham as their spiritual progenitor: 'in you all the *families* [plural] of the earth will be blessed' (Gen. 12:3); 'you shall be the father of a *multitude* of nations' (Gen. 17:4).

Second, as with the majority interpretation, Wright does not explain how or why Paul ignores the explicit requirement for circumcision laid on Abraham's 'seed' in Genesis 17:9ff.[15]

Third, Wright's reading of 'Christ' as a corporate figure in Galatians 3:16 is unsustainable. 'Christ' elsewhere in Galatians, and especially in this chapter, is clearly an individual (e.g. 3:1,13,24). There is of course a corporate solidarity between Christ and believers in Paul's mind, but when Paul wishes to refer to such solidarity he indicates it explicitly by phrases such as 'in Christ' (e.g. 3:14,26,28). There is no such phrase in Galatians 3:16. Paul does not say 'which is in Christ' – as he would if he were referring to the people of God. Rather he says 'who is Christ' – most obviously referring to the individual Christ.[16]

An Alternative Interpretation: The 'Many Nations' Versus the Unique Redeemer

In view of the problems with existing solutions to the puzzle of Galatians 3:16, we will here present an alternative solution.

The nature of the contrast

Our thesis is this: Paul's contrast between plurality and singularity is a contrast between the 'many nations' of whom Abraham is father in Genesis 17:1–6, and the more specific 'seed' of Abraham in Genesis 17:7ff., which is one particular nation: Israel, ultimately fulfilled in Christ.

Paul's use of his source text

Our solution seeks to explain Galatians 3:16 as a careful reading by Paul of the whole of Genesis 17.

The problem posed by Genesis 17: Paul needs to engage with Genesis 17, because it seems to represent a fatal blow to his cause. Paul's argument in this part of Galatians rests on the notion of a 'covenant' with Abraham characterized entirely by divine promises. For Paul, this promissory 'covenant' stands in opposition to the 'law' – a law which came after the covenant and which imposed obligations which stand in opposition to the promises (Gal. 3:15–18). This notion of a covenant founded entirely on divine promises is derived from Genesis 15, which Paul has already cited (Gal. 3:6//Gen. 15:6). Genesis 15 depicts a covenant with Abraham whose obligations are entirely on God's side.[17] God promises to give Abraham land, offspring and thus inheritance; Abraham's part in the covenant is simply to believe the promises.

Genesis 17, however, seems to pose a problem for Paul's claim. Genesis 17 reiterates the promises of Genesis 15, but then expands on Genesis 15 in two crucial ways.[18] First, Genesis 17 adds a reference to the *international* blessing which will come through Abraham.[19] According to Genesis 17, Abraham is not to be the father of a single nation only; he will in fact be the father of 'many nations'. Second, Genesis 17 describes an explicit *obligation* laid upon Abraham and his 'seed': circumcision. The fact that circumcision is an obligation is reinforced by the threat that members of Abraham's household will be 'cut off' if they are not circumcised (Gen. 17:14). This obligatory character of circumcision in Genesis 17 surely contributed to the move by a number of Jewish writers to conflate Genesis 17 with the Mosaic covenant, thus identifying Abraham as the supreme law-keeper (e.g. *Jub*. 15:25–32, Sir. 44:19–20). This close association between circumcision and law-keeping is, indeed, a factor in the argument of Galatians (2:12,16; 5:3; 6:13; cf. Acts 15:5).

Genesis 17, then, links Abraham's international fatherhood to an obligation of circumcision, which in turn suggests a requirement for law-keeping. Hence one could easily imagine an argument from Paul's opponents on the basis of Genesis 17: Abraham is the father of many nations, Abraham and his seed were obliged to be circumcised (and thus keep the law), therefore any Gentile who wishes to have Abraham as his father must also be circumcised and keep the law.[20] So Paul, who wishes to maintain that the Gentiles are *not* obliged to be circumcised or to come under the law, must deal with this text. How does he do so?

The 'many' and the 'seed' in Genesis 17: Our claim is that Paul, by making a point about *plurality* and *singularity*, is in fact emphasizing a distinction which is present in the text of Genesis 17 itself: the distinction between the plurality of the 'many nations' of Genesis 17:1–6 and the singularity of the 'seed' of Abraham in Genesis 17:7ff.

Plurality is, indeed, a striking feature of the first six verses of Genesis 17. We may note the following features of vv. 1–6:

1. The use of the emphatic phrase: 'I will multiply you greatly' in v. 2.
2. The threefold use of the plural 'nations' in vv. 4, 5, 6.
3. The twofold use of the term 'many'/'multitude' to refer to those nations in vv. 4, 5 (Hebrew noun *hāmôn*, translated with Greek noun *plēthos* and adjective *polys*)
4. The change of Abram's name to Abraham in v. 5, which includes a suggestion of the word 'many' (Hebrew *'abrāhām* suggests a conflation of *'abrām* and *hāmôn*).

5. The promise that 'kings' will come from Abraham (v. 6), implying a plurality of nations, each governed by an individual ruler.

This description of the plurality of nations in vv. 1–6 points to a projected eschatological future in which the blessing referred to at the opening and closing of the Abraham cycle (Gen. 12:3; 22:18) has finally flowed to the rest of the world.[22]

Genesis 17:7, on the other hand, returns to the more immediate promise of land to Abraham and his singular 'seed' (vv. 7–8), which is followed by the introduction of the covenantal obligation of circumcision (vv. 9–14). Circumcision is envisaged as an obligation for Abraham's *singular* household (vv. 12–13) and for a *singular* 'people' (v. 14). The circumcision of the 'seed' envisages an immediate and concrete situation, as opposed to the projected future plurality of nations. Indeed, Abraham himself immediately fulfils the obligation of circumcision among the members of his household (vv. 22–7).

Thus there is a distinction in Genesis 17 itself between the future, worldwide plurality of nations of whom Abraham will be father, and the more immediate, particular singular nation which constitutes Abraham's 'seed' and which has special responsibilities and obligations.[23] As Watson observes: 'The initial apparently universal scope of God's covenant with Abraham gives way to a covenant sign which radically demarcates Abraham's seed from all other nations.'[24]

Paul's reading of Genesis 17: Paul's reference to plurality and singularity in Galatians 3:16, then, is not an alien concept imposed on the text of Genesis 17. Rather, Paul is using the word 'seed' to point out a feature of this text already pregnant with contrasts between plurality and singularity. Indeed, Paul refers explicitly to two key terms from his source text: not only the term 'seed' (*sperma*), which denotes singularity, but also the term 'many' (*polys*), which denotes plurality.[25] Although interpreters invariably notice that the term 'seed' occurs in Genesis 17, they consistently fail to notice that the equally significant term 'many' also occurs in Genesis 17.

Let us return to examine Galatians 3:16 directly. Paul says: 'Now it is to Abraham that the promises were spoken – and to his seed. It does not say, "and to the seeds" (*kai tois spermasin*), *as referring to many* (*epi pollōn*), but as referring to one (*hōs eph' henos*): "and to your seed" (*kai tō spermati sou*) – who is Christ.'

Paul is here pointing out the distinction in Genesis 17 between the plural 'many' nations of whom Abraham will ultimately be the father (Gen. 17:1–6), and the singular 'seed' of Abraham which stands under the obligation (Gen. 17:7ff.). The singular 'seed' of Abraham is the only entity in Genesis 17 that stands under Abraham's obligation of circumcision (and, consequently, of law). This obligation is not laid on the future projected 'many' nations of whom Abraham will ultimately be the father. Indeed, as Paul points out, the only way in which the 'many nations' could unambiguously be identified with the 'seed' in this instance would be if the term 'seed' itself were plural. Since it is not plural, Paul argues, Genesis 17 cannot be used to support the view that the 'many nations' must be circumcised in order to receive the promises.

The significance of 'Christ'

At the end of Galatians 3:16, Paul adds the phrase, 'who is Christ'. Paul is thereby claiming that this collective 'seed' of Abraham in Genesis 17 – Israel, the 'seed' which stands under the covenantal obligation – is ultimately fulfilled in the person of Christ. We have already seen that there is a scriptural precedent for narrowing the Abrahamic 'seed' to an individual, representative messianic king (cf. 2 Sam. 7:12–14, Ps 89:3–4, cf. Ps. 17.4). Thus it makes sense to view Christ as the fulfilment of Israel and her obligations.

Nevertheless, there remains a possible problem for our interpretation. If our interpretation is correct, Paul is *not yet* using the concept of the 'seed of Abraham' to speak of Gentile believers in corporate solidarity with Christ, as he does at the end of the chapter. Can our interpretation explain this transition from Christ as an 'exclusive' seed of Abraham (Gal. 3:16) to a more 'inclusive' seed of Abraham (Gal. 3:28–9)?

Indeed it can, because the transition is entirely in line with Paul's description of Christ elsewhere in Galatians. Paul in Galatians consistently describes Christ from two related perspectives: *first,* Christ is individual who acts *exclusively,* by his death, to redeem others by taking on their sin and curse; and *consequently,*

Christ is the *representative* of a new people, standing in corporate solidarity with those whom he has redeemed. Christ's exclusive role precedes his inclusive role; Christ's substitution precedes believers' participation. This can be seen in the following places in particular:

1. In Galatians 1:4, Christ is introduced in terms of his exclusive role: Christ 'gave himself for (*hyper*) our sins to deliver us from the present evil age'.
2. In Galatians 2:19–20, Paul claims that he lives his life by faith in the Son of God who acted *for* him: Christ 'loved me and gave himself for (*hyper*) me'. Christ's exclusive act is the ultimate basis for Paul's claim to be *included* in Christ: i.e. that he has been 'crucified with Christ' and that Christ lives 'in (*en*)' him.
3. In Galatians 3:1, Christ is introduced as the one 'publicly portrayed as crucified'. Christ's *exclusive* death for sins is the starting point for the chapter which ultimately ends portraying believers as *included* in Christ (Gal. 3:28–9).
4. In Galatians 3:13–14 – immediately preceding the passage we are discussing – Christ is *first* described as a substitute who 'redeemed us from the curse of the law by becoming a curse for (*hyper*) us'; *consequently* Christ is described as the source of Gentile inclusion in Abraham's blessing which comes 'in' (*en*) him.[26]
5. In Galatians 4:4–5, Christ is described first as the one 'born under the law' (v. 4) – i.e. subject to the obligations on Israel. The purpose for Christ's subjection to these obligations was that he might 'redeem those who were under the law' (v. 5). Again, Christ acts exclusively: he was born 'under law' so that believers do *not* have to be 'under law' (cf. Gal. 4:21; 5:18). Nevertheless, as a *consequence* of his redemptive act, believers may participate in Christ's sonship, Christ's Spirit and Christ's inheritance (vv. 6–7).

Paul's references to the 'seed' in Galatians 3 follow the same pattern. The 'seed' is first understood exclusively as Christ (v. 16), the individual 'seed' to whom the promises were initially directed. This seed, when he came, took upon himself the curse of the law (cf. v. 14), and so annulled the power of transgression, sin and law (see vv. 19, 22–3). Yet as a result of Christ's action as the exclusive 'seed', those who are justified by faith in Christ may be included in him (v. 28) and thus share in his status as 'seed' (v. 29). This means that Gentile believers – i.e. the 'many nations' – can lay claim to Abraham's inheritance according to the promise (Gen. 15) without being subject to Abraham's obligations (Gen. 17).

The purpose in Paul's overall argument

The purpose of Galatians 3:16 in Paul's overall argument, then, is to dissuade his Gentile readers from identifying themselves with the wrong parts of the story of Abraham and his 'seed'. They should only identify themselves with the future projected 'many nations' to whom the promises were ultimately applicable (Gen. 17:1–6), not with the immediate 'seed' to whom the promises were initially spoken (Gen. 17:7ff). The singular 'seed' of Genesis 17 is one particular nation: Israel, which – unlike the 'many nations' – was subject to circumcision and the law. Ultimately, the obligations laid on Israel devolved onto Christ. Like Israel, Christ was born under the law. Unlike Israel, however, Christ brought redemption by giving himself over to crucifixion for sins, so putting an end to the obligation of the law and circumcision.

Thus Paul's Gentile readers should not consider themselves subject to the obligation laid on Abraham's 'seed' in Genesis 17. Ultimately, of course, Gentile believers do become the 'seed' of Abraham by faith *in* Christ (Gal. 3:29) – but only after the obligations have been fulfilled and the promises have been achieved by Christ (Gal. 3:16). Believers are 'seed of Abraham' only in the sense of being heirs according to Abraham's promise (cf. Gen. 15), not in the sense of being subject to Abraham's obligation (Gen. 17).

Conclusion: A More Coherent Account of Galatians 3:16

There are two broad lines of scholarly interpretation of Galatians 3:16, both of which present us with severe problems. In view of these problems, we have offered here an alternative interpretation of Galatians 3:16, by paying closer attention to features of Genesis 17 itself. We have argued that Paul is carefully rereading the text of Genesis 17 in a new, yet surprisingly coherent, fashion, interpreting it in light of the death of Christ. Christ, according to the Scriptures, is the 'seed' who alone bore the curse of the law for the sake of others – the exclusive 'one' who died on behalf of the 'many'.

8

Taking with One Hand, and Giving with the Other? The Use of Psalm 68:18 in Ephesians 4:8

Martin Foord
Trinity Theological College, Western Australia

The Problem

An infamous exegetical puzzle is the use or perhaps misuse of Psalm 68:18 in Ephesians 4:8: 'When he ascended on high he took captivity captive; he gave gifts to people.'[1] Here Paul[2] appears to cite Ps. 68:18 (MT 68:19; LXX 67:19) but modifies the psalm's wording from 'you received gifts among people' to 'he gave gifts to people'. The change of the verb 'received' (MT לָקַחְתָּ; LXX ἔλαβες) to 'gave' (ἔδωκεν) looks like no minor adjustment but a veritable reversal of the text's original meaning.

Is this not a clear case where an OT text is pulled from its original context and used to make a point quite alien to its fundamental meaning? Joseph Fitzmyer frankly declares: 'Here Paul completely disregards the original context of the Psalm.'[3] In his commentary on Ephesians, Peter O'Brien canvasses five attempts to explain the change of wording and then finally concludes: 'None of the above-mentioned suggestions fully solves this difficult crux.'[4]

However, there seems a way to explain the use of Psalm 68:18 in Ephesians 4:8 where the OT context is respected and the change of wording is understandable. The key is grasping a particular way NT revelation relates to the OT. Let us explore Paul's change of wording, first with a survey of various solutions found in the Christian tradition. Then, second, we will examine both Psalm 68 and Ephesians 4:7–11 in order to make sense of their connection.

Various Solutions

In the history of exegesis, a variety of solutions have been proposed to explain Paul's change of wording. Let us survey some chief contenders.

Different perspectives of time

One of the earliest explanations comes from Jerome.[5] He contended that the change of 'receiving' to 'giving' reflects a perspective of time. When Psalm 68 was written Christ had not yet ascended to 'receive' gifts. But when Ephesians was written, Christ had already ascended and 'received' gifts and now 'gave' gifts.[6] This solution was followed by the Frankish monk, Bishop Atto of Vercelli (fl. 924–61).[7]

There are two problems with this explanation. First, it seems to ignore the original meaning of the psalm. Psalm 68:18 is not talking about Jesus but YHWH receiving tribute gifts as the ark of the covenant came into Jerusalem. Second, it does not explain how Paul could change the wording of the OT text to suit what appears to be a very different theological point he is making.

Giving faith, receiving the Spirit

A second solution is that of Bishop Theodoret of Cyrus (c. 393–c. 457 AD). He believed the change of 'receive' to 'give' simply conveys the idea that when Christ 'receives' faith from a person he then 'gives' grace to them: 'Both things happened: receiving faith he gives grace in return.'[8]

This resolution suffers from the same two problems as the first: it pays no attention to the original context of Psalm 68:18, which is not talking about receiving faith from people, but YHWH receiving gifts of tribute. And, second, how can Paul change the wording of Psalm 68:18?

'To receive' is 'to give'

A third explanation focuses on the meaning of the verb 'to receive'. It is argued that this word in both Greek (λαμβάνω) and the Hebrew (לָקַח) can also mean 'to give'. John Chrysostom (c. 347–407) famously said: 'The one [word] is the same as the other.'[9] It is also the solution of various post-Reformation, continental theologians like the Dutch thinkers Hugo Grotius[10] and Johannes Coccejus,[11] the English Puritans Paul Baynes[12] and John Owen,[13] as well as the nineteenth-century systematician Charles Hodge.[14] Grotius enlists Exodus 25:2 and 1 Kings 17:10 as examples where לָקַח is better understood as 'to give'.[15] John Owen avers that לָקַח can mean 'to receive in order to give'.[16] However, the chief difficulty with this solution is that Ephesians 4:8 does not use lamba&nw as a translation of לָקַח but δίδωμι. Moreover, the LXX translates לָקַח as λαμβάνω not δίδωμι.[17]

Different words, same sense

A fourth explanation is particularly common in the sixteenth and seventeenth centuries. It argues that despite Paul not using the exact words of Psalm 68:18 he preserved their same sense. This solution is found in commentators across a variety of traditions, such as the Roman Catholic opponent of Martin Luther, Thomas Cardinal Cajetan (1469–1534),[18] the Strasbourg Reformer Martin Bucer (1491–1551),[19] the Bernese Reformer Wolfgang Musculus (1497–1563),[20] the Zurich Reformer Heinrich Bullinger (1504–75),[21] and the seventeenth-century Scottish minister and biblical commentator James Fergusson of Kilwinning (1621–67).[22]

In what way do these commentators think Paul's words have the same sense as Psalm 68:18? First, they believe Paul relates the psalm to Christ via typology. Psalm 68 portrays God as a conqueror of Israel's enemies, which is a type of Christ who conquered the true enemies of sin, death and the devil in his ascension. Second, they argue that the change from 'receiving' to 'giving' respects the meaning of the psalm as a whole. In Psalm 68 YHWH not only receives gifts in v. 18 but also gives blessings to his people, not least the plunder of God's enemies.[23]

> God gives the desolate a home to live in (Ps. 68:6, NRSV)
> The women at home divide the spoil [of God's enemies] (Ps. 68:12, NRSV)
> [God] gives power and strength to his people (Ps. 68:35, NRSV)

So these commentators believe Paul is not changing the words of Psalm 68:18, but rather alluding to the general thrust of the psalm itself.

John Calvin mentions this solution as possible but then concludes: 'I am inclined to a different opinion, that Paul purposely changed the word, and employed it, not as taken out of the Psalm, but as an expression of his own, adapted to the present occasion.'[24] Calvin maintained that this 'same sense' solution does not fit with the flow of Paul's argument in Ephesians 4. He averred that Paul did not wish to convey that Christ received and then gave gifts. Such an idea is 'forced and utterly at variance with the apostle's purpose'.[25]

The Jewish interpretation

A final and more recent explanation focuses on the reading of Psalm 68 found among Jewish commentators after Christ. They interpreted Psalm 68:18 as a reference to Moses 'ascending' Mount Sinai to receive the 'gifts' of God's words, the Decalogue. This is reflected in the Targum of Psalm 68:18: 'You ascended to the expanse, O prophet Moses, you led captivity captive, you taught the words of the Law, you gave gifts to the sons of men. But as for the rebellious who are becoming proselytes (and) are turning in repentance, there rests upon them the shekinah of the glory of the LORD God.'[26] Of great interest here is that 'received' has become 'gave', just like Ephesians 4:8.

Therefore, because of the similarity between the Targum and Ephesians 4:8, scholars like George Caird,[27] Markus Barth,[28]

Andrew Lincoln[29] have proposed that Paul in Ephesians 4:8 was countering this Jewish interpretation of Psalm 68:18. The apostle was showing that it was Jesus, not Moses, who 'ascended' to heaven. Hall Harris argues that Jesus then 'descended' in the person of the Holy Spirit at Pentecost.[30] Hence, the traditional order of Christ's descent then ascent is reversed. Christ first ascends to the Father's right hand; then, second, descends at Pentecost.

Rudolph Schnackenberg[31] and Thurston Moritz[32] give a similar proposal. They believe Paul is simply repeating a pre-existing Christian response to the Jewish reading of Psalm 68:18. Both draw attention to the introductory formula of Psalm 68:18 in Ephesians 4:8: διὸ λέγει. The only other place where Paul uses it is in Ephesians 5:14, where he appears to introduce an early Christian hymn.

However, there are two particular difficulties for these solutions that draw upon Jewish exegesis. First, the Targums come from the fourth or fifth centuries after Christ, long after Paul wrote.[33] They may reflect an earlier text form of Psalm 68:18, but that is highly speculative. Indeed, Frank Thielman rightly notes it is just as likely Ephesians 4:8 influenced the Targum text, as vice versa.[34] Second, the wording of Targum Psalm 68:18 is very different from Ephesians 4:8. Third, and more importantly, there is nothing in Ephesians about the superiority of Christ to Moses.[35] If Paul was seeking to confront a Jewish reading of Psalm 68 one would expect some explicit indication in the near context, let alone the epistle as a whole.

Towards a Solution

The Μυστήριον *and the OT*

When seeking to explain the use of Psalm 68 in Ephesians 4:8 it is critical to examine the text in light of the epistle as a whole. How does Ephesians speak about itself in relation to the OT? A crucial clue is given in the letter's use of 'mystery' (μυστήριον).[36] In 1:9 we learn that the 'mystery' is a new revelation about God's purpose to sum up all things in Christ. The reason it is a 'mystery' is precisely because this information had been kept secret in the past. So 3:5

states that the 'mystery' (of Gentiles being made co-heirs with Jews in God's people) 'was not made known' in 'former generations'. This point is vital because it shows that the mystery's content cannot be found literally in the OT itself. Rather, Paul says in 3:3 that the 'mystery' was revealed to him 'by revelation' (κατὰ ἀποκάλυψιν). Paul did not discover it by his own ingenuity. It was a secret that could only be divulged to him by someone else, in this case Christ. As Frank Thielman rightly says: 'No amount of exegetical study of the [OT] Scriptures would have yielded this insight; God had to make it known to Paul personally.'[37]

If the 'mystery of Christ' is not found in the OT this says much about Paul's use of the OT in Ephesians. Take, for example, Paul's teaching about Christ as the head of his body the church in Ephesians 5:22–32. He relates it to Genesis 2:24: ' "For this reason a man will leave his father and mother and be joined to his wife, and the two will become one flesh." This is a great mystery (μυστήριον), and I am applying it to Christ and the church' (NRSV). Paul's new teaching about Christ and the church cannot be found literally in Genesis 2:24. It was given to him via revelation. But it is harmonious with the OT. Indeed, the new revelation about Christ and the church renders a new fuller meaning to Genesis 2:24 via typology. Human marriage as described in Genesis 2:24 is an analogue of Christ and the church. Knowledge of the 'mystery of Christ' has enabled a new reading of an OT text.

It would appear that Paul does something similar with Psalm 68:18 in Ephesians 4:8. He is not deriving his teaching about Christ's ascension and spiritual gifts from Psalm 68 itself. Rather he is starting with the revealed 'mystery of Christ' and then shedding new light back onto Psalm 68. Paul is giving a novel fuller reading of Psalm 68 that is determined by the mystery of the gospel. How so? First, let us look at Psalm 68 itself, and then, second, examine how Paul uses it in Ephesians 4:8.

Psalm 68 as a whole

In his Psalms commentary, Hans-Joachim Krauss says: 'There is in the Psalter scarcely a song that, in its textual corruption and disconnectedness, presents the interpreter so great a task as Psalm

68.'[38] Indeed, Mitchell Dahood declares that Psalm 68 is 'Widely admitted as textually and exegetically the most difficult and obscure of all the psalms'.[39] On the other hand, Allan Harman can conclude: 'There is no more triumphant song in the whole of the Psalter than Psalm 68.'[40]

The psalm presents legendary difficulties due to its frequent *hapax legomena,* strange expressions and awkward syntax.[41] However, despite murky details, Psalm 68 as a whole has a discernible gist: *the establishment of God's rule.* This includes both the defeat of God's enemies and the ensuing blessings for God's people. An important image of God's rule in Psalm 68 is the ark of the covenant and its place on Mount Zion.[42] Hence, the psalm begins with the statement:

> Let God rise up, let his enemies be scattered;
> let those who hate him flee before him. (Ps. 68:1, NRSV)

Here is a wish for God to intervene against his enemies. These words recall the movement of the ark after Sinai in Numbers 10:35:
Whenever the ark set out, Moses would say,

> 'Arise, O LORD, let your enemies be scattered,
> and your foes flee before you.' (Num. 10:35, NRSV)

And a similar cry is found in Psalm 132:8, a psalm about the building of the temple:

> Rise up, O LORD, and go to your resting-place,
> you and the ark of your might. (Ps. 132:8, NRSV)

Thus in Psalm 68 the ark is associated with God's rule; a rule entailing the conquest of enemies.

What is the basic movement of Psalm 68 as a whole?[43] After a prayer for God to establish his rule (vv. 1–6) it recounts God's past interventions to rule from Sinai to Jerusalem (vv. 7–18). The psalm then moves into a paean of praise because God is a saviour who rescues his people from their enemies and death (vv. 19–23). What follows is a picture of the procession of musicians and singers who accompanied the ark to Jerusalem (vv. 24–7). The psalm finally closes with a prayer for God to establish his rule again, but this time not only over his own people but over the whole world (vv. 28–35). Thus, Psalm 68 recounts that YHWH has faithfully intervened to rule in the past. And it cries out for him to intervene finally and rule the entire world.

Verse 18

But what of v. 18, which Paul deploys in Ephesians 4:8? It occurs in the section of the psalm that recounts God's past interventions from Sinai to Jerusalem (vv. 17–18). This narration contains three moments. The first is when God leads his people from Sinai to Canaan (vv. 7–10). The second concerns God's giving of the promised land to Israel (vv. 11–14). And then the third climaxes with YHWH coming to dwell on the mountain he has selected (vv. 15–18). This last section most likely refers to the ark being brought to Jerusalem (recounted in 2 Sam. 6; 1 Chron. 15).

Enthronement on Mount Zion: Verse 18 occurs in the final scene when YHWH comes to dwell on his chosen mountain as the ark enters Jerusalem (vv. 15–18).[44] It depicts God as a successful conqueror accompanied with a multitude of chariotry (v. 17).[45] Then v. 18 gives this interpretation of YHWH's arrival at his mountain:

> When you ascended on high,
> you took many captives;
> you received gifts from people,
> even from the rebellious –
> that you, LORD God, might dwell there. (Ps. 68:18, NIV)

Here, the arrival of the ark in Jerusalem is interpreted as God ascending to his mountain sanctuary in triumph over his enemies. Psalm 68 throughout contains verbal echoes from the Song of Deborah in Judges 5, one being found in v. 18 with the phrase 'took captivity captive' (שָׁבִיתָ שֶּׁבִי). It alludes to Judges 5:12 where this phrase refers to Israel's victory over her enemies. In other words, Psalm 68:18a affirms that God's enemies have been unable to prevent the ark coming from Sinai to Zion.[46] Now 'Sinai has been moved to Zion'. And now in Zion YHWH dwells as a victorious ruler.

The gifts: It is upon his ascension to his mountain dwelling that YHWH is given gifts 'among men' (בָּאָדָם). What are these gifts? A variety of proposals have been made. Martin Bucer believed the gifts were the Israelites whom God made as his own people.[47] Bucer did not read v. 18 as reference to the ark coming to Zion, but of God freeing his people from the Egyptians. Others have argued that the gifts were the Levites originally given to God, which he in return gave to Israelites (Num. 8:19; 18:6).[48] This proposal is made by those who construe v. 18 as about Moses' ascent of Sinai to receive the Decalogue. An ancient and long-lasting interpretation is that the gifts are the plunder or spoils taken from God's defeated enemies.[49] The final and most plausible suggestion is that the gifts are tribute gifts that people bring to show their recognition that YHWH is king.[50] The same idea arises later in the psalm:

> Because of your temple at Jerusalem
> kings bear gifts to you. (Ps. 68:29, NRSV)

This is the theme that lies behind the Magi bringing gifts to Jesus. However, the idea of tribute gifts in Psalm 68:18 needs nuancing by the biblical narrative of the ark coming to Jerusalem in 2 Samuel 6 and 1 Chronicles 15. Once the ark had arrived in Jerusalem David and the leaders of Israel gave gifts toward the building, and ongoing life of the temple (1 Chron. 29:1–9). David himself had accumulated an extensive store of silver and gold items from his military victories. And he 'dedicated these articles' to YHWH (2 Sam. 8:9–11). They became gifts to be placed in the temple treasuries once it was built (1 Chron. 28:12). Hence, Solomon used the gifts of David and the leaders of Israel for the building of God's temple, and he placed David's dedicated articles in the temple treasuries (1 Kgs 7:51; 15:15; 2 Chron. 5:1; 15:18). Some of these 'dedicated articles' were used for the repair of the temple (1 Chron. 26:27). In other words, once the ark was in Jerusalem we see the theme of gifts being given both for the building and maintenance of the temple.

This understanding of 'gifts' fits well with Psalm 68:18 when it says:

> you received gifts from people,
> even from the rebellious –
> that you, LORD God, might dwell there. (Ps. 68:18, NIV)

The purpose (לִשְׁכֹּן) of the bringing of gifts is so that YHWH might dwell in Jerusalem in a temple soon to be built.

Psalm 68:18 in Ephesians 4:8

The common theme: We can now turn to Ephesians 4:8. Ephesians 4 commences with an exhortation to unity (4:1–6). Paul then turns to the maintenance of this unity through the diversity of grace that Christ gives to each member of the church: 'But each of us was given grace according to the measure of Christ's gift' (Eph. 4:7, NRSV). It is Christ's giving of grace to all in the church that provides the reason for quoting Psalm 68:18:

> Therefore it is said,
> 'When he ascended on high he made captivity itself a captive;
> he gave gifts to his people.' (Eph. 4:8, NRSV)

And Paul proceeds to interpret his use of Psalm 68:18 in the following verses: '(When it says, "He ascended", what does it mean but that he had also descended into the lower parts of the earth? He who descended is the same one who ascended far above all the heavens, so that he might fill all things) (Eph. 4:9–10, NRSV).

A vital point is Paul's association of Christ's ascension with YHWH's ascension to Mount Zion in Psalm 68:18. Christ's ascension is now 'far above all the heavens, so that he might fill all things'. This recalls the language of Ephesians 1:20–22 where Christ's resurrection and ascension establish his rule over all things: 'God put this power to work in Christ when he raised him from the dead and seated him at his right hand in the heavenly places, far above all rule and authority and power and dominion, and above every name that is named, not only in this age but also in the age to come (Eph. 1:20–21, NRSV).

Hence, the line of thought becomes clear: the resurrection and ascension establishes Christ's rule over all things. Both Psalm

68:18 and Ephesians 4:8 are concerned with the establishment of kingly rule. In Psalm 68, God's rule is established in the ark's ascension to Mount Zion. In Ephesians, Christ's rule is established through his ascension to heaven.[51] Paul has not arbitrarily plundered Psalm 68 but deployed it via typology giving full respect to its original meaning.

Christ's giving: However, the question still remains: Why the change of 'received gifts' to 'gave gifts'? It must be recognized that Christ's 'giving' in Ephesians 4:7–10 is critical to its argument. The verb 'gave' is used three times and the noun 'gift' twice:

> But each of us was given grace [ἐδόθη] according to the measure of Christ's *gift* [τῆς δωρεᾶς]. (Eph. 4:7, NRSV, emphasis added)
> Therefore it is said, 'When he ascended on high he made captivity itself a captive; he gave gifts [ἔδωκεν δόματα] to his people.' (Eph. 4:8, NRSV, emphasis added)
> The gifts he *gave* [ἔδωκεν] were that some would be apostles, some prophets, some evangelists, some pastors and teachers. (Eph. 4:11, NRSV, emphasis added)

Hence, Paul's use of 'gave' instead of 'received' is significant. It thus seems overly forced for Paul to use Psalm 68:18 to convey that what YHWH receives he also gives. In Psalm 68 YHWH gives because he is 'good' (v. 10), 'almighty' (v. 14), and the Creator (vv. 33–4). The emphasis is that God gives because of who he is, not because he receives people's gifts.

Therefore, it would seem that Paul has deliberately changed 'received' to 'gave' (as Calvin suggested) so as to emphasize *the difference and superiority of Christ's ascension* compared to the ark's ascension to Zion.[52] The former is superior because Christ as ruler not only receives tribute gifts but also shares them with his people. And if we understand the tribute gifts of Psalm 68:18 to be those donations used for the building and maintenance of the Jerusalem temple (as argued above), then this fits neatly (via typology) with what Paul says earlier in Ephesians about the church as a temple that is being built: 'In him [Christ] the whole structure [of the body] is joined together and grows into a holy temple in the Lord; in whom you also are built together spiritually into a dwelling-place for God (Eph. 2:21–2, NRSV).

Christ's gifts are for the building of the true temple, namely the church. Such a reading also properly makes sense of the verses that follow Ephesians 4:8–10, which focus on the building of the church.

Conclusion

What then is to be concluded from this enquiry? It appears that when Paul used the word 'gave' instead of 'received' he was *not changing* Psalm 68:18 but *interpreting* it (as John Calvin originally argued). The reason Paul draws on Psalm 68:18 is because its theme is crucial to his argument. Psalm 68:18 is concerned with the establishment of YHWH's rule through ascension. Paul shows that this is a type of Christ. His rule was established in his grander ascension higher than all the heavens. Now as the conquering and reigning king, Christ in generosity builds his church through giving 'gifts' of the Holy Spirit to his people. Hence, Paul's use of Psalm 68:18 in Ephesians 4:8 is neither arbitrary nor forced. It respects both the original intention of the psalm and its new (typological) meaning in the light of the revealed mystery of Christ.

9

The Use of the Old Testament in Philippians

Mark J. Keown
Laidlaw College, Auckland, New Zealand

When discussing Paul's use of the Old Testament, it may seem strange to focus on a letter which has few intertextual links to the OT. However, it is equally instructive to explore letters with few explicit references to the OT, such as Philippians and 1 Thessalonians, to understand Paul's use of the OT. This I will do in this chapter. First, I will look at the OT data in Philippians. Second, I will discuss the implications of this material for Paul's perspective on the OT. Finally, I will look briefly at the use of the OT in the NT church.

The Data

First, I will briefly note the use of the OT in Philippians in comparison with other undisputed Pauline epistles. According to Silva, Romans has forty-two undisputed OT citations including four which align with the MT, fifteen where Paul does not use the MT or LXX, and two that are disputed. Thirty-six are from the LXX (86 per cent). Of these LXX references, thirteen line up with the MT and twenty-three do not.[1] First Corinthians includes sixteen citations, one which correlates with the MT and not the LXX, seven of which are neither LXX nor the MT, and two debated references. On eight occasions, Paul uses the Greek OT (50 per cent). Of these, seven align with the MT and one does not.[2] Second Corinthians has thirteen citations, of which four cohere neither with the LXX nor the MT while two others are debated. The other seven are from the LXX (54 per cent), six of which are in line with the MT and one which is not.[3] Galatians includes eleven citations, one of which is the same as the MT, two which parallel neither the MT nor the LXX, and one which is debated. He uses the LXX on the other seven occasions (64 per cent); five times in line with the MT and two which line up with the LXX but not the MT. In the four epistles mentioned above then, there are eighty-two citations, of which fifty-eight are undisputedly in line with the LXX (71 per cent). Aside from citations which align with both LXX and MT and disputed ones, only six of the eighty-two citations in these letters correspond to the MT.[4] This indicates that for Paul, his 'go to' OT for letter-writing was a Greek version of the Scriptures. In stark contrast to these other epistles, 1 Thessalonians and Philemon include no explicit citations of the OT.[5]

Turning to Philippians; like the Thessalonian letters and Philemon (and Titus), according to Ellis, Silva and Hays, Paul makes no direct citations of the OT.[6] However, unlike the Thessalonian correspondence, Philemon (and Titus), there are still a good number of points where the OT is important to Paul's thought in Philippians.[7] It is also arguable that Paul cites the OT in Philippians, even if unconsciously, or in a manner that his readers may not have understood without assistance. Most if not all of Paul's echoes and allusions to the OT align with the LXX, with Daniel 12:3 in Philippians 2:15–16 possibly drawing on both the LXX and MT. We will briefly discuss these references here.

Philippians 1:19 and Job

There are two passages in Philippians which could be regarded as including direct OT quotes (Phil. 1:19; 4:5), albeit both very brief. The first is Philippians 1:19 where Paul appears to cite two sequences of Greek words in succession which can both be found in Job in the LXX. The first of the two is the words οἶδα γὰρ ὅτι, 'for I know that', which is found four times in the LXX, three in Job (Deut. 31:29; Job 9:28; 19:25; 30:23).[8] In each case, death is the subject of the knowledge indicated by the verb οἶδα, 'I know', although in varying ways.

In Deuteronomy 31:29 the context is the writers' knowledge of what will come after death: 'For I know that *after my death* you will transgress in lawlessness and turn aside from the way.' In Job 9:28 Job responds to Bildad of God, 'I shake in all my parts, for I know that you will not leave me alone as innocent.' He goes on in the next verse to say, 'but since I am ungodly, because of this *why have I not died*?' In Job 30:23, the phrase introduces Job's certainty of death destroying him: 'for *I know that death will destroy me*, for the earth is the house for all who are mortal.'

Of particular interest is the LXX of Job 19:25 in which Job states, οἶδα γὰρ ὅτι ἀέναός ἐστιν ὁ ἐκλύειν με μέλλων ἐπὶ γῆς. The whole verse reads 'for I know that he who is eternal is about to deliver me upon the earth, to raise up my skin that is suffering these things, for according to the Lord these things have been accomplished in me'.[9] While the MT varies considerably from this, the LXX is particularly pertinent to Philippians 1:19 speaking of the eternal God delivering Job from suffering, and raising him. This has parallels to the situation in Philippians where Paul speaks of his hope of release from suffering and ultimate eternal salvation (and/or deliverance). With what follows from Job 13:16, this parallel is suggestive that Paul is using this introductory formula intentionally. Whether or not the Philippians would have noted this is questionable; however, as I will argue further below, with assistance, they may indeed have.

The final part of Philippians 1:19 includes a sequence of five Greek words found in the LXX of Job 13:16: τοῦτό μοι ἀποβήσεται εἰς σωτηρίαν. In Job 13:16 these words come in Job's defence to his accusers whereby he urges them to be silent so that he can speak and plead his case before God. Job states 'this will turn out to me for deliverance', indicating his confidence that God will vindicate him despite his great suffering. Job also portrays himself as being in prison (Job 13:27).[10] In Philippians, the words are found in Paul's report of his situation in prison[11] where he states his confidence that the prayers of the Philippians, and the help granted by the Spirit (or the supply of the Spirit) will turn out for his σωτηρία.[12] Σωτηρία here can refer to his vindication or deliverance from the trial,[13] to his ultimate eschatological salvation,[14] or is a play on words or intentional ambiguity to encompass both ideas.[15] Most likely, the latter is in mind as Paul only ever elsewhere uses σωτηρία of eschatological salvation,[16] and is ultimately pointing to his being vindicated before God whatever the outcome of his trial. However, he is also likely pointing to his release from prison, something he is certain will be accomplished (see Phil. 1:24–6).[17]

It is correct to note that the situations in Job and Philippians are not completely congruent. For example, in Job, Job is presenting his defence before his fellow Jewish opponents and proposes to give his defence to God rather than imperial authorities.[18] However, there are also resonances. Both Job[19] and Paul are facing serious suffering from opponents (esp. Phil 1:20–23,30). They are both in a situation of defence: Job before his accusers and Paul before the Roman authorities. Both hope to find vindication from God. The congruence between the two contexts makes it likely that Paul's use is intentional; he is consciously identifying in his suffering and struggle with Job. Like Job, Paul believes that God will bring about his vindication. This then should be treated as an intentional quote[20] or at least an echo.[21]

Bockmuehl rightly notes that '[g]iven the absence of OT quotations from Philippians and the likely background of Paul's original audience, it is not clear to what extent the apostle could have expected his readers to understand such specific allusions'.[22] On its own it is unlikely.[23] However, as we will discuss below, there are reasons to argue that they would have heard or been made aware of the echo.

Philippians 4:5

A second passage that may be an explicit quote from the LXX is Philippians 4:5. Placed without connective (asyndeton), after his appeal for constant rejoicing in the Lord, and before his injunction to pray continually, is the cryptic clause ὁ κύριος ἐγγύς, 'the Lord is near'. The majority of interpreters see here an eschatological assurance, a reference to the impending Parousia of Christ.[24] This is not without warrant, with eschatological assurances scattered through the letter indicating that one of the sub-themes of the letter was to give eschatological hope to the Philippians.[25] There are several such futuristic eschatological assurances in the immediate context (see esp. Phil. 3:20–21; 4:3, cf. 1:6,10–11,19–23,28; 2:10–11,16; 3:10–14; 4:17). Further, it can be argued that while the LXX references use both κύριος and ἐγγύς together to yield the same overall translation 'the Lord is near' (further below), the word order differs and, unlike Philippians 4:5, there is no use of the article with κύριος in the LXX.

However, with the slight differences noted, the Greek clause is found in Psalms 33:19 and 144:18 (ἐγγὺς κύριος), both in the context of seeking God in prayer. Psalm 33 (34, MT) is a Davidic hymn of praise to God for deliverance from enemies and in which David urges reverence for God. In Psalm 33:16–17 (34:15–16, MT) the psalmist writes, 'the eyes of the Lord are over the righteous, and his ears to their prayer (δέησις)'; whereas God opposes evil-doers and destroys their memory. In v. 18, the righteous cry out to God in prayer and God hears their prayers and delivers them from their suffering (θλῖψις). Verse 18 states that 'the Lord is near (ἐγγὺς κύριος) to those that are of a contrite heart, and will save the lowly in spirit' (τοὺς ταπεινοὺς τῷ πνεύματι σώσει). This deliverance is further explained in vv. 19–22. The language and ideas common with Philippians are striking, especially the theme of prayer and the use of δέσις and ταπειν– (humility) language (cf. Phil. 2:3,8; 4:12).

Psalm 144 (145, MT) is another Davidic hymn of praise to God proclaiming that generations will sing of his great power, acts and character (vv. 1–6). God is extolled for his compassionate character (esp. v. 8, cf. Phil. 2:1). God's holy people will speak of the greatness of his everlasting kingdom (vv. 9–13). In vv. 14–16, God supports all those who are falling and broken, he watches over all *providing for them* (cf. Phil. 4:19) and filling all living things with pleasure. Verse18 (Ps. 145:18, MT) reads: '*The Lord is near* (ἐγγὺς κύριος) to all that call upon him, to all that call upon him in truth'. In v. 19 the psalm goes on to describe how God responds, blessing those who fear him, hearing their petition (δέησις) and saving (σώζω) them. God 'guards' (φυλάσσω, cf. φρουρέω, Phil. 4:7) those who love him, while destroying sinners (cf. Phil. 1:28; 3:19).

Both these references to 'the Lord is near' suggest that God is close to respond to his people in prayer. If Paul is drawing on one or other of these, perhaps from his memory from liturgical tradition, then it should be connected to what follows rather than an eschatological assurance, i.e. the Lord is near to answer prayer.[26]

Despite the slight differences to the LXX, I am persuaded that this is the correct reading of Philippians 4:5, i.e. it should be read as a prelude to Paul's injunctions to pray in 4:6–7, rather than as a reference to the future coming of Christ. As such, with the reference to Job 13:16 in Philippians 1:19, this may be an echo drawn from Paul's remembrance of Israel's liturgical tradition.

While it is unclear whether the Philippians would recognize the earlier echoes in 1:19, it is more likely that ὁ κύριος ἐγγύς would be noticed as it is drawn from songs which were likely sung in the context of the new Christians' worship (cf. 1 Cor. 14:26; Eph. 5:19; Col. 3:16).[27] As such, it should arguably be seen as an OT citation, although very brief. With the prayer-appeal that follows, it would have drawn the readers to the liturgical tradition of Israel and the new church, and brought to mind the promises of Psalms 33 and 144 (LXX).

Isaiah 45:23–4 in Philippians

In Philippians 2:10–11 (cf. Rom. 14:11), Paul uses a clear allusion to the LXX of Isaiah 45:23–4 which reads in Greek: ὅτι ἐμοὶ κάμψει πᾶν γόνυ και ἐξομολογήσεται πᾶσα γλῶσσα τῷ θεῷ λέγων Δικαιοσύνη καὶ δόξα πρὸς αὐτὸν ἥξουσιν, 'because to me every knee will bend and every tongue will confess to God saying righteousness and glory will come to him'. Philippians 2:10–11 picks up a number of the same words (πᾶν γόνυ κάμψῃ . . .καὶ πᾶσα γλῶσσα ἐξομολογήσηται . . . δόξαν θεοῦ πατρός, cf. Rom. 14:11).

Various elements of the language of Isaiah 45 also turn up in Philippians 1:27–30 and 3:17–21 including: the language of salvation (Isa. 45:15,17,20,21,22; Phil. 1:28; 3:10); ἀντικειμαι, 'opponents' (Isa. 45:16; Phil. 1:28, cf. ἐξθρος in Phil. 3:18); the language of shame (Isa. 45:16,17; Phil. 3:19c); 'walk' language (Isa. 45:16; Phil. 3:17,18);[28] the nations or the far reaches of the earth of which the Gentile Philippians form a part (Isa. 45:16,20,22); and idolatry (Isa. 45:20; Phil. 3:19b). There is also a range of other possible connection-points to Philippians from Isaiah 45:15–25 including speaking (λαλέω; Isa. 45:19; Phil. 1:14); δικαιοσύνη, 'righteousness' (Isa. 45:19,23,24; Phil. 1:11; 3:6,9); δικαιόω, 'justified' (Isa. 45:25; Phil. 3:9), proclaiming truth (cf. 1:18), δόξα, 'glory' (Isa.

45:24,25; Phil. 1:11; 2:11; 4:19,20, cf. κενοδοξία, 2:3), and 'descendants of the children of Israel' (Isa. 45:25; Phil. 2:15). This suggests that Isaiah 45 was important for Paul as he constructed Philippians.

Philippians 2:14–15

Another likely allusion to the LXX is found in Philippians 2:14–15 where Paul uses and transforms ideas and language drawn from the wilderness. These include γογγυσμός, 'grumbling', and the church as 'God's children' (τέκνα θεοῦ) rather than Israel, while describing the social setting in Macedonia as γενεᾶς σκολιᾶς καὶ διεστραμμένης, 'a crooked and depraved generation' (cf. Exod. 16:2–12; Num. 14:27; 16:41; Deut. 32:5). The reference to universal submission to Christ (ὑποτάξαι αὐτῳ τὰ πάντα) alludes to Psalm 8:7 (πάντα ὑπέταξας ὑποκάτω τῶν ποδῶν αὐτοῦ).

Other possible allusions and echoes: There are also a range of other possible allusions and echoes in Philippians noted by different interpreters. In Philippians 1:11 the clause καρπὸν δικαιοσύνης, 'fruit of righteousness', may allude to or echo the LXX of Proverbs 3:9 (καρπῶν δικαιοσύνης) and/or Proverbs 11:30 or Amos 6:12 (καρπὸν δικαιοσύνης).[29] The threefold use of this clause in the LXX may indicate it is well known and Paul is appropriating it here intentionally.

In the Christ-hymn, in describing Christ as a human and slave (μορφὴν δούλου λαβών, 2:7), Paul may be alluding to or echoing the Servant Song which refers to the humanity and servanthood of the figure of Isaiah 53:3,11 (cf. Phil. 1:1).[30] Paul's appeal to the Philippians to shine as stars in the universe and to 'hold forth the word of life'[31] possibly alludes to the LXX and MT of Daniel 12:3 (καὶ οἱ συνιέτες ἐκλάμψουσιν ὡς ἡ λαμπρότης τοῦ στερεώματος καὶ ἀπὸ τῶν δικαίων τῶν πολλῶν ὡς οἱ ἀστέρες εἰς τοὺς αἰῶνας και ἔτι, 'those who are wise shall shine like the brightness of the sky, and those who lead many to righteousness, like the stars for ever and ever' (NRSV).[32] Κενὸν ἐκοπίασα, 'labor in vain' in Philippians 2:16 may allude to Isaiah 49:4 (Κενῶς ἐκοπίασα) and/or Isaiah 65:23 (οὐ κοπιάσουσιν εἰς κενὸν). In Philippians 3:19, καὶ δόξα ἐν τῇ αἰσχύνῃ αὐτῶν, 'and their glory is in their shame', may allude to Hosea 4:7 (τὴν δόξαν αὐτῶν εἰς ἀτιμίαν θήσομαι, 'I will turn their glory into shame').[33]

It is noted by most scholars that βίβλῳ ζωῆς, 'the book of life' in Philippians 4:3 recalls the idea of God's scroll of his people in the OT, especially βίβλου ζώτων, 'the book of the living', in Psalm 69:28 (cf. Exod. 32:32; Isa. 4:3; Exod. 13:9; Dan. 12:1; *1 Enoch* 47.3; 1 QM 12:3).[34] Some also contend that the appeal to continue in obedience in Philippians 2:12 may be an allusion to Deuteronomy 31:27, 'If you have been rebellious against the Lord while I am still alive and with you, how much more will you rebel after I die!'[35] The string of cultic commendations of the gift from Philippi draws on OT passages. The language of sacrifice (θυσία) and 'acceptable' (δεκτός) is common.[36] Most especially, ὀσμὴν εὐδίας, 'fragrant offering, is found thirty-six times in the OT.[37] While Paul is not necessarily drawing on any one reference, it remains an allusion. Although not exactly parallel, κακοὺς ἐργάταj, 'evil workers' in 3:2, may echo the phrase οἱ ἐργαζόμενοι τὴν ἀνομίαν, 'workers of iniquity' of the psalmists' enemies (Pss 5:6 [5:5, MT]; 6:9 [6:8, MT]; 13:4 [14:4, MT]; 35:12 [36:12, MT]).[38]

Other ideas

Other important OT ideas are drawn on and developed in the light of the coming of Messiah Jesus. These include the description of believers, Gentile and Jew, as 'holy ones' or 'saints' (ἅγιος, Phil. 1:1; 4:21). The language of the Jewish sacrificial system mentioned above in terms of 4:18 also features in 2:17 (σπένδομαι ἐπὶ τῇ θυσίᾳ). Paul draws on priestly language (λειτουργ–) in terms of the service of the Philippians (2:17,30) and Epaphroditus (2:25).

In Philippians 3:2–6 Paul applies characteristic Jewish ideas and language to Judaizers including 'dogs', and 'workers of 'evil' (above). He uses paronomasia describing circumcisers as mutilators in Philippians 3:2. He then describes the church as 'the Circumcision'; Israel by faith has gone global (3:3). 'Worship in the Spirit of God' is the language of the temple.[39] He then catalogues his own credentials with reference to his circumcision, citizenship of Israel, tribal affiliation to Benjamin, his genuine Hebrew heritage, and his history as a Pharisee (Judaism), the law, and zeal recalling Phinehas and other zealous Israelites (e.g. Num. 25:11).

Other OT ideas pepper the text. These include the language of God and his fatherhood, Lord, Jesus as Christos, peace (Shalom), thanksgiving, joy, gospel, creation (Phil. 1:5–6; 2:7; 4:12,15), the day of the Lord, glory, praise, the word, prayer, the Spirit, salvation, the fear of God, holiness language, worship, resurrection, eternal destruction, idolatry (3:19), heaven, and church (ἐκκλησία, 3:6; 4:15).[40]

Summary

In conclusion we can note several things. Although there are only two or three possible citations in Philippians, there is substantial material in the letter that draws on the OT and Jewish tradition. Aside from the possibility that Paul drew on a blend of the LXX and the Hebrew in Philippians 2:15–16a, he draws exclusively from the LXX. With the material summarized earlier from other Pauline letters, this indicates that for Paul his 'Bible' or 'Scriptures' was Greek OT. He was comfortable infusing it into his letters even to Gentile readers like the Philippians. Paul seems relaxed to see the Greek translation of the OT as 'inspired' and important for Christian life and growth (esp. Rom. 15:4; 1 Cor. 10:6; 2 Tim. 3:16).[41] This has interesting implications for a Christian view of the LXX and translations today.[42] Whether or not Paul's readers recognized every nuance of his use of the OT, Paul appears confident that the readers/hearers of Philippians had now come to know the story of Israel sufficiently well to read it in the light of Christ. Whether they could or would have discerned these is a debatable point. To this we now turn.

Paul's Fresh View of the OT

In his use of the OT in Philippians outlined above, writing some thirty years after his conversion, Paul gives strong indications of a redefined view of the OT. First, having once zealously persecuted Christians for blasphemy (Phil. 3:5–6), his perspective is now profoundly christological and christotelic. Jesus is Messiah (*Christos* thirty-seven times). He is Lord (fifteen times). He is God made human in human form (2:6–7). He is servant (2:7; 3:10,21). He is crucified (2:8; 3:10), raised (3:10,21), and exalted (2:9–11). Everything is about Christ. Most importantly, Isaiah 45:23 is read through this lens with Jesus in the place of God.[43] Outrageously for a fierce monotheistic Pharisee (Phil. 3:5), Jesus is now named alongside the Father as God and object of worship and obedience. All of Scripture is now read through this understanding. Salvation history from creation (1:5–6; 2:7; 4:12,15) to redemption (1:6,10,22–3,28; 3:10–14,19–21; 4:3) is read through the lens of the pivotal moment in history, Christ (esp. 2:6–11). Life in the present is obedience to Christ, service, and mission, which at its heart, is proclamation of Christ (1:5,7,12–18,27; 2:14–16a,19–30; 3:10–17; 4:2–3).

Second, his Christ-centred view has transformed his soteriology and ecclesiology which are now defined not by the requirement that Gentiles Judaize to be saved and integrated into God's people (as Paul held previously), but they must believe in Jesus Christ as Lord (3:1–9). Those who preach Judaizing are 'dogs, evil workers, and mutilators' who deny the complete sufficiency of Christ (3:2). Now that Messiah has come and is being preached, belief in Jesus alone draws people into saving relationship with Yahweh (3:9). Those 'in Christ' are God's people (1:1). They are 'holy ones' or 'saints', sanctified by Christ (1:1). God's appointed King, Jesus, is the one that they serve (1:1), just as he served God (2:7). They are recipients of the Spirit who is 'God and Christ with them' enabling them through suffering (1:19). It is Christ they live for (1:21). They work and suffer for Christ's sake (2:29–30). Their values are to be cross-shaped, rather than law-shaped (2:1–11). This is the basis of their unity (2:1–4). Salvation is defined in relation to Christ with believers saved (1:28; 2:12) and those who deny and reject him are destroyed (1:28; 3:19). As such, believing Jew and Gentile now come together as one people in Christ (cf. Gal. 3:28) – together, they are God's children (Phil. 2:15). They are 'the circumcision' who worship by the Spirit (3:2–3). They will together experience God's salvation (1:28; 4:3). For Paul, Israel has been radically transformed from a people descended from Abraham by physical descent, to a people descended from Abraham by faith (Rom. 4;

9 – 11; Phil. 3:9). Paul's reading of the OT has undergone a radical metamorphosis so that now the Jewish Scriptures are consistently and creatively read through Christ.

The Old Testament in the Lives of the Philippians

As far as we are aware, the Philippian church was entirely Gentile in composition. Assuming the historicity of Acts 16, Luke's use of 'place of prayer' (Acts 16:13) suggests that there was no Jewish synagogue in Philippi[44] and those with an interest in Judaism appear to be all women;[45] at least on the day Paul met them.[46] That they gathered outside the city (Acts 16:13) could indicate their desire to be near water for cleansing purposes,[47] or indicate the marginalization of the Jews from Philippi.[48] Further indication of Jewish marginalization is found in the charges against Paul and Silas in Acts 16:20–21 which, aside from the charges of advocating non-Roman customs and causing trouble, stresses their Jewishness.[49] These hints could indicate that Jews were not welcome in Philippi. This could relate to the Claudian Edict to expel the Jews from Rome in AD 49, with Philippi either emulating this and expelling the Jews from the city (Suetonius, *Claud*. 25.4), and/or refusing entry to Jews who were scattered by the edict (cf. Acts 18:2). This is important for our discussion of the use of the OT in Philippians, as it decreases the potential of the Philippians hearing the echoes and allusions Paul includes in the letter.

Whether or not the town was anti-Semitic, the first converts on Paul's initial journey were an Asian woman, possibly a fortune-telling, pagan slave girl,[50] and the Roman jailor's family. Undoubtedly these are all Gentiles.[51] The names of the Philippians from Paul's letter also indicate Gentiles – Greeks Epaphroditus, Syntyche, Euodia, and possibly Syzygos (below), along with a Latin, Clement. The key point is that, although we cannot completely rule out some Jews being added to the church over time, unlike any other known Pauline community of faith this church appears to be completely Gentile.[52] Only Lydia, and any other subsequent God-worshipping or Jewish converts, would have any understanding of the LXX, aside from that gleaned from the reading and preaching of the word by the Philippian Gentile converts in Philippi, when travelling or in contact with other Christians in travel, or gleaned through visiting itinerant Christians familiar with the LXX. We cannot be sure that Lydia's understanding was great considering that she was an Asian woman who had not yet converted and had been in a Jewish context in which men did not look favourably on women studying the Torah. In the intervening years, she may have built on that foundation and learnt more of the LXX from a Christian perspective. However, she is not mentioned in Philippians, and we cannot be sure she is in the church at this time. As such, we cannot assume that, without some assistance, these Gentile hearers of Paul's letter would pick up the echoes and cross-references from the LXX when first read. Indeed, I would suspect that at a first hearing, most would be missed without assistance. However, NT letters were not read in a vacuum and there are good reasons to argue that, while at first hearing these may not be discerned, with the assistance of the bearers of the letter and as the letter sat in the community they would be noted.

First, assuming some of the church had access to the LXX through copyists or otherwise, it is not unlikely that some in the Philippian church, particularly the educated, had devoted great time to its study. If the letter is written from Rome as is likely,[56] it would be twelve or so years since the church's initial establishment.[57] This is sufficient time for the educated in the church like Epaphroditus or the Latin Clement, well versed in literary analysis through their rhetorical training, to have spent a great deal of time in study in the LXX.[58] We cannot underestimate the ability of the learned in Paul's churches to gain a quick and deep knowledge of the Jewish Greek Scriptures. Some of the believers in Philippi may have come into contact with other Christians in their own travels, enhancing their understanding.

Second, in Philippians 3 Paul states that there is a threat to the church from a heresy that involves circumcision and so some degree of Judaizing (3:3).[59] These are then possibly unbelieving Jews,[60] some pneumatic Judaizing threat perhaps similar to the problem of 2 Corinthians 10 – 13,[61] or as is more likely and is more commonly held, Judaizers.[62] Paul states in Philippians 3:1 that he has warned them previously of this problem,[63] either in person, through co-workers, or in earlier letters sent to Philippi (cf. Polycarp, *Phil.* 3:2).[64] There was likely much engagement with the OT

Scriptures in this safe-guarding process, a time in which the Philippians would have gained a thorough understanding of Israel, the church, and the Greek Scriptures. It is not implausible that Paul's own copy of the LXX was copied and used in the church by its first converts, perhaps in the initial visitation or while Timothy and Silas were in Macedonia.[65]

Third, there is Epaphroditus who was likely the bearer of the letter and perhaps Paul's secretary (Phil. 2:25–30).[66] It is likely that the reading of the letter was accompanied by significant embellishment and explanation.[67] There is also the mysterious γνήσιε σύζυγε, 'loyal companion', who may be Epaphroditus (a note of commendation for the reader and letter-bearer),[68] but could equally be Luke or another Pauline co-worker familiar with the LXX.[69] Indeed, if this person is Luke, his writings demonstrate a deep familiarity with the Greek OT. It is not implausible that the reading of the letter was an opportunity to educate the recipients, enabling them to recognize and discuss the echoes and allusions in the letter. In this way, perhaps they developed a rudimentary early Pauline 'biblical theology', reading the Greek OT through the lens of Christ.

Fourth, even with the likelihood that these points were not picked up by the hearers, Epaphroditus, Timothy, who is co-sender and possibly Paul's amanuensis (Phil. 1:1),[70] is soon coming to Philippi (2:23). Finally, Paul himself states his emphatic confidence of impending release and forthcoming trip to Philippi (1:23–6; 2:24).[71] Without question, at this point, any OT connections would be well understood by the Philippians.

All this suggests there was a good likelihood that, while the Philippians may or may not have initially 'heard' the echoes and allusions to the OT in Philippians, they would have quickly become aware of them through the assistance of others, and/or over time as they continued to grow in their knowledge of the Scriptures with the words of Philippians in their minds.

Conclusion

In conclusion I suggest that Paul used citations, allusions, and echoes to the OT intentionally in Philippians. Further, the Philippians likely came to know these through their own observation or through the help of others, especially the letter-bearer Epaphroditus, other Pauline co-workers like Luke and Timothy, and finally Paul himself. Preferring the LXX for communication, this letter like others demonstrates that he now creatively and consistently reads the OT through the lens of Christ. We should do the same. The use of the LXX reinforces that the Greek OT was understood as inspired (2 Tim. 3:16), was the 'Bible' of the early church, and was critical for the equipping of the new converts including the Gentiles. Contemporary biblical studies research and theological education should pay equal attention to the LXX and the MT.

Non-Pauline Letters

10

The Appropriation of Scripture in 1 Peter

Allan Chapple
Trinity Theological College, Western Australia

As Martin Hengel rightly observes, 'the history and theology of earliest Christianity are "mission history"[1] and "mission theology".' This means that the NT documents are to be seen both as products of mission and as instruments of mission: they have a missionary origin and they serve missionary purposes. But they are not all products of the same mission. In addition to the one we know most about – that of Paul – there were several other streams of mission in the apostolic generation.[2] Hence the topic allocated for this lecture: 'the appropriation of Scripture in the missions of the apostles'. Given the limitations of our evidence, I have decided that the most satisfactory way into the subject is to focus attention on one mission-document in particular – and 1 Peter seems ideal for our purpose. An encyclical or diaspora letter[3] to believers throughout Anatolia (1:1), it gives us a valuable window into early Christianity outside the Pauline mission.[4] One of its most striking features is the extensive use it makes of the OT.[5] It thus enables us to investigate 'the appropriation of Scripture' in the mission of an apostle who is often significantly underestimated.[6]

First Peter is best seen as a paraenetic letter,[7] whose chief aim is stated as follows: 'I have written to you briefly, encouraging – or, exhorting – and testifying that this is the true grace of God. Stand fast in it' (5:12). Here Peter identifies the overriding theme of the letter as χάρις, God's 'true grace'.[8] In 1:10–12 we discover that 'grace' is closely connected with the idea of 'salvation', and that this is what is announced in the gospel. One of the letter's principal tasks is thus to remind its readers of the saving work of 'the God of all grace' (5:10) – what he has done, is doing, and will do to deliver believers from sin, to make them his own, and to bring them to eternal glory. It does this so that they will 'stand fast' in this grace and salvation. What makes this exhortation necessary is the fact that they are suffering serious opposition.[9] They are in fact 'elect rejects': as a result of the changes their conversion has made to their way of life (1:18; 4:3–4), they are now aliens in their own society (1:1,17; 2:11).[10] 'Christian existence is lived out between divine election and social ostracism. Each dimension conditions the other, for the Christian community's conflicts with the surrounding world result from the act of God that separates them from the world and makes them into the people of God.'[11]

The readers will 'stand fast' by living in confident trust, joyful hope, and genuine love (1:6,8,13,21,22; 3:8; 4:8,19; 5:7), as well as by persisting in doing good in the face of harsh and unjust treatment (2:12,15,20; 3:13–17; 4:19). In all of this they will be expressing the new identity that God in his grace has given them. Spelling out this identity is one of Peter's primary objectives.[12] The letter is thus teaching its readers how to inscribe the narrative of their life as the elect but suffering people of God within the meta-narrative of God's saving work, declared in Scripture and the gospel.[13] As embodied within 1 Peter, these linked narratives are set out in ways heavily influenced by the OT.

So pervasive is the letter's use of the OT that studies of this subject regularly employ such language as 'teems', 'lavish', 'rich profusion', 'saturated', 'abundant use' and 'abounds'.[14] It clearly reflects a mind 'deeply steeped' in the Scriptures, 'soaked in the scriptural heritage of Israel'.[15] Its author 'is first and foremost a theologian of Scripture'.[16] The density of its OT quotations and allusions ranks 1 Peter alongside such OT-rich works as Romans, Hebrews and Revelation.[17] Depending on how 'quotation' is defined, there are said to be anywhere between nine and twenty OT quotations in 1 Peter.[18] Again, while the number given varies depending on the definition being used, there is general agreement that the letter also contains a great many allusions to the OT.[19] Third, we must also take account of what are variously referred to as 'echoes' or 'biblicisms': that is, the use of language that expresses a particular biblical theme or that just sounds biblical.[20] These are so extensive that Carson observes: 'If one were to extend beyond allusions (however defined) to echoes picking up OT language and themes, scarcely a verse in this epistle would be exempt.'[21]

This brings us to the point where we can ask three basic questions about Peter's use of Scripture: Which parts of the OT does he use? How does he use them? And why does he use them as he does? We will begin with the third question, because Peter provides us with a clear answer to it. We will then consider the other two questions before we return for a final look at the third one.

Why, then, does Peter use the OT as he does? Seeking an answer to this question takes us to 1:10–12, where Peter states the convictions that underlie his use of Scripture.[22] He is convinced that Scripture speaks of Jesus Christ (1:11) and of the salvation he has won for his people, of the grace that they receive because of him (1:10). So what the gospel declares has been announced in Scripture: for Peter, the OT prophets and Christian evangelists speak the same message. This unity reflects the ministry of the Spirit. As the Spirit of Christ,[23] he speaks through the prophets (1:11).[24] And the Spirit of prophetic testimony is the Spirit who has been sent from heaven, through whom the gospel is now proclaimed (1:12).[25] He imparts the testimony of the prophets and he also empowers the proclamation of the evangelists. And both of these dimensions of his work are focused on the gospel. Scripture is the Spirit's advance testimony (προμαρτυρόμενον, 1:11) to Christ and the gospel. So the word of God to Israel is one with the gospel message that the readers have embraced (1:25). The chief difference between them is one of perspective: the prophets anticipate the promised Saviour and his salvation, while the gospel announces them. The prophetic message is thus to be understood as a proleptic form of the gospel. For Peter, this means that the gospel is the hermeneutical key to the OT Scriptures.

This gospel is first and foremost the gospel of Christ – so in Scripture the Spirit of Christ speaks of Christ (1:11). His testimony concerns Christ's sufferings (τὰ εἰς Χριστὸν παθήματα)[26] and also what Peter calls 'the subsequent glories' (τὰς μετὰ ταῦτα δόξας).[27] This plural is best understood as referring to the glories of Jesus' resurrection and exaltation (1:21; cf. 3:22) and of his return (4:13), as well as to the glory that belongs to the readers because of him – the glory that rests on them now through the Spirit (4:14), and the glory that will be theirs when Jesus Christ is revealed (1:7; cf. 5:1,4,10).[28] This reminds us that the gospel of Christ is also the gospel of salvation – so Peter sees the Spirit as giving advance testimony in Scripture not just to the glories in which believers share but also to their salvation as a whole (1:10). The prophets speak of the grace that is for them (τῆς ἐις ὑμᾶς χάριτος, 1:10) – the grace they receive in the present (1:2; 3:7; 4:10; 5:12), as well as the grace they will receive when Jesus Christ is revealed (1:13).

By announcing the truths of the gospel in advance – speaking through the Spirit of this time of salvation and also of the one through whom it came about – the prophets were (according to Peter) serving his readers (1:12). This statement is important for two reasons. It means that the readers 'stand in a position that even the greatest of the ancient prophets did not have'.[29] In their own society, they may be oppressed and marginalized – but as God's elect they are in a very privileged position, seeing and hearing what the prophets longed to see and hear (cf. Matt. 13:16–17; Luke 10:23–4).[30] It also explains why Peter appropriates the OT to instruct and exhort his readers. Through the prophets, the Spirit spoke in advance of the gospel events and the gospel era. The Scriptures thus speak especially to those who live in this eschatological time (ἐπ' ἐσχάτων τῶν χρόνων, 1:20). More than that, the readers' embrace of the gospel has now inserted them into the meta-narrative of God's saving work.

So what is the relationship between the initial stages of this narrative and the events of the gospel era? That is, what is the relationship between Scripture and the gospel, between Israel and Peter's readers?

Peter's convictions in this matter are reflected in the way he begins the letter. He describes his readers as the ἐκλεκτοί (1:1), language that began to be used of Israel in light of the exodus and the Sinai covenant.[31] The parallel with Israel is extended when he says that his readers constitute a διασπορά (1:1).[32] Both of these foreshadow what we will see again in 2:9–10, where language that the OT applies to Israel is used of the readers. Achtemeier sees this as fundamental to the letter as a whole: 'Israel has become the controlling metaphor for the new people of God, and as such its rhetoric has passed without remainder into that of the Christian community.'[33]

But why is this so? Why does Peter take this approach? We get some indication of the answer by observing what he does in 1:2. There the readers learn that they have been chosen 'for obedience and the sprinkling of the blood of Jesus Christ' (ἐις ὑπακοὴν καὶ ῥαντισμὸν αἵματος Ἰησοῦ χριστου).[34] This is best seen as an allusion to the covenant ceremony in Exodus 24, where the people of Israel pledge their obedience to YHWH (vv. 3, 7) and are then sprinkled with the blood of the covenant (v. 8).[35] So Peter has used a pivotal event in the story of Israel to describe the position of his readers: they are the people of the new covenant, bound to God as Israel was. And as we are about to see, Peter continues to do this, drawing especially on the foundational stage in Israel's story, from redemption in Egypt to inheritance in Canaan. This tells us why Israel is the 'controlling metaphor' for the Christian community. Peter believes that in accordance with God's purpose (κατὰ πρόγνωσιν θεου, 1 Pet. 1:2), Israel finds the climax of her story in the Jesus of the gospel. It is as though the gospel casts its shadow backwards into the OT story: 'The Israel into whose history Peter writes his audience is *Israel as interpreted* by the suffering, death, resurrection, ascension and pending revelation of Jesus Christ.'[36] So Peter is reading Scripture eschatologically, in light of its fulfilment in the gospel events.

He is also reading it typologically, discerning the patterns in Israel's story which point forward to their fulfilled embodiment in the gospel era.[37] Both of these reflect his christocentric approach to the OT – as does the fact that he reads it ecclesiologically. For Peter, Scripture speaks of the eschatological people of God because it speaks of the one in and by whom they are saved (1:10-12). 'The author's christocentric and ecclesiocentric reading strategies intertwine, for he is convinced that the communities he addresses have come to share in the vocation and destiny of their Lord.'[38]

In this sense, what God said to Israel and did with Israel had Christ and the church in view. More of this below, after we consider our other two questions: namely, which parts of the OT does Peter use? And how does he use them?

According to the most thorough study of Peter's use of the OT, 'the Scriptures are broadly represented, four books of the

Pentateuch (Gen., Ex., Lev., Dt.), four of the latter Prophets (Is., Hos., Ezek., Mal.), and three of the Writings (Ps., Prov., Job), although the distribution is unevenly concentrated in just three, Isaiah (twenty-one), the Psalms (eleven), and Proverbs (six).'[39]

We may compare this with Paul's use of the OT, in around one hundred citations in the Pauline canon.[40] As is the case with 1 Peter, most come from Isaiah (twenty-three) and the Psalms (nineteen), and then we have fourteen from Deuteronomy and twelve from Genesis.[41]

We cannot form a proper appreciation of Peter's 'appropriation of Scripture' by confining our attention to where he quotes it; we must also take account of his allusions to the OT. Some of these consist of references to OT people and events – to Noah and the flood (3:20); to Abraham and Sarah (3:6) – rather than to particular OT passages or themes. For the latter, five principal sources have been proposed. First of all, there is Psalm 34 (Ps. 33 LXX), which Peter cites in 3:10–12. Almost a century ago W. Bornemann found six quotations from this psalm as well as some forty-two allusions to it in the letter.[42] Schutter's careful analysis of Bornemann's case argues instead that there is only 'one explicit allusion, one very weak implicit allusion, and a handful of iterative allusions'.[43] This subject has now received extended discussion in a 2008 doctoral thesis for the University of Exeter.[44] Susan Woan thinks that both Bornemann and Schutter go too far, if in opposite directions, and concludes: 'on over twenty occasions in the course of 1 Peter, resonance with Psalm 34 occurs . . . When one excludes echoes from the reckoning on the grounds of uncertainty, there are still eight instances when Psalm 34 is cited.'[45]

However, five of these eight instances are only 'weak allusions'. These involve basic biblical themes or terminology that is widespread in the LXX, and it is difficult to see how they would point the reader to this psalm in particular. This is true also of the 'significant allusion', which involves only two quite common words.[46] This leaves us with a strong allusion to Psalm 33:9 LXX in 2:3, and the citation of Psalm 33:13–17a LXX in 3:10–12. It is therefore difficult to conclude that this psalm has had a major influence on the contents of our letter.[47]

A second proposed source for Peter's OT allusions is Zechariah 9 – 14, according to a doctoral thesis submitted to the University of St Andrews in 2010.[48] Kelly Liebengood makes a good case for seeing 'the shepherd tradition of Zechariah 9–14' behind 2:25, and Zechariah 13:7–9 behind the letter's references to fiery trials (1:6–7 and 4:12).[49] Apart from these allusions, he relies on three rather doubtful 'echoes', and seeks to show that Zechariah 9 – 14's 'eschatological program' underlies that of 1 Peter as a whole, shaping its theology of Christian suffering.[50] It is difficult to escape the conclusion that if Zechariah had been so fundamental to Peter's thought, Liebengood would have made use of it in a way that is both more frequent and more obvious.[51]

We come now to a third possible source of Peter's OT allusions. A 1967 study by Danker finds evidence of the influence of Malachi.[52] He finds five allusions,[54] and also five thematic parallels. To this we can add the possible allusion in 2:9 to Malachi 3:17 (εἰς περιποίησιν).[55] The case he makes is not compelling. None of the thematic parallels would be evident unless Peter's readers were already committed to finding connections with Malachi, for they concern themes that are often discussed in Scripture. And the allusions are neither numerous enough nor close enough to lead the reader to look for wider thematic links with the book of Malachi in particular.[56]

Fourth, in a 2001 study, Sharon Clark Pearson argues that the letter has been heavily influenced by Isaiah: '1 Peter is an address built upon the themes, concerns and language of the canonical book of Isaiah in general and Deutero-Isaiah in particular.'

The principal thrust of her argument is that the 'broad themes' of the letter – 'humiliation / vindication, mercy, hope, and eschatological joy' – come from Deutero-Isaiah.[57] At one level, this reads Peter accurately.[58] As we have noted, Schutter finds twenty-one quotations of or allusions to Isaiah in the letter.[59] But there are two problems with Pearson's claim. Her 'broad themes' are not just central in 1 Peter; they are fundamental biblical motifs. As a result, they are found in too many other sources for their use in 1 Peter to be regarded as due especially to Isaiah. Second, the same is true of the language and themes of 1 Peter in general: they reflect the influence of other OT materials as well as a range of early Christian traditions, and cannot be traced to Isaiah in particular.

Another version of this approach is found in Mark Dubis, who argues that 'the most important theological motif in 1 Peter

[is] the motif of exile and restoration'.[60] In part this is based on his contention that 'the suffering/glory pattern that dominates 1 Peter (1:6-7, 11, 21; 4:13; 5:1, 4, 10) is fundamentally an exile/restoration pattern'.[61] This in turn rests on his view about the way the letter uses Isaiah: 'First Peter's numerous references to Isaiah 40-55 suggest both the importance of this exile/restoration theme,[62] as well as a key source of this theme.' Several responses to this view are in order.[63] First, the prescript's reference to the readers as παρεπιδήμοις διασπορᾶς (1 Pet. 1:1) is sufficient to indicate that they are being seen as exiles – a perspective that is also found elsewhere in the letter.[64] Second, however, there is one very notable sense in which the situation of Peter's readers differs from that of the Babylonian exiles: their sufferings are not God's judgement upon their sins.[65] On the contrary, by the death of Jesus they have been delivered from sin and brought to God (2:24; 3:18). This can only mean that there is a sense in which their 'exile' is over: 'Peter is clearly affirming that restoration has *already occurred* in and through Jesus: they are a newly formed people (1.3, 23), redeemed by the unblemished lamb (1.18-19), declared to be a people of God again (2.9-10), healed (2.24), and returned to the eschatological shepherd (2.25) – all images that come from the OT prophets and point to restoration.'[66]

Third, to the extent that their 'exile' is at an end, the readers' sufferings cannot simply be regarded as 'exilic', as Dubis calls them.[67] Fourth, it is thus difficult to see how Peter's suffering/glory pattern can be an exile/restoration pattern. This raises the question of whether there is another, better way of understanding this pattern – a question that is also raised by a study that builds on Dubis' work.

Like Dubis, Andrew Mbuvi recognizes that the exile/restoration theme in Isaiah 40 – 55 is developed in terms of a new exodus.[68] He acknowledges that the exodus 'provides the linguistic framework within which the present situation of the believers can be reinterpreted and actualized, just as prophets like Isaiah were able to recast the anticipated restoration from Babylonian exile as a "New Exodus"'. Yet he immediately goes on to claim that 'the exodus "echoes" in 1 Peter are subsumed into the exile imagery, which itself is expressed in light of the Second Temple mindset of the "continuing exile"'.[69]

It is difficult to follow his logic here. If exile and restoration are seen in terms of a 'new exodus', then it is not exile but exodus that is the more fundamental concept of the two.[70] We will return to this point shortly – but first we must consider where and how Peter makes use of Isaiah.

There is, first, the quotation of Isaiah 40:6–8 in 1:24–5. This confirms the point made in v. 23: that the word of God is enduring. In contrast to the fleeting impermanence of all human life and activity, God's word remains forever. Peter's reason for making this point is pastoral: because the readers' new life as God's reborn children (ἀναγεγεννημένοι, 1:23) is as secure and lasting as the word which generates it, new ways of relating (ἀλλήλους ἀγαπήσατε ἐκτενῶς, 1:22) within the family of believers (εἰς φιλαδελφίαν, 1:22) are now possible and expected.[71] In making this point, Peter says that the enduring divine word that Israel heard through Isaiah – the declaration of God's saving purpose; the promise of his saving intervention (Isa. 40:1–5,9–11) – is now heard in the gospel (1 Pet. 1:25). What does he mean by this? How are we to understand the continuity between Isaiah's message and the gospel? It is not just that the situation of Peter's readers is very similar to that which evoked the prophet's words.[72] His point is that the gospel announces what Isaiah promised: the gospel of Zion (Isa. 40:9) is now heard in the gospel of Christ. The prophetic word anticipates the gospel word and finds its intended fulfilment in that word.

The next use of Isaiah is in 2:4–10, a passage full of OT citations and allusions.[73] Isaiah 28:16 is quoted in 2:6, and Isaiah 8:14 in 2:8.[74] Both are seen as referring to the Lord Jesus, the λίθον ζῶν (2:4). He is either the object of believers' faith (ὁ πιστεύων ἐπ' αὐτῷ, 2:6) or the occasion of unbelievers' stumbling (2:8). However, Peter is not primarily making a christological point here, for his Christology is in the service of his paraenesis. He is calling his readers to keep coming to the Lord (2:4) and to keep believing in him (2:6–7).[75] He intends to assure them that by doing so, they will not be put to shame (οὐ μὴ καταισχυνθῇ, 2:6); instead, they will receive honour from God (2:7).[76] This is despite the hostility and rejection they experience in their own society, for they belong to Jesus, the 'elect reject' (2:4). To be his is to share not only his rejection but also his election: 'Jesus is the λίθος ἐκλεκτός, the believing community is the γένος ἐκλεκτόν.'[77] So like him, they are precious to God (παρὰ Θεῷ ἐκλεκτόν ἔντιμον, 2:4) – no matter what their society says or does to them. In making this point, Peter uses Isaiah 43:20–21 (along with Exod. 19:6) in 2:9. The τιμή his readers have already (2:7) is that they are God's γένος ἐκλεκτόν, his λαὸς εἰς περιποίησιν. Their role as a redeemed people, called out of the darkness of paganism into God's light, is to proclaim his ἀρεταί, his glorious deeds. In all of this they are the people of the promised new exodus (Isa. 43:14–21), the 'eschatological covenant community'.[78]

Peter turns to Isaiah again in 2:21–5, where he both quotes and alludes to the fourth of the Servant Songs (Isa. 52:13 – 53:12).[79] This is seen as speaking of Jesus' sufferings, which Peter views as both redemptive (2:24) and exemplary (2:21–3). We are meant to be healed by his wound (2:24) and also to follow in his steps (2:21).[80] Although Peter is addressing Christian slaves (2:18), what he says applies to all his readers: Christ suffered for us all and set an example for us all (2:21). There is a close connection between these two: what he achieved by his sufferings frees us to follow his example – frees us, that is, to live rightly before God (τῇ δικαιοσύνῃ ζήσωμεν, 2:24). 'In Jesus Christ, the obedient, suffering servant of God, obedient, suffering servants have both an enabler and an exemplar.'[81]

Again, it is important to note that Peter is not primarily making a christological point here; rather, he 'deploys christology in the service of his instruction about Christian life and witness in the world. This is christology in the service of ecclesiology.'[82]

In Jesus, Peter's readers are to see the pattern of their own life as God's people. He is a model of how to remain faithful in the face of harsh and unjust treatment. Instead of threatening or retaliating, he entrusted himself to the God who judges justly (2:23), and so he was raised from death and glorified (1:21). He is thus not only their model but also the guarantee of their vindication by God. The pattern of suffering and glory that we see in him also characterizes his persecuted people.[83]

Next we find the use of Isaiah 8:12–13 in 3:14–15.[84] Here Peter applies a YHWH-text to Jesus Christ. His point is that his readers should be honouring Christ as Lord rather than fearing their opponents – just as Isaiah was to fear YHWH and not Israel's enemies (Isa. 8:6–13). The Lordship of Jesus has a direct and powerful impact upon their situation: 'Because Jesus is Lord, the dominant religious and political powers of this world are not ultimate. God remains in control, even when his people suffer . . . As God exalted Christ, so God will also vindicate those who honor Christ as Lord in the face of hostile opposition.'[85] Once again, Peter is not spelling out a christological point per se. Rather, he is employing the Christology with which they are familiar to urge his readers to stand firm in the face of suffering.

More could be said about Peter's use of Isaiah, but this is sufficient to make it clear how important this major OT work is to him.[86]

We now come to consider a fifth source for Peter's OT allusions. These are his references to the foundational events of Israel's story: the exodus, wilderness wanderings, and entry into the promised land.[87] That the letter is likely to contain such allusions is suggested by two passages in particular. The first is 1:15–16, which quotes a core principle of the Sinai covenant-legislation: 'You shall be holy, because I am holy.'[88] The second is 2:9, where Peter applies terms from Exodus 19:6 to his readers: like Israel at Sinai, they are God's βασίλειον ἱεράτευμα and ἔθνος ἅγιον.

This exodus-theme is clearly present in 1 Peter 1. As we have seen already, v. 1's ἐκλεκτοί is language that the OT applies to Israel because of the exodus and the Sinai covenant, and 1:2 alludes to the covenant-ceremony Moses performed at Sinai (Exod. 24:3–8). We see this exodus-theme once more in the reference to believers' 'inheritance' (κληρονομία, 1:4), a term the LXX often uses to speak of the promised land. We see it next in the reference to 'redemption' (ἐλυτρώθητε, 1:18), one of the principal ways in which the OT speaks of YHWH's mighty deed of salvation at the exodus.[90] The language of 1:19 is an obvious reference to the sacrificial system that was at the heart of the cult YHWH prescribed at Sinai.[91]

Once we see the exodus-theme in these passages, other passages which contain no explicit reference to it can now be seen as likely allusions. There are seven of these in 1 Peter 1. First, mention of God's πολὺ . . . ἔλεος (1:3) takes us to YHWH's revelation of his glory to Moses: κύριος ὁ θεὸς ... πολυέλεος ... καὶ ποιῶν ἔλεος εἰς χιλιάδας (Exod. 34:6–7). Second, while the OT knows many instances of God's 'salvation' (σωτηρία, 1:5, 9), the exodus is the first and most significant of them.[92] Third, the use of ἀγαλλιᾶσθε (1:6,8) can be related to the exodus-theme.

The OT records many instances of rejoicing, especially in the Psalms, a great many of which are focused on God's saving work.[93] Of particular importance for our purposes is the reference to the exodus in Psalm 104:43 LXX: καὶ ἐξήγαγεν τὸν λαὸν αὐτοῦ ἐν ἀγαλλιάσει καὶ τοὺς ἐκλεκτοὺς αὐτου ἐν εὐφροσύνῃ? Like Israel, Peter's readers are God's ἐκλεκτοί (1:1; 2:9), his λαός (2:9–10), and like Israel, they rejoice at God's saving work (1:5–6). Fourth, mention of the readers' πειρασμοί (1:6; 4:12) echoes the way the OT refers to YHWH 'testing' his people in the wilderness.[94] Fifth, the call to 'gird up the loins' of the mind (1:13) is reminiscent of an instruction given to the Israelites at the first Passover (Exod. 12:11). Sixth, reference to their παροικία (1:17; cf. 2:11) echoes what is said of Israel in Egypt.[95] Finally, the readers have 'consecrated' or 'purified' themselves (ἡγνικότες, 1:22), reminding us of the provisions of the covenant legislation given at Sinai.[96]

There are at least thirteen such allusions – the use of terminology that the LXX applies to the events of the exodus-period – throughout the remaining four chapters of the letter.[97] In 2:4 we find a word (προσέρχομαι) that is used of Israel's access to YHWH in the Sinai cult.[98] The priestly offering of sacrifices (2:5) is obviously one of the fundamental elements of that cult.[99] Although 2:9's use of the phrase λαὸς εἰς περιποίησιν is likely to be derived from Isaiah 43:21, the concept involved goes back to the exodus events.[100] Addressing the readers as πάροικοι in 2:11 can be seen as comparing them with Israel in Egypt.[101] The reference in 2:12 to the ἡμέρᾳ ἐπισκοπῆς reminds us of YHWH's 'visitation': that is, his intervention to rescue his people from Egypt.[102] The description of believers as δοῦλοι Θεοῦ (2:16) uses a term applied to the Israel of the exodus.[103] When Peter calls Jesus the ποιμήν (2:25) and the church God's ποίμνιον (5:2,3) he is using language that the OT applies to Israel in the time of Moses.[104] To inherit a εὐλογία (3:9) is to receive what the Sinai covenant held out to Israel.[105] In 3:18 we learn that Christ's death was intended to 'bring' us to God. This uses a word (προσάγω) that has a prominent role in descriptions of the Sinai cult.[106] The use of γογγυσμός in 4:9 harks back to Israel's behaviour in the wilderness.[107] In 5:3 Peter employs a term (κλῆρος) that is used frequently in the LXX of the division of the land between the tribes.[108] The use of ταπεινόω in 5:6 echoes a prominent description of Israel's plight in Egypt.[109] This word is also used in the Sinai legislation to speak of Israel's observance of the Day of Atonement.[110] This verse also features an expression – God's 'mighty hand' (τὴν κραταιὰ χεῖρα) – that the OT uses especially of YHWH's works at the time of the exodus.[111]

While not all of these allusions are equally strong or obvious, there are too many to be overlooked. It seems clear that the foundational events in Israel's story play a critical role in Peter's understanding of his readers and their situation. Although his use of Isaiah is unquestionably prominent and important, there is, as we have seen, some difficulty aligning the situation of his readers with that of the Babylonian exiles. We are now in a position to suggest a more satisfactory alternative. As we have noted, Peter sees his readers as poised between redemption (1:18) and inheritance (1:4). This means that they are like Israel in the wilderness, with Egypt behind them and blessing in the promised land ahead of them.[112] There were two phases in Israel's experience of salvation: as Moses addressed them at Sinai and in the plains of Moab, they had already been saved out of slavery and death in Egypt but had not yet been saved into their promised rest in the land. So it is with Peter's readers, who live between the salvation that is already in effect (1:9; 2:2; 3:21) and the salvation that is still to come (1:5).

This brings us to another parallel with Israel in the wilderness. Their journey from Egypt to Canaan was a story with two sides. They faced significant threats and real hardship, but they were also under the care of YHWH, who in these struggles both tested them and protected them. Peter's readers too are experiencing significant suffering but are also cared for by God (5:7). For them too this in-between time is a story with two sides: they are both tested (1:6; 4:12) and protected (1:5). And their story involves both suffering on the one hand and glory and joy on the other (1:6,8; 4:14). Yes, their sufferings will give way to glory and joy when Jesus Christ is revealed – but that glory and joy are being experienced already, in the midst of their struggles. It is thus not Israel in exile but Israel in the wilderness that provides the closest model for Peter's readers: 'Israel's Exodus provides all the means of expressing the unique, paradoxical condition of the people of God.'[113]

It is worth noting that Peter's use of the exodus-theme is especially characteristic of the first major section of the letter (1:3 – 2:10), where he is concentrating on the question of his readers' true identity, before he turns in the rest of the letter to focus on how they should respond to the challenges and struggles confronting them.

What are we to say about the parallels between Israel's story and the situation of Peter's readers? Our search for an answer takes us back to 1:10–12. In view of what Peter says there, we can hardly regard these parallels as just a happy coincidence. He is convinced that we must read the OT as prophetic of Christ and the salvation he has won for the people of God. To make the same point from a different angle, we are to read the OT through the lens of the gospel. As we noted above, for Peter the gospel is the hermeneutical key to the OT. And now that we have surveyed his use of the OT, we are in a position to draw some firm conclusions about what this conviction means.

To read Scripture through the lens of the gospel is, first, to read it as 'christotelic': that is, as embodying a narrative that reaches its τέλος, its intended climax, in the person and work of Christ. Scripture is, above all, prophetic testimony to Christ in his sufferings and glories (1:11). Hence, for example, the way Peter uses Isaiah 53 in 2:21–5. But as we have seen, his dominant note is paraenetic rather than didactic or polemical. So in his use of the OT, he is not usually making a christological point as such. Christology is more his foundation than his focus – it is generally what he argues from rather than what he argues for. His principal objective is identity-formation: he aims to give his marginalized readers a secure sense of who they are before God and because of Christ. This means that his use of Scripture combines 'christological-prophetic interpretation and paraenetic application'.[114] It is because he wants his readers to understand themselves as God's elect community (1:1; 2:9) that he points to Christ's status as the rejected Elect One (2:4). As we discover from 2:6–8, Peter finds this status attested in Scripture, which he reads as Spirit-given testimony to the glories of Christ's person and work. The OT is not only christotelic, however. Peter sees it as testifying also to the status of his readers as the eschatological covenant community (2:9–10).

Second, then, to read Scripture through the lens of the gospel is to read it as 'laocentric', that is, as focused on the people of God.[115] We learn from 1:10 that Scripture is prophetic not only of Christ but also of the salvation of his people. Their status as God's people is determined by him and his saving work: they are who they are in and because of him. He is God's elect (2:4) – and in him, they too are elect (1:1; 2:9). He is the living stone (2:4) – and in him, they too are living stones (2:5). Christology and ecclesiology belong together. So, according to Peter, Scripture concerns the grace God displays towards the readers (τῆς εἰς ὑμᾶς χάριτος, 1:10) as well as the glories he confers upon Jesus Christ. That is why Peter looks to his Bible to find appropriate characterizations of his readers and their way of life. 'Reading Israel's Scriptures in light of what God has accomplished for the world in the death and resurrection of Christ, the author fashions for his predominantly Gentile communities a new identity as the people of God, both by appropriating for them significant scriptural designations typically reserved for Israel and by allowing the words of Scripture to address their lives directly.'[116]

This laocentric reading of the OT grounds Peter's ethics as well as his ecclesiology. He is seeking to make clear both the new identity of his readers and the new way of life that flows from that identity. He is thus reminding them of the word of God, the gospel by which his readers have been given new life as the people of God (1:23–5; 2:9–10). He is also reminding them of the will of God, by which the life of God's people is to be governed (2:15; 4:2,19). Peter shows us that both of these have their roots in the OT Scriptures (1:14–16; 23–5).

Third, to read Scripture through the lens of the gospel is to read it eschatologically. Because God's saving work has reached its τέλος in Christ, we have come to what Peter calls the 'last of the times' (ἐπ' ἐσχάτων τῶν χρόνων, 1:20). This means that we are living in the eschatological 'now' (1:12; 2:10,25; 3:21). This is the era of the gospel, when what the Scriptures attest reaches its fulfilment (1:12). It is the era of God's mercy to the Gentiles, who are now incorporated into his people (2:10). It is the era when the eschatological Shepherd is rescuing his straying sheep (2:25). It is the era of salvation, when believers, poised between redemption (1:18) and inheritance (1:4), begin to participate in the salvation of the end times (3:21; cf. 1:5). There is thus a fullness in the eschatological present that surpasses what we find in the earlier stages of the story. But that is because the OT story prepares us for an end it does not by itself contain. It is an unfinished story that finds its intended climax in Jesus Christ and his gospel. If we are to read it rightly, therefore, we must read it in light of the end announced in the gospel.

Fourthly, when we read Scripture as christotelic, laocentric and eschatological, we also read it typologically. This is what is happening in Peter's frequent references to the exodus story. These make it clear that he sees 'a typological connection between the church and the people that was formed at Sinai under the Old Covenant'.[117] What God is doing now through the gospel is patterned upon what he has been doing all along in the story of Israel: the end is foreshadowed in the journey that brings us to the end. We can see another kind of typological connection in Peter's use of such OT material as Psalm 33 LXX and Isaiah's fourth Servant Song. He wants his readers to grasp that their suffering 'takes its meaning from the pattern of the Suffering and Vindicated Righteous that runs like a thread through the fabric of Israel's Scriptures and that comes to decisive expression in the career of Christ'.[118]

We can sum this up by saying that God was at work in Israel with Christ and the church in view – providing that we do not take this to mean that Israel's story has been replaced by a different one. Here a typological reading of the OT involves both unity and distinction. It emphasizes the continuity in God's saving work with his people, from the beginning through to the end.[119] But this work was always aiming at the climax which it has now reached in Jesus Christ. So in addition to the unity of this work, a typological reading also acknowledges the fullness that marks the eschatological era. The eschatological 'now' both fulfils and surpasses all that prepared for it.

As we come to the end of our study of 1 Peter, many questions remain: what versions are Peter's OT citations drawn from, and how closely does he follow them? How does Peter's use of the OT compare with that of other NT writers – or that of the Qumran community and other Jewish groups? . . . and so on. But I hope that what we have done is sufficient to give us a deep appreciation of this important product of early Christian mission which is also an important NT witness to Jesus Christ.

11

God Has Spoken: The Renegotiation of Scripture in Hebrews

Matthew R. Malcolm
Trinity Theological College, Western Australia

Post-Crisis Conceptual Renegotiation

What does 'the holocaust' *mean*?

According to the edition of the *International Standard Bible Encyclopedia* which was published by Eerdmans in 1939,[1] 'the holocaust' simply refers to the whole burnt offering of a heifer, into which cedar-wood and hyssop and scarlet were cast. But that was 1939. Perhaps not many of us begin with that image in our heads when we hear the word today.

Language use changes after a triggering crisis – like a world war . . . or the execution and claimed resurrection of a would-be Jewish messiah. Old words become filled with new meaning; old texts receive new light; old concepts undergo *renegotiation*.[2] Indeed, a term sometimes used in the field of cultural and cognitive linguistics for such conceptual and linguistic change is renegotiation. In his inaugural address as professor at Monash University in 2011, Farzad Sharifian spoke of 'the role of culture in shaping language and its influence on all levels of language'.[3] According to Sharifian, the cultural conceptualizations that underlie language are 'constantly negotiated and renegotiated through generations of speakers within a cultural group, across time and space'.[4]

Sometimes, as with the Holocaust, that renegotiation occurs suddenly.[5] There is now no return to a pre-Holocaust unmarked use of the imagery of 'holocaust'. A cultural crisis has precipitated a juncture, causing widespread renegotiation of that image, so that for most people it is now impossible to hear the term *only* with its previous meaning.

It is essential to recognize that a very similar thing has taken place in the NT, such that when we speak of 'appropriation' of Scripture in the NT, it does not mean an innocent 'interpretation' of what Scripture had always 'meant'; but rather, a post-crisis renegotiation of Scripture, given the believed resurrection of Jesus from the dead. What once referred to David can no longer only be heard within previously existing parameters, now that Jesus is believed to have received Davidic vindication. What once referred to the Spirit as an impersonal power or emanation can no longer only be heard within previous parameters, now that Jesus is believed to have received the promises to David and poured out the living Spirit on all flesh.

At one and the same time, Scripture provides the conceptual resources in the enacting of the crisis events associated with the emergence of Christianity, and those key events prompt renegotiation of the Scripture-based conceptualizations. For example, Psalm 22 provides the words for Jesus' lament on the cross; and Jesus' lament on the cross transfigures the way that Psalm 22 must now be heard for those who follow him.[6]

Therefore, in considering the NT appropriation of scriptural resources, there are three complex stages to consider: first, the varied *initial readings* of the Scriptures before Christ; second, the *crisis* of the Christ event itself, including the actions and teachings of his life, as well as the claims and experiences of his death, resurrection, and ascension as Spirit-sending Lord; third, the *renegotiation* of Scripture in the light of this culture-shifting crisis.

This essential point is missed by biblical commentators as varied as Gerd Lüdemann and Lee Strobel, who are looking for a one-to-one correspondence between prophecy and fulfilment across Old and New Testaments.

Lüdemann states: 'The evangelist Matthew would have us believe that Isaiah 7:14 foretold the virgin birth of Jesus; but since the announcement of this forthcoming birth refers to an event during the reign of king Ahaz (741-725 BCE), Jesus cannot have [been] the child referred to.'[7] Lee Strobel states: 'I concluded that the odds of forty-eight Old Testament prophecies' coming true in any one individual are the same as a person randomly finding a single predetermined atom among all the atoms in a trillion trillion trillion trillion billion universes the size of our universe.'[8]

But such one-to-one correspondence is unhelpfully simplistic.[9] We should not think that the NT writers were oblivious to the fact that the psalmic son was originally heard to refer to the Davidic king, or that the Isaianic Servant was perhaps originally heard to refer to Israel. But that was before the crisis of the Christ event. And the experiences of the Christ event directed that Scripture be revisited, and heard and appropriated in startlingly radical ways. The NT disciples are like those who have been surprised by the ending of an Agatha Christie novel, and are now able to reinterpret the prior material that they had once known from a different perspective. They find meaning where they had found little before; they notice details that had passed by them previously; they amplify significant silences; they draw new connections.

My interest in this chapter is to see how this has happened in the book of Hebrews, as suggestive scriptural figures have been renegotiated, post-Christ event, as the triadic utterers[10] of divine speech: God, the Son and the Holy Spirit.

Post-Crisis Renegotiation of Conceptualized Figures in Hebrews

Initial readings

God

Conceptualizations of God in the OT and early Jewish witness cannot be considered adequately here; nevertheless, for the purposes of this chapter, it is enough to consider that prior to the NT, it was uncontroversial to consider God as the divine initiator and appointer of Israel's identity, including Israel's ideal leadership. It is he who announces 'You are my son' in Psalm 2, or 'You are a priest' in Psalm 110. It is he whose initiative has been flamboyantly defied by the corrupt Jerusalem leadership portrayed in *PsSol* 17:6:

> In their pride they [gloriously] set up their own royal house.
> Their arrogant substitution desolated David's throne
> and they did not glorify your honourable name.

God is the rightful appointer, whose initiative should be respected.

Son

Although Psalm 2 is extremely important in Hebrews and other early Christian literature, Sam Janse has recently argued that messianic readings of this psalm were not as prevalent as one might expect in earlier Jewish material. In Qumran literature, for example, the 'son' of Psalm 2 appears to be interpreted communally and eschatologically, rather than as a singular messianic figure.[12] However, *PsSol* 17:21–32 certainly draws on the language of Psalm 2 to depict a Davidic Messiah who will reign, purge, destroy, gather, judge and purify. This figure is a 'son' (17:21) in the pattern of Psalm 2 (17:24), who is sinless (17:36) and possessing of a holy spirit (17:37), but is by no means to be thought of as divine.

There was, then, a range of conceptions of 'sonship' prior to Jesus, even when the focus is limited to the meaning of the figure in Psalm 2.

Spirit

Max Turner points out that, prior to Jesus, 'By far the most widespread understanding of the Spirit in Judaism was as something like what later came to be called the "Spirit of prophecy".'[13] Drawing on scriptural precedent, the Spirit was represented (in part) in early Judaism as a 'channel of communication between God and a human person'.[14] So, for example, we read in 1 Chronicles 12:18 that the Spirit enabled Amasai to address David with words given by God.

Indeed, at numerous points in the NT, it appears conventional to ascribe OT scriptural revelation to the activity of the Spirit. Mark has Jesus discussing Scripture in the temple, arguing a point with reference to the agreed conviction that David spoke by the Holy Spirit (Mark 12:36). Exactly the same pattern is seen in the speech by Peter in Acts 1:15. Their arguments depend upon this agreed assumption.

Of course, such usage does not demand that the Spirit be viewed as a distinct member of the Godhead. Rather, as Turner comments: 'if one were to ask Jewish readers of the Hebrew Bible, most would have been liable . . . to explain the Spirit as God's *own* life and vitality in action.'[15] So, in considering readings of the Jewish Bible before Jesus, it is relevant that God could, among other images, be uncontroversially viewed as *appointer*; the son could, in various ways, refer to the *Davidic king* or his messianic heir or communal eschatological heirs; and the spirit could be viewed, at least, as the agent or enabler of *divine communication*. None of this is sufficient to explain the sudden and focused use of triadic categories in the NT, but it provides a partial and necessary background.

Crisis

This brings us to the triggering crisis of the Christ event. The occasion of Jesus' baptism seems a prime candidate to prompt consideration of just what caused a sudden and apparently promiscuous renegotiation in the conceptualizations of these three scriptural figures of God, Son and Spirit, by the time of the earliest Christian literature. However, given the somewhat impenetrable mystery surrounding Jesus' baptism, which is only accessible through tantalisingly brief later testimony, I will limit my attention to an element of that occasion that *is* penetrable by historical Jesus scholars: Jesus' own belief that God addressed him as son. As sceptical a scholar as Maurice Casey is able to affirm Jesus' experience at this point as formative:

> The image is quite violent, as anyone who has experienced a flapping pigeon descending on them will be unable to forget. The way it is put cannot be due to the early church, and must be accepted into the historical record . . . 'my son the beloved' in first-century Judaism means that Jesus was a faithful Jew chosen by God to do for Israel something that mattered . . . it is probable that the auditory part of the vision is as genuine as the event itself.

Formative for Jesus' ministry was this conviction that he had been addressed by God as son. All four evangelists refer to this event in some capacity, and all make reference to the Spirit in this context. We have in this event a perceived voice from God, a perceived appointment as son, and perceived testimony of the Spirit – experienced by Jesus, and passed on to his followers, as of formative significance.

The evangelists unanimously consider the ministry that began with this event to have climaxed with this son's resurrected vindication (e.g. Mark 15:39; 16:6–7). The NT more broadly evidences the claims that this vindication entailed the confirmation of sonship (Rom. 1:4) and the dispensation of the Spirit (Acts 2:32–3). This was the triggering crisis of the Christ event, as perceived by the very earliest followers of Jesus.

Renegotiation

After the crisis of this Christ event, we encounter renegotiated triadic conceptualization[17] in the NT. In a shift that is radical, and yet bears a significant degree of continuity with the Scriptures themselves, we encounter the *God* who appoints; the *son* who obeys; and the *Spirit* who bears witness. They are the same figures, but their parameters have been renegotiated. My brief observations will be limited to the book of Hebrews.[18]

God

God is the main character of the book of Hebrews. He is the one in relation to whom the other characters are identified. It is he who says, 'You are my Son' (1:5). It is he who says, 'You are a priest' (5:6). In this sense, the conceptualization of God in Hebrews bears strong continuity with the pre-existing view of God as appointer, apart from a very focused orientation towards the Son.

Son

This Son is, of course, Jesus, the second main character in the book of Hebrews. He is presented as the author, sustainer and climactic figure of all history, who responds obediently to God's appointments. In response to the call to sonship, he ascends, through his suffering, to God's right hand (2:9). In response to the call to priesthood, he perfects, through his sacrifice, his brothers and sisters (7:26–8). There is continuity here with the OT conception of the 'son' as the king who executes God's will; but this conception has clearly been radically enlarged beyond the bounds of early Jewish interpretation, by the crisis of the Christ event itself.

Spirit

Schenck rightly reflects on the role of the Holy Spirit in Hebrews:

> The Holy Spirit speaks a contemporary meaning to the audience in Heb. 3:7 in the words of Ps. 95:7-11, and in Heb. 10:16-17 he witnesses to a truth of the new covenant by way of Jer. 31:33-34. What both of these instances have in common is a direct and contemporary application of the words to the situation of the audience. It would thus appear that the author primarily located messages addressed by the Holy Spirit in the present, with the audience as addressee in such instances.[19]

Again, this bears continuity with an OT conception of the Spirit as the agent of divine communication; but again, the Christ event has radically enlarged this conception, such that the Spirit personally speaks his communication.

Thus in Hebrews we encounter the appointing *God* of the OT, but now he is oriented specifically towards his son; we encounter the obedient *son* of the OT, but now he is both all-surpassingly perfect and a perfector; and we encounter the communicative *Spirit* of the OT, but now he communicates in person, rather than just in abstract agency. These three OT figures have been renegotiated, via the Christ event, to become something larger than they could possibly have been perceived to be before. The writer to the Hebrews has returned to the Scriptures, and found room there for the crisis-triggered expansion of these three figures.

Triadic Conceptualization and Macro-Rhetoric in Hebrews

Finally, I want to move to consider the impact of this triadic conceptualization on the macro-arrangement of Hebrews.

Numerous commentators, whether for thematic or text-linguistic reasons, have perceived an overarching threefold division in Hebrews.[20] While affirming the complexity of the literary devices noted especially by Vanhoye and Guthrie, such an overall sweep is still useful. Keeping in mind Guthrie's insistence that attention be paid to the author's use of parallelism in particular, I see the following overlapping threefold sweep as reasonable:[21]

1:1 – 4:16:	God has spoken in the divine son
4:14 – 10:25:	The son is a superior high priest
10:19 – 13:25:	Let us persevere

This much is not new. What I wish to add is the observation that in the first two of these divisions, one finds a repeated rhythm in which God, Jesus and the Holy Spirit are said to speak portions of Scripture in turn, in a manner that fits their respective post-crisis characterizations.

In the first division, *God* is said to have spoken the words of Psalm 2 to Jesus, 'You are my son' (1:5), as well as a series of other passages, climaxing with Psalm 110, 'Sit at my right hand' (1:13). After some further explication, including conspicuously unattributed[22] words of Scripture, *Jesus* is said to have spoken Scripture to his 'Father' in obedient response, climaxing with the words, 'Here I am, and the children God has given me' (2:13) – an affirmation which is immediately developed in relation to his bodily ('flesh and blood') death. Subsequent to this, the *Holy Spirit* is said to speak the words of Scripture to these children of God, calling for obedience of heart: 'do not harden your hearts as in the rebellion' (3:8), an exhortation which is unpacked throughout the rest of the division.

In the second main division, we find a similar progression. *God* is said to have spoken the words of Psalm 2 and Psalm 110: 'You are my son'; 'You are a priest forever' (5:5-6). After an extensive explication, including further words of Scripture attributed to God, *Christ* is said to have spoken the words of Scripture in obedient bodily response: 'a body you have prepared for me'; 'I have come to do your will' (10:5–9). Subsequent to this, the *Holy Spirit* is said to speak the words of Scripture to 'us', promising obedience of heart: 'I will put my laws in their hearts, and I will write them on their minds' (10:16).

1:1 – 4:16 *God has spoken in the divine son*		**4:14 – 10:25** *The son is a superior high priest*		**10:19 – 13:25** *Let us persevere*
1:5–2:9	*God*: 'You are my son' (Ps. 2); Sit at my right hand' (Ps. 110)	4:14 – 9:28	*God*: 'You are my son' (Ps. 2); 'You are a priest forever' (Ps. 110)	
2:10 – 1:8	*Jesus*: 'Here I am, and the children;' flesh and blood death	10:1 – 14	*Christ*: 'A body you have prepared for me'	
3:1 – 4:11	*Holy Spirit*: 'Do not harden your hearts'	10:15 – 18	*Holy Spirit*: 'I will put my laws in their hearts'	

This rhythm – of God speaking Scripture to the son; Jesus speaking Scripture to God; and the Holy Spirit speaking Scripture to the children – illustrates the pervasive influence of the renegotiated conceptualizations at the core of the emerging Christian movement. T*hey have the capacity to articulate and structure formational Christian discourse*. If it is true, as cultural linguistics holds, that we ought to pay attention to 'the role of culture in shaping language and its influence on *all levels* of language',[23] then we should not be surprised by this influence of a cultural crisis both on terminology, and even on discourse structure. Indeed, it is strikingly fitting that an arrangement in which Scripture is uttered in turn by God, Jesus and the Holy Spirit, should flow from the homiletic voice of one who is persuaded that at the climax of history, *God has spoken*.

Or to come at it the other way, it is extraordinarily significant for the examination of the emergence of Christianity that before Christian literature was produced – certainly before the letter to the Hebrews was produced – a seismic cultural change had already taken place; one that was powerful enough to cause the renegotiation of central devotional imagery: *God has spoken in utterances by God, by Jesus and by the Holy Spirit.*

Appropriation Today

12

Reading the New Testament from the Outside

Rory Shiner
Providence Church, Perth (W.A.), and Macquarie University, Sydney

D.W.B. Robinson on Reading the New Testament as Gentiles

> 'My job, I used to say, was to land the students on the moon: they might have to find their own way back to earth!'[1]

This is how the Australian New Testament scholar and churchman Donald Robinson understood his role in teaching the Moore College Special Doctrine Course of the 1950s and 1960s. The course, originally intended as a general introduction to theological studies for Anglican ordination candidates in the Diocese of Sydney, quickly became a medium by which generations of students were taught Robinson's distinctive biblical-theological approach to understanding the whole of Scripture. Thus, while Robinson's own work is not widely known, through students such as Graeme Goldsworthy, William Dumbrell and P.T. O'Brien, many of his ideas have been developed and disseminated to a wide audience.

The approach to biblical theology taught in Robinson's classes has since moved beyond the academy and become a staple feature of catechesis in a large number of churches and ministries – especially in conservative evangelical circles.[2] Through the popular writings of authors such as Goldsworthy and Vaughan Roberts literally thousands of students and ordinary Christians have been taught a grasp of the overall unity of Christian Scripture in a form that is comprehendible, transferable, and on the broad question of the unity and diversity of the testaments, satisfying.[3] For many within evangelicalism, it has spelt a welcome departure from both pietistic, devotional readings of the OT on the one hand and from dispensationalism, its heirs and successors on the other. For many Christians, the effect has been to make the Scriptures (and particularly the OT) closer, more accessible and, in a word, *their* book – a book that tells *their* story.

If the works of authors like Roberts and Goldsworthy have helped to make Christians feel at home in the world of the Bible, Robinson saw his own task as (at least initially) rather the opposite. He wanted, as in the quote above, to 'land his students on the moon' – that is, for them to feel the strangeness, the alienness, the otherness of the biblical narrative and, in particular, to unsettle their sense that even the NT was *their* book – at least in the terms it might be traditionally understood. Robinson's grasp of the shape of the OT's narrative and theological structure actually raised tensions and problems as much as it raised solutions for contemporary Bible readers. Whereas biblical theology itself seeks to read the Bible from the inside, in its own categories with within itself its own dynamics, Robinson was exercised by the possibility that, at the end of the project we might find ourselves reading the Bible (and especially the NT) *from the outside,* ultimately strangers to its own inner dynamics.

This chapter is in reality a piece of Australian church history, coyly smuggled into a biblical studies publication. It tells the story of Donald Robinson's role in the development of biblical theology in Australia, itself an important and influential stream of what Goldsworthy has identified as the Modern Evangelical Biblical Theology Movement.[4] By telling this story, I hope to offer some insights into the origins and development of Robinson's work and, by doing so, to open up some lines of critical evaluation.

Once the story is told, I will venture beyond my competency and into the main subject of this book by exploring some of the tensions Robinson himself saw in his work. In particular, I want to explore Robinson's concerns about whether contemporary Christians should read the NT as if we were still *within* its story (including the expectation of an immanent Parousia and the Jew–Gentile dynamics of the nascent church), or whether we in some sense stand apart from the biblical drama and read the Bible from the *outside*.

Donald Robinson's biblical theology

Donald Robinson joined the Moore College faculty in 1952, after three very fruitful years at Queen's College, Cambridge, where he completed a theological tripos in New Testament and had been deeply impressed by (among others) C.H. Dodd and C.F.D. Moule.

Robinson had read Dodd's *Apostolic Preaching and its Developments* and *Parables of the Kingdom* before arriving at Cambridge, and managed to attend Dodd's lectures and his NT seminars in Dodd's final years at Cambridge. Robinson had been struck by Dodd's attention to the promise and fulfilment themes in Scripture, and his general grasp of the 'sub-structure' of NT theology.

In 1949, Moule's special NT doctrine course for that year was on the church. It was a topic that initially disappointed Robinson, who had hoped for something (like the atonement), which would be, in his words, 'closer to the heart of my evangelical priorities'.[5] However, in beginning to read around the subject, including early work by F.J.A. Hort and more contemporary work by R. Newton Flew, J.Y. Campbell and G. Johnston, Robinson was to discover a wealth of linguistic, theological and biblical-theological work on the *ekklesia* in the Old and New Testaments that would greatly fire his interest in the theme.

Evangelicalism has always been disposed to biblical scholarship that emphasized the unity of Scripture. In Cambridge, Robinson discovered a suite of scholars who, while not themselves evangelical, fuelled in Robinson a passion to pursue the unity of Scripture in a way that was both critical and, at the same time, conducive to faith.

If figures such as Dodd and Moule provided the basic architecture for Robinson's approach to the NT, it was against the 'almost continuous' conversation with Fr Gabriel Hebert in the years 1952–60 that Robinson's biblical theology course was hammered out. Hebert and Robinson had first met in 1952 at a theological conference of evangelicals and Anglo-Catholics at St Paul's College, Sydney University. The younger Robinson and more senior Hebert remained in conversation over biblical themes from that day onward. Despite their variant churchmanship, both shared deep convictions about the nature of theological education, about the general NT presentation of Christ as fulfilment of OT types, and specifically shared a distinct three-stage schema of promise and fulfilment, to which we turn below.

(As an historical aside, I cannot resist noting here that Leon Morris's dispute with C.H. Dodd on *propitiation* and J.I. Packer's response to Gabriel Hebert in his *'Fundamentalism' and the Word of God*[6] have marked out both Dodd and Hebert in popular evangelical historiography as *bêtes noires* of the movement; in Robinson's story, by contrast, both are crucial allies.)

The Moore College Special Doctrine course

It was with these conversation partners that Donald Robinson developed the Moore College Special Doctrine course. Owing largely to the experience with ecclesiology under Moule at Cambridge, the course itself focused on the people of God as a prominent biblical theme. It explored major OT covenants, especially with Noah, with Abraham and the Sinai covenant with Israel via Moses. It took the promises of Genesis 12 to Abraham and his seed and saw its outworking through the redemption from Egypt and the possession of the land. And it framed the NT as grounded in the claim that all this is fulfilled in Christ.

The most distinctive feature of Robinson's work lay in a three-stage schema for the biblical narrative. Though originally interested in 'covenant' as a unifying strategy, Robinson had concluded that covenant itself was captured within a wider promise and fulfilment structure, grounded specifically in the kingdom of God. However, Robinson saw a promise and fulfilment shape *within* the OT itself. The promises to Abraham, Moses and David were, for Robinson, actually fulfilled in the historical reality of the reign of Solomon. The nature of the promises to David's son in 2 Samuel 7, the exalted language of Solomon's reign in 1 Kings 3 – 8, and the superlative terms of Psalm 72 all confirmed for Robinson that, according to these accounts, in Solomon the promised kingdom of God had come.

Thus, while the NT was indeed an account of fulfilment, it is more specifically fulfilling those promises made in the devastation of exile. These promises are grounded in, but expanding on the promises that sustained the biblical narrative up to the point of Solomon's reign. The promises that come in the exile amount to 'an experience of God's kingdom – in a form which would transcend the temporal blessings of the old Exodus and the old kingdom of David'.[7] (Robinson was pleased to note Hebert had a similar division in his book *Christ the Fulfiller*,[8] though he was not aware of a direct debt to this aspect of his work.)

Israel and the nations

Robinson of course rejected the dispensationalist account of Scripture which was then a live option in evangelical circles. More strikingly, however, Robinson's studies lead him to a firm rejection the supercessionism, which was dispenationalism's normal alternative. That is to say, for Robinson '[t]he popular view that God rejected the Jews and that the gospel became a wholly Gentile matter is so far at variance with the NT as well as with the expectation of the Old Testament that a complete reappraisal of the New Testament is called for.'[9]

On the one hand, dispensationalism maintained a distinction between Israel and the Gentiles, but by what Robinson considered a sleight of hand, rearranged the timetable to place Israel's salvation in the future, beyond the age of the church. On the other hand, much mainstream Christian thought simply accepted the idea that God's dealing with Israel qua Israel had ended with the birth of the church. In contrast to both, Robinson contended that:

> What neither position allows for, but what I believe to be the teaching of the NT, is that God's distinctive promises to Israel are in the NT fulfilled, not to all believers, but to Jewish believers who constitute the restored remnant of Israel and that Gentile believers are the inheritors of other promises altogether, that is, the promises made in the Old Testament to the nations who should come to Israel's light.[10]

For Robinson, this one observation led to a steady stream of scholarly work in which all the major sections of the NT were interrogated in order to establish if this dynamic shed light on the texts. The results were startling. Were 'the saints' in Paul a specific title for Jewish Christians, on whom Gentile believers were now dependent for blessing and judgement? Was the Jerusalem church owed tribute, not just on account of the famine, but for its spiritual prestige? Would the wealth of the nations brought to the Jerusalem church precipitate the parousia? Was 'the Israel of God' not 'the church' but in fact those Jewish missionaries on whom Gentiles could reliably depend for the gospel and the traditions? And so on.

The dissemination of Robinson's biblical theology

As Robinson assumed the role of bishop in Parramatta in 1972 and Archbishop of Sydney from 1981 to 1992, it fell to others to disseminate his ideas. Robinson's influence on a generation of biblical scholars was significant, with Paul Barnett, Peter O'Brien, John Painter, William Dumbrell and Bruce Kaye all conscious of a deep debt to his approach. However, in terms of his biblical theology proper, the task of making that accessible to a wide and popular audience fell almost single-handedly to Graeme Goldsworthy. If Robinson promised to take his students 'to the moon', Goldsworthy was determined to land Robinson's teachings in the lives of ordinary believers.

As his 2012 *homage* to Robinson makes clear, it was the three-stage schema that most impressed Goldsworthy.[11] While the work of Vos, Clowney and VanGemeren offered various epocal divisions of Scripture that were in their own way informative and helpful, it was Robinson's schema alone that seemed to Goldsworthy to have unearthed a division intrinsic to the Scriptures themselves.

Unresolved tensions: Robinson's critique of Robinson's biblical theology

In 1996, Moore College hosted a school of theology on the topic, 'Biblical Theology and the Pastor'. Among the presentations was a paper by Donald Robinson in which, after tracing the history of his influential course, he goes on to indicate what he himself saw as the tensions or loose ends in his proposal. Thus, as it happens, the first published critique of Robinson's biblical theology is from Robinson himself.

The nature of his critique is telling. The first concern Robinson raises is the fairly standard concern of any biblical-theological proposal; namely, whether it leaves some parts of Scripture uncomprehended. For Robinson, while he was satisfied that his schema accounted well for the main part of the OT (namely, the Torah, the Former, and the Latter Prophets), he wondered out loud whether it could account for wisdom literature on the one hand and apocalyptic on the other.[12] While gesturing to Goldsworthy's work on wisdom literature, Robinson raises a particular concern about the psalms that is instructive:

> Whatever else [the psalms] do, they remind us that the OT pattern of promise, redemption, kingdom, etc. was not play acting, not a charade . . . The events may indeed have happened to them tupikos (figuratively?) as St Paul says, any may have been recorded for our benefit ('upon whom the ends of the ages have come') rather than for theirs, but God was God, and faith and hope were real – so real that the Psalms have always been accepted by the Christian church as voicing the Christian response, individual and corporate, to all that God says to us in and through Christ . . .The whole biblical story becomes our own, from Abraham, through redemption in the exodus, the day of temptation in the wilderness, as pilgrims through this barren land, and in the fruition of God's presence and rule in the prophetic hope of the city of God and our dwelling in the house of the Lord forever.[13]

The fascinating point here is that, for Robinson, Christian liturgical use is relevant in assessing how the Scriptures should now be received by Christians. Robinson's work, with its fresh originality, its tendency to minority readings and its determination to let the Bible speak 'on its own terms' has sometimes encouraged a 'Year Zero' approach to reading the Bible, cut free of the history of reading that has gone before it. And yet here, for Robinson, 'the fact that the Psalms have always been accepted by the Christian church as voicing the Christian response' is for him sufficient reason to think that they should *continue* to do so, and to be the means through which 'the whole biblical story becomes our own'.[14]

Robinson was undoubtedly concerned that 'the whole biblical story' should become 'our own' as contemporary Christians. And yet, as Robinson recognizes in his 1996 paper, two factors in particular alienated contemporary Christians from the biblical story: first, our status as Gentiles reading the story and, second, our position as seemingly outside the eschatological expectations of the NT.

On the first question (reading as Gentiles), Robinson's rigorous rethinking of Jew–Gentile dynamics within the NT was the catalyst for much of his most creative and sometimes ground-breaking exegetical studies. But its net import was to raise more questions than answers for the contemporary Gentile reader of the NT. His readings would often place the Gentile reader on the passive, rather than active, side of the story – as the receiver of Israel's blessings, rather than the disseminator of them. So, for example, the Gentile reader is receiving the blessings of the Great Commission as a restored Israel now fulfils its vocation; but it was not at all clear to Robinson that the Gentiles ought to participate in this same vocation. Whole books, such as 1 Peter, become problematic as in Robinson's estimation they are not addressed to Gentiles and deal with privileges and an identity that continue to be distinctively Israel's. And many of Robinson's exegetical conclusions address situations that are seemingly impractical and unreal for contemporary Gentile churches. Ought we to have within our congregations a locus of 'saints' (that is, Jewish Christians) from whom we can receive instruction? Where should the synagogue fit within the evangelistic programme of a local church? Are we obliged to take the gospel to the local Jewish community first? How could we Gentile Christians pay homage to the spiritual prestige of the Jerusalem church when none (in the shape of the first-century's version) exists?

These questions remain unresolved. Goldsworthy's earlier work did not engage this particular tension. I note, however, that in Goldsworthy's most recent work, he has conceded that Robinson's exegetical case on this matter is unanswered and that 'there are no grounds in the Old Testament for supposing that the Gentiles would one day replace Israel as the people of God'.[15]

He has not returned to his teacher's conviction that an important distinction between Israel and the church remains within the NT documents, and has even now distanced himself from aspects of his earlier work in which he has conflated Israel and the church, in light of Robinson's cogency on this matter.[16]

For Robinson the second main tension – that of our relationship with NT eschatology – is in fact related to the Jew–Gentile question. Robinson took for granted that the NT envisioned an imminent eschaton and that Paul in particular expected the collection from the Gentile churches would, once delivered to Jerusalem, precipitate the salvation of Israel in the terms of Romans 9 – 11 and that the Parousia would follow.

This is bracing stuff in the context of conservative evangelical thought! The vast majority of evangelicals have developed strategies to accommodate the apparently unfulfilled eschatological expectations of the NT (from pious readings of the imminence of the end for each person, through to the more baroque eschatological schemes of premillenialism). Robinson's own take is striking for the taken-for-granted way in which he offers it – the NT writers taught and expected an end that, in the end, did not happen. For him, attempts to stretch out 'this generation' to two millennia was unconscionable,[17] and the contemporary Christian must therefore grapple with two alternatives:

> are we latter day Christians to see ourselves and still *within* this Christian movement as depicted in the NT, still in this 'this is that' era, still within the dynamics of Jew/Gentile relations, apostolic commissions, and expectations of the parousia of Christ in 'this generation' . . . ? Or are we to see ourselves as standing *outside* the whole biblical drama, from Abraham to parousia, accepting it as divinely revealed paradigm in history of God's redemptive purpose for mankind, and, dare I say it, as providing the data-base, or mine of revelatory information, from which systematic theologians can draw the substance of their systematic constructions to comfort and enlighten Christians in their walk with God in this world?[18]

Robinson notes that Christians have assumed the first answer is correct, though the tradition has acted as if the second situation were the reality. The surprising thing is that Robinson, rather than chastising the church for the second approach (mining the NT for 'revelatory information'), actually offers it as a live option. On the surface, this would seem to undermine the very thing a generation of enthusiastic adopters first found attractive in Robinson's proposals: namely, a means by which they might frame their faith as within the biblical story. To entertain this kind of rapprochement between the biblical story and more traditional dogmatic theology seems, on the surface, to be a proposal to sell the farm.

The dissemination of biblical theology emanating from Robinson's work did not, on the whole, question where we stood within Scripture's story – assuming a perspective from within the now-not yet eschatology of the first Christians. But for Robinson, it was an acute issue. Could we really read the NT as if that eschatological perspective was our own? To suggest that, having understood the biblical story on its own terms, we now discover that its terms are not our terms and our job was now to mine those texts for the materials on which systematic constructions could be formed would be, to many, to exactly rob the biblical-theological project of the very thing that attracted them to it in the first place. Perhaps the theology of Karl Barth was a model Robinson had in mind: clearly dogmatic rather than biblical theology, and yet a theology that entered into the 'strange new world of the Bible' and remained highly sensitive to the particularities of Israel and so on. Maybe?

In his 1996 paper, Robinson names two authors whose work offered promise for resolving the tensions he was aware of in his treatment of the NT: G.B. Caird's *New Testament Theology*[19] and N.T. Wright's *The New Testament and the People of God*.[20] As Wright's work builds on Caird's, I will limit myself to Wright and ask the question: What solutions might Wright offer to the tensions of which Robinson was aware?

First, on eschatology, Wright has mounted a vigorous case to locate much of the eschatological material in Jesus and Paul as pointing neither to an end still future to us, nor to an end of the space–time universe that demonstrably did not happen, but rather to the events culminating in CE 70 with the destruction of Jerusalem by the Romans.[21] This approach has the obvious advantage of dismissing what Robinson felt was the unconscionable stretching of 'this generation' to include us, while at the same time avoiding the conclusion that Jesus and Paul were mistaken on such a fundamental issue. Wright's contention that that CE 70 is the major (though not only) eschatological event to which the NT documents point also allows him to say something more nuanced about the story of Israel than simply 'it was replaced'. It is curious that, as far as I am aware, Robinson does not explore the events of CE 70 in this connection, as it would appear to offer such an elegant solution to the tension.

Second, Wright's analogy of contemporary Christians as participating in the fifth act of an as yet incomplete drama similarly holds promise of a resolution to Robinson's unresolved tension.[22] On the one hand, it has the potential to relieve contemporary Christians of the burden of trying to imagine they exist within certain dynamics of the NT that simply do not pertain today (a prestigious Jerusalem church, Jewish Christians fulfilling a special role within Gentile congregations, etc). Yet at the same time it allows Christians to participate within the biblical narrative, rather than having to stand outside the whole drama and access it in an unstoried way.

A final comment on Wright: his work, despite its highly sensitive and nuanced approach to the identity and vocation of Israel, does at certain key points argue that the church *in some* sense takes on the privileges, identity and vocation of Israel.[23] While positively this makes lighter work of the task of seeing the whole biblical story as our own, it would need, for me at least, to offer a sufficient answer to Robinson's contentions regarding: (a) the fact that the OT offers no grounds for supposing that gentiles will ever become 'Israel' as such; and (b) the continued distinctions between Israel and the Gentiles that seem to be evident within the NT itself.

Conclusion

The conservative biblical theology movement has naturally emphasized the unity of the testaments and presented the NT as a nearly self-evidently fulfilment of what the OT had always meant. Especially in circles where supersessionism is taken for granted, the biblical story can then be approach from Genesis to Malachi as our story, or the story of God and his people, of whom we (Gentiles) are straightforwardly members. In this book several authors, though varied in their approaches, have questioned those sorts of assumptions and instead argued for what Matthew R. Malcolm has called a 'post-crisis conceptual renegotiation' of Scripture in the light of the 'culture-shifting crisis' of the death and resurrection of Christ. In a sense, Robinson's questions regarding contemporary readings of the NT are similarly 'post-crisis' readings. Does the loss of a prestigious Jerusalem church, the loss for most churches of a Jewish–Christian core ('the saints'), and the apparently unfulfilled eschatological expectations within the NT mean that we need to renegotiate the NT itself?

As for the OT, for Robinson it is *Israel's* story, not ours. We find ourselves in it, not as agents within Israel's life, but rather as those Gentiles who stand, one day, to be on the receiving end of Israel's blessings, should Israel manage to fulfil her vocation. We do not read it innocently, like the first-time reader of a detective novel for whom the identity of the murderer is genuinely open. Likewise, a Gentile Christian reader of the OT is not wondering whether Israel will fulfil her vocation, understanding it to have been fulfilled in Christ. Perhaps, therefore, there is something disingenuous with the idea that a Gentile Christian 'starting' with the OT and reading forward toward fulfilment. A Gentile Christian 'starts', as Robinson would put it, with 'gospel' and 'apostle', by which an ambassador of the newly reconstituted Israel comes to them (literally, in the first century, or via the NT ever since) with the message of the Creator God of Israel and his call for them to turn from idols to serve the living and true God and to wait for his Son from heaven. In this way is a Gentile included in the Messiah – not by imagining themselves to have been under the privileges and trauma of the Torah, but as late-comers, included by grace and recused, not from the curse of the Torah, but from idolatry.

This analogy might help: ever since the completion of C.S. Lewis' *The Chronicles of Narnia,* publishers had been divided over whether to present the box-set in order of publication (placing *The Lion, the Witch, and the Wardrobe* first) or according to the internal chronology of the books themselves (with The Magician's Nephew and its creation stories leading the series). McGrath, in his recent biography of Lewis, has argued for the coherence of the former, noting that the implied reader of the *The Lion, the Witch, and the Wardrobe* is meeting Aslan for the first time, and is assumed not to be aware of the stories told in *The Magician's Nephew*.[24] The reader of *The Lion, the Witch, and the Wardrobe* would then turn to *The Magician's Nephew* curious to know more of the origins of the Aslan they have now met.

Is this truer to how a Gentile encounters Jesus Christ, and through him, the OT Scriptures? We do not follow Israel's story with Israel, but through Christ. Through the gospel we are called out of our own particular story of idolatry (Gal. 4:8) and incorporated into the story of Israel's God and Israel's Messiah, not as if now Israelites, but as the Gentile beneficiaries of Israel's vocation, now fulfilled in Jesus. And, in this way, we now access the story of the OT as the reader of the *The Lion, the Witch, and the Wardrobe* might access *The Magician's Nephew* – curious of the origins of the One they have encountered.

Conclusion

The Appropriation of Scripture in the Emergence of Christianity

Matthew R. Malcolm
Trinity Theological College, Western Australia

Scripture is used in the NT in startling ways, which attest to the major hermeneutical impact of the Christ event. Contributions in this volume have provided various models to describe this feature of early Christianity, drawn from fields such as linguistics, cultural memory and anthropology. This has resulted in varied characterizations of what is taking place in the use of Scripture by Jesus and/or the NT writers: 'reschematization'; 'renegotiation'; 'reconstruction' and other terms have been suggested. There has been no attempt to harmonize this terminology, because the aim of this volume is not to advocate for a single model or set of terms; but to demonstrate, using the varied expertise of contributors – each with distinctively useful categories – a broadly concordant approach to the topic, which carries discussion further.

It should be noted immediately that there are numerous fresh contributions to scholarship to be found in this volume that do not fit within the narrow identification of the theme above. These would include Hurtado's proposal regarding 'at the right hand'; Deines' intriguing consideration of the family of Jesus; Chapple's advocacy of the primacy of the exodus–wilderness experience as a motif of 1 Peter; Windsor's fresh reading of Galatians 3:16; and other proposals. These should be seriously considered and evaluated. In this conclusion, however, it will be worthwhile to focus more narrowly on the cohering theme that is essential to the volume, and consider how each contribution relates to it.

The volume opens with a substantial study by Larry Hurtado, immediately drawing our attention to case studies of the appropriation of Scripture in earliest Christianity. Hurtado argues that the earliest Christians' sudden novel interpretations of their Scriptures occur in response to christological convictions that arise from their experiences – especially visions of the risen Jesus. He suggests that the NT readings of these key texts can by no means be explained with reference to standard methods or interpretations prior to Christ. He uses such terms as 'innovative', 'remarkable', 'novel', 'creative' and 'astonishing' to describe early Christian reading, concluding that it is not only radical in relation to contemporary interpretation, but that at times it clearly 'exceeds' any original meaning of the source text. It is important to Hurtado to note that this radical rereading of Scripture does not emerge at the end of a long evolutionary process, but as early as can be traced or conceived, being already assumed as traditional in Paul's letters from the fifties CE.

Hurtado's interest in the 'cognitive processes involved in the earliest Christian exploration and appropriation of particular OT texts' relates closely to a number of other contributions to this volume, including that by Malcolm and Malcolm. This second chapter continues the opening section of the volume on 'appropriation and interpretation'. Malcolm and Malcolm argue that Luke presents Jesus as initiating his disciples into rereading Scripture in the light of the 'triggering event' of his coming. Approaching Scripture with such a 'reschematization' results in a fresh construal of its meaning and focus, which nevertheless bears some continuity with its pre-Christian heritage. Here, the insights of cognitive and cultural linguistics are seen to suggest precise terminology for the phenomenon that we see in the NT's surprising appropriation of the Scriptures. This analysis also suggests that the initial impetus for the innovative interpretation of Scripture identified by Hurtado above comes from Jesus himself (at least according to Luke).

This perspective, that Jesus is the source of the NT's radical reading of Scripture, is given a great deal of further consideration in the chapter by Roland Deines. While Deines argues that Jesus introduces a heretofore unseen perspective on the meaning and focus of the Scriptures, he is careful to insist that this arises from an approach to Scripture that Jesus shares with his contemporaries: Scripture provides lenses through which the world is seen and evaluated and understood. Expecting his hearers to share this readiness to interpret present people and events in the light of scriptural precedents, Jesus authoritatively presents himself as the climactic destination of biblical patterns and promises. This 'bold' christological appropriation opens 'the possibility that the evangelists or their sources actually *learned something from Jesus' own handling of Scripture*'.

With this in mind, the subsequent two chapters of the book can be read as an intriguing exploration of the disciples putting into practice what they had learned from their master. Donald S. West's chapter considers how the Jerusalem church appropriates a text from the prayer book of Israel (Ps. 2) for its own devotional life. To relate this to Deines' chapter, one could say that because Christians continue to operate with 'biblical lenses', they appropriate both form and content of OT prayers in a way that allows adaptation in the light of their present life-situation. Furthermore, the nature of that adaptation is now inexorably shaped by 'the light of the coming of the Messiah'.

In Benjamin L. Sutton's chapter, a 'social memory' analysis of Acts 10 illuminates how Jewish 'cultural memory', encapsulated in Scripture, becomes re-evaluated and redirected in the light of the Christ event and its aftermath. Sutton's description of how a 'striking new experience (vision from God)' leads to a crucially reformulated conviction is evocative of Hurtado's conception of early Christian appropriation of Scripture. Similarly, Sutton's point that Peter must re-evaluate his previously accepted schema ('cultural memory') in the light of the coming of Jesus reminds very much of Malcolm and Malcolm's chapter, although with illumination from a different adjacent field.

The volume then moves to a focus on Paul, beginning with Mark A. Seifrid's chapter. This contribution involves the most lengthy exegetical analysis of the volume. Seifrid aims to show how in practice, Paul's 'encounter with Christ' has resulted in a new sense of personal identity, and a new understanding of Scripture. For Paul, while the Scriptures precede and promise Christ, it is Christ who surprisingly 'figures out' the Scriptures (specifically, the law). For the Galatians, this perspective requires application to their own sense of identity: in accordance with Paul's (re)reading of Scripture, they are to understand their identity as granted from God in Christ, rather than generated or maintained by visible boundary markers.

The next two chapters focus in on particular Pauline usages of Scripture. Given that so far the volume has especially emphasized the surprising elements of the NT's use of Scripture, it is notable that these two chapters argue for Paul's awareness of contextual concerns. Lionel Windsor argues that Paul's rereading of Scripture in the light of Christ remains respectful of the context from which the citation is drawn, in the instance of Galatians 3:16. While Paul's use of the passage from Genesis is certainly novel in terms of application, it is important to Windsor that it is not ignorantly torn from its context, but draws sensitively from a text 'already pregnant' with possibility.

Martin Foord argues that Paul respects the context of the psalmic text that he cites in Ephesians 4, but feels at liberty to reinterpret the text's meaning in the light of the subsequent revelation of the Christ event. Some might respond that this 'reinterpretation' involves unacceptable change (from 'receiving' to 'giving' gifts); but the acceptability or otherwise of Paul's reinterpretation depends upon one's assessment of whether the subsequent triggering revelation was in fact from the same divine author. It is certainly Paul's assumption that this is the case. In this regard, Foord proposes the motif of the revealed 'mystery' as a key to Paul's use of the OT: what God had formerly disclosed as a 'mystery', he has now brought to plain fulfilment in Christ. This validates the revisiting and reconsidering of the earlier revelation, in which the content of the gospel had been cloaked in mystery.

The final contribution on Paul is that by Mark J. Keown. In contrast to the chapters by Windsor and Foord, which focus on individual citations, this contribution surveys the whole letter of Philippians. Keown finds that Paul 'creatively and consistently reads the OT through the lens of Christ'. This, of course, is consonant with what one finds in the rest of this volume. Keown furthers the discussion by considering how this might have been perceived in Gentile churches, pondering whether in receiving instruction from Pauline co-workers, 'perhaps they developed a rudimentary early Pauline "biblical theology", reading the Greek OT through the lens of Christ'.

Moving beyond the Pauline Corpus, Allan Chapple considers the appropriation of Scripture in 1 Peter. Chapple finds that in this letter, the gospel of Jesus Christ functions as the hermeneutical key to the OT. Intriguingly (and in agreement with Hurtado's findings), he points out that a christological reading is assumed rather than argued, issuing without defence in the use of Scripture for ecclesiological and ethical purposes. Specifically, elements of Israel's experience in advance of Christ's initial coming are able to be viewed as patterns informing the readers' experience in advance of Christ's second coming. To put it differently, the scriptural patterns of wilderness identity, agreed to have been fulfilled in Christ, provide a template for the experience of those who now belong to Christ.

Matthew R. Malcolm's chapter moves to consider the book of Hebrews. Adapting certain terminology from the field of cultural linguistics, he describes the hermeneutical phenomenon under discussion as involving the three stages of *initial readings* of Scripture prior to Christ; the *crisis* of the Christ event; and the post-crisis *renegotiation* of Scripture that ensues. With regard to Hebrews, this can be seen in the way that 'suggestive scriptural figures have been renegotiated, post-Christ event, as the triadic utterers of divine speech: God, the Son, and the Holy Spirit'. Such a remarkable rereading of Scripture attests to the major transforming impact of the Christ event upon the writers of the NT.

The volume concludes, perhaps surprisingly, by questioning the extent to which current-day Gentile churches may appropriate Israel's scriptural story as their own. This chapter, by Rory Shiner, focuses in on one historically situated reader of Scripture, to consider how the questions raised in this volume might be pondered: Is it in fact the case that largely Gentile churches are to consider themselves invited into messianic Israel's rereading of her Scriptures? Do Gentiles read these Scriptures as 'insiders' or 'outsiders'? As readers of this volume witness the serious grappling with such questions in this chapter, they may find themselves articulating their own answers – perhaps with fresh insights and terminology from the volume itself.

This, of course, is an important outcome of the volume. While at one level it is an exploration of the hotly debated topics of the *emergence of Christianity* and the *New Testament's use of the Old Testament*, it is also unavoidably an invitation for Christian readers of

Scripture to evaluate consciously the intersection of their own reading, interpretation and identity. If it is indeed the case that *the New Testament writers follow the lead of Jesus himself, in creatively rereading their Scriptures in the light of the Christ event,* the impacts of this for contemporary use of the Scriptures must be engaged.

Endnotes

[1] Most famously, Maurice Casey, *From Jewish Prophet to Gentile God: The Origins and Development of New Testament Christology* (Cambridge: James Clarke, 1991).

[2] See, for example, ch. 15 of N.T. Wright, *The New Testament and the People of God* (London: SPCK, 1992).

[3] Larry W. Hurtado, *Lord Jesus Christ: Devotion to Jesus in Earliest Christianity* (Grand Rapids, MI: Eerdmans, 2003).

[4] Personal correspondence.

[5] www.bibleinterp.com/opeds/oldt314159.shtml (accessed 6 December 2013).

[6] Personal correspondence. The reference to 'Guidance' is an attempt to characterize positively that which is sometimes negatively referred to as 'law'. It is capitalized to signify that it represents 'Torah'.

[7] Personal correspondence.

[8] Personal correspondence. Casey's statement need not be taken as an endorsement of the veracity of the resurrection, but presumes belief in Jesus' resurrection on the part of the disciples.

[9] These contributions were prompted by an international symposium, for which funding was kindly granted by the Australian College of Theology.

1. Two case Studies in Earliest Christological Readings of Biblical Texts

[1] E.g. Daniel Patte, *Early Jewish Hermeneutic in Palestine* (Missoula: Scholars Press, 1975); David Instone Brewer, *Techniques and Assumptions in Jewish Exegesis Before 70* CE, *TSAJ* 30 (Tübingen: Mohr Siebeck,

1992); and, more briefly, Donald Juel, *Messianic Exegesis: Christological Interpretation of the Old Testament in Early Christianity* (Philadelphia: Fortress Press, 1988), pp. 31–57. For a recent discussion of Qumran *pesher* exegesis, see Timothy H. Lim, 'Biblical Quotations in the Pesharim and the Text of the Bible: Methodological Considerations', in *The Bible as Book* (ed. E. Herbert and Emmanuel Tov; London: British Library, 2002), pp. 71–9; Timothy H. Lim, *Pesharim* (London: Sheffield Academic Press, 2002). On the relevance of Qumran texts more generally for use of OT in the NT, see, e.g. J.A. Fitzmyer, 'The Use of Explicit Old Testament Quotations in the Qumran Literature and in the New Testament', in *Essays on the Semitic Background of the New Testament* (Missoula: Scholars Press, 1974), pp. 3–58; and now George J. Brooke, 'Shared Exegetical Traditions Between the Scrolls and the New Testament', in *The Oxford Handbook of the Dead Sea Scrolls* (ed. Timothy H. Lim and John J. Collins; Oxford: OUP, 2010), pp. 565–91.

2 For an earlier study addressing similar questions and focused on Ps. 110, see Martin Hengel, 'Psalm 110 und die Erhöhung des Auferstandenen zur Rechten Gottes', in *Anfänge der Christologie: Festschrift für Ferdinand Hahn zum 65. Geburtstag* (ed. Cilliers Breytenbach and Henning Paulsen; Göttingen: Vandenhoeck & Ruprecht, 1991), pp. 43–73.

3 Juel, *Messianic Exegesis*, p. 140.

4 Key previous studies include David M. Hay, *Glory at the Right Hand: Psalm 110 in Early Christianity* (Nashville: Abingdon Press, 1973); Michel Gourgues, *A la Droite de Dieu: Résurrection de Jésus et actualisations du Psaume 110,1 dans le Nouveau Tesetament* (Paris: J. Gabalda, 1978); William R.G. Loader, 'Christ At the Right Hand – Ps. CX.1 in the New Testament', *NTS* 24 (1978): pp. 199–217; Martin Hengel, 'Setze dich zu meiner Rechten!', in *Studien zur Christologie: Kleine Schriften IV* (WUNT 201; Tübingen: Mohr Siebeck, 2006), pp. 281–368, originally in *Le Trône de Dieu* (ed. Marc Philonenko; WUNT 69, 1993), pp. 108–94, English trans. ' "Sit At My Right Hand!" The Enthronement of Christ at the Right Hand of God and Psalm 110:1', in *Studies in Early Christology* (Martin Hengel; Edinburgh: T&T Clark, 1995), pp. 119–225 (which I cite here).

5 Loader, 'Christ at the Right Hand', p. 199. Similarly, Juel, *Messianic Exegesis*, p. 136, noted that Ps. 110:1 in particular 'decisively shaped hymnic and confessional language' in the early years of the young Christian movement.

[6] Citations: Matt. 22:44; Mark 12:36; Luke 20:42; Acts 2:34; 1 Cor. 15:25; Heb. 1:13. Allusions: Matt. 26:64; Mark 14:62; 16:19; Luke 22:69; Rom. 8:34; Eph. 1:20; Heb. 1:3; 8:1; 10:12. In addition, there are citations in *1 Clem.* 36:5 and *Barn.* 12:10, and further allusions in *1 Clem.* 36:5; *Pol. Phil* 2:1; *Apoc. Pet.* 6; *Sib. Or.* 2:243; *Apoc. Jas.* 14:30.

[7] Acts 2:33; 5:31; 7:55–6; Col. 3:1; Heb. 1:3; 12:2; 1 Pet. 3:22.

[8] Citations: Heb. 5:6; 7:17,21. Allusions: Rom. 11:29; Heb. 6:20; 7:3,11. Two allusions listed in the twenty-seventh edition of Nestle-Aland no longer appear: Col. 3:1 (referring to Christ 'seated on the right hand of God') and Heb. 3:15 (which refers to another priest in the likeness of Melchizedek). Both arguably could be included, however, as instances where the influence of Ps. 110 is likely. We should also note the frequent citations of and allusions to other OT texts, e.g. the Nestle-Aland list shows ten citations of various verses in Ps. 118, and another eight allusions to it.

[9] Hengel made this point earlier, noting that by the date of 1 Corinthians and Romans, 'The time of its [Ps. 110:1] effectiveness in forming and influencing christology was already past' ('Sit at My Right Hand!', p. 137).

[10] This has been the dominant view for some time now. See, e.g. the discussion by Artur Weiser, *The Psalms: A Commentary* (London: SCM, 1962; German original 1959), pp. 692–7.

[11] So, e.g. Weiser, *The Psalms*, p. 694; also Hay, *Glory at the Right Hand*, pp. 19–20.

[12] John J. Collins, *The Scepter and the Star: The Messiahs of the Dead Sea Scrolls and Other Ancient Literature* (New York: Doubleday, 1995), p. 142. He also observed (p. 151 n. 32) that the proposal by Bernard Duhm (*Die Psalmen* [Tübingen: Mohr, 2nd edn, 1922], pp. 398–400) that Psalm 110 originated as Maccabean propaganda 'is now universally rejected'.

[13] Cf. Bradley H. McLean, *Citations and Allusions to Jewish Scripture in Early Christian and Jewish Writings through 180* CE (Lewiston: Edwin Mellen Press, 1992), p. 77, who lists allusions to Ps. 110:1 in *1QS* 3:17 and *T. Reu.* 6:8. But I can see no basis for positing an allusion in either text. McLean posits an allusion to Ps. 110:4 in *T. Mos.* 6:1, presumably based on the reference to kings who will rule over the Jewish people and who will be called 'priests of the Most High God', commonly thought to refer to the Hasmonean rulers.

[14] Cf. however, Rikk Watts, 'The Psalms in Mark's Gospel', in *The Psalms in the New Testament* (ed. Steve Moyise and Maarten J.J. Menken;

London: T&T Clark, 2004), pp. 25–45, citing p. 38, who posits influence of Ps. 110 in *11QMelch* and the Similitudes of *1 Enoch*. But any such influence is hardly obvious. Of course, the enthronement scene in Dan. 7:10–14 may also be relevant for the Similitudes.

15 Hay, *Glory at the Right Hand*, p. 23. 'God' is one of several variants here, however, along with 'the Father', and 'the Saviour'. For the Greek text and variants, see Sebastian P. Brock, *Testamentum Iobi* (PVTG 2; Leiden: Brill, 1967), and Robert A. Kraft (ed.), *The Testament of Job* (Missoula: Society of Biblical Literature & Scholars Press, 1974).

16 James R. Davila, *The Provenance of the Pseudepigrapha: Jewish, Christian, or Other?* (JSJSup 105; Leiden: Brill, 2005), pp. 195–9, citing p. 199. Certainly, the variants cited in the preceding note seem to reflect Christian vocabulary. The recent study by Maria Haralambakis, *The Testament of Job: Text, Narrative and Reception History*, LSTS 80 (London: Bloomsbury, 2012), focuses on reception-history of the text and offers no firm view of original provenance.

17 Cf. Robert A. Kugler, 'Testaments', in *The Eerdmans Dictionary of Early Judaism* (ed. John J. Collins and Daniel C. Harlow; Grand Rapids, MI: Eerdmans, 2010), pp. 1295–7, who notes 'a weak consensus at best' for a first-century CE date, goes with that view.

18 Hay, *Glory at the Right Hand*, p. 26. Hengel ('Sit at My Right Hand!', p. 179) referred to the Similitudes as the only unambiguous witness to the messianic reading of Ps. 110 in second-temple Judaism, judging (p. 186), 'The influence of Ps. 110 and Isa. 11:1ff. upon the Similitudes cannot be overlooked.' Nevertheless, he concluded that Ps. 110 had 'only a limited impact upon the content of the preserved Jewish apocalyptic texts from Hellenistic Roman times'.

19 The references to *2 Enoch* 11 (24:1) and *3 Enoch* 10:1; 48C.5 are not clearly allusions to Ps. 110, and in any case take us far too late to be of any use in mapping pre-Christian usage of the text.

20 David L. Washburn, *A Catalog of Biblical Passages in the Dead Sea Scrolls* (Atlanta: Society of Biblical Literature, 2002), lists no citation or allusion. Collins (*The Scepter and the Star*, p. 151 n. 34) claimed echoes of Ps. 110 in the *Apocryphon of Levi (4Q540-541)*, but he does not specify them and I cannot detect any. Cf. Hengel ('Sit at My Right Hand!', p. 184): 'Unfortunately we know nothing about the interpretation of Ps. 110 and Dan. 7 in Qumran.'

21 Hay, *Glory at the Right Hand*, p. 27.

[22] Washburn (*A Catalog of Biblical Passages in the Dead Sea Scrolls*) has eight and a half pages of references to Genesis, and the Qumran texts include portions of commentaries on Genesis (4Q252, 4Q254), multiple copies of Genesis, and 'rewritten' material from Genesis (1QApGen).

[23] The evidence is gathered in H.L. Strack and Paul Billerbeck, *Kommentar zum Neuen Testament aus Talmud und Midrasch* (Munich: C.H. Beck, 1922–8), 4/1: 452–65. For a more recent attempt to use rabbinic texts critically, see David Instone-Brewer, *Traditions of the Rabbis From the Era of the New Testament, Vol. 1: Prayer and Agriculture* (Grand Rapids, MI: Eerdmans, 2004); but cf. also reviews, which pose questions about the success of his venture: www.bookreviews.org/pdf/4659_4763.pdf (accessed 6 May 2014); www.bookreviews.org/pdf/4659_4764.pdf (accessed 6 May 2014).

[24] Strack and Billerbeck, *Kommentar zum Neuen Testament aus Talmud und Midrasch*, 458–9.

[25] Hay, *Glory at the Right Hand*, p. 30.

[26] On the same logic, we would have to presume that the citation of Exod. 3:6 in Mark 12:26 presupposes that the Exodus text was already understood in second-temple Jewish circles as a reference to the resurrection of the dead, but this is neither attested nor asserted by scholars.

[27] Adela Yarbro Collins, *Mark: A Commentary, Hermeneia* (Minneapolis: Fortress Press, 2007), pp. 579–80.

[28] In his review of Hay's book, Joseph A. Fitzmyer (*CBQ* 36 [1974], pp. 594–5) likewise expressed doubt that the messianic reading of Ps. 110 can be affirmed with any confidence.

[29] Juel, *Messianic Exegesis*, p. 139. Yet, although he granted that '[t]here is little direct evidence in extant texts for a messianic interpretation of Psalm 110:1', Juel also judged that the reference to Ps. 110:1 in Mark 12:35–7 'seems to presume widespread agreement that the psalm speaks of the Davidic Messiah' (p. 138 n. 10).

[30] Hengel ('Sit at My Right Hand!', p. 137–63) stresses this as well in a much more detailed discussion of all the NT references than I can provide here.

[31] Paul's combination of wording from Ps. 110:1 and Ps. 8:6 (which is also alluded to in 15:27) is noted by many, e.g. Anthony C. Thiselton, *The First Epistle to the Corinthians: A Commentary on the Greek Text* (Grand Rapids, MI: Eerdmans, 2000), p. 1234; Richard B. Hays, *Echoes of Scripture in the Letters of Paul* (New Haven, CT: Yale UP, 1989), p. 84. Because this is an allusion in 1 Cor. 15:25 and not an exact citation,

it is not discussed in Christopher D. Stanley, *Paul and the Language of Scripture: Citation Technique in the Pauline Epistles and Contemporary Literature*, SNTSMS 74 (Cambridge: CUP, 1992), which I consider an unfortunate decision, precisely because Stanley sought to portray the various direct and indirect ways that Paul (and ancient authors more generally) cited and/or alluded to familiar texts.

32 Given that these two psalms are also linked in other NT texts (Eph. 1:20–22; Heb. 1:13 – 2:9), it is often suggested that Paul and other NT writers draw on an early Christian 'testimony' tradition/collection: e.g. Martin C. Albl, *'And Scripture Cannot Be Broken': The Form and Function of the Early Christian Testimonia Collections*, NovTSup, 96 (Leiden: Brill, 1999), pp. 221–8.

33 Jan Lambrecht, 'Paul's Christological Use of Scripture in 1 Cor. 15.20-28', *NTS* 28 (1982): pp. 502–27, esp. pp. 508–11.

34 Lambrecht, 'Paul's Christological Use of Scripture in 1 Cor. 15.20-28', p. 511.

35 Gordon Fee, *The First Epistle to the Corinthians*, NICNT (Grand Rapids, MI: Eerdmans, 1987), p. 756.

36 Hengel, 'Sit at My Right Hand!', p. 207. See his wide-ranging examination of various traditions about heavenly thrones, pp. 185–212. Cf. Collins, *The Scepter and the Star*, pp. 136–53. The unnamed figure of *4Q491^{c}* (*4QSelf-Glorification Hymn*) makes claims of having 'a mighty throne in the congregation of the gods', being exalted above all others, etc. (and note also *4Q427/4QHodayot*, in which a figure claims uniquely exalted insights and status). If these texts refer to a human being (Messiah? The Teacher of Righteousness?), they would give us an interesting comparator for the exalted claims for Jesus in the NT. On these texts, see Martin G. Abegg, Jr, 'Who Ascended to Heaven? 4Q491, 4Q427, and the Teacher of Righteousness', in *Eschatology, Messianism, and the Dead Sea Scrolls* (ed. Craig A. Evans and Peter W. Flint; Grand Rapids, MI: Eerdmans, 1997), pp. 61–73.

37 I cite the translation in Florentino García Martínes and Eibert J. C. Tigchelaar, *The Dead Sea Scrolls Study Edition*, Vol. 2 (Leiden: Brill, 1998; Grand Rapids, MI: Eerdmans, 2000), p. 981.

38 Cf. Hengel, 'Psalm 110', pp. 45–51; and his fuller/later discussion of Rom. 8:34 in 'Sit at My Right Hand!', pp. 137–63.

39 I return to the Greek phrasing in this and other NT confessional references later in this chapter.

[40] So, e.g. Hengel, 'Psalm 110', p. 46; Gourgues, *A la droite de Dieu*, pp. 53–7, 210–12. See also the analysis of the verse and the rhetorical structure of the larger context by Robert Jewett, *Romans: A Commentary. Hermeneia* (Minneapolis: Fortress Press, 2007), pp. 532–4. Though critical of some proposals that an early catechetical tradition underlies a large part of Rom. 8 or that vv. 31–4 reflects a two-strophe hymn, Jewett (pp. 532–3) judges it 'quite likely' that 'early kerygmatic material' is cited in v. 34, citing also Henning Paulsen, *Überlieferung und Auslegung in Römer 8*, WMANT 43 (Neukirchen-Vluyn: Neikirchener Verlag, 1974), p. 171.

[41] In Rom. 8:34 some manuscripts (e.g.) A et al.) have 'Christ Jesus' and others (e.g. B D 1739 et al.) have 'Christ'. But on either reading Paul clearly refers to Jesus as Messiah. On Paul's messianic christology and his use of 'Christ', see now Matthew V. Novenson, *Christ Among the Messiahs: Christ Language in Paul and Messiah Language in Ancient Judaism* (New York: OUP, 2012).

[42] Jewett, Romans, p. 542, citing Horst Balz, 'ἐντυχάνω', *EDNT* 1:461 (pp. 461–2).

[43] Jewett, *Romans*, p. 542.

[44] E.g. *Num.R.* Hukkat 19.33; *Esther R.* 7.13; *Lam.R.* Introduction, p. 24, these and other texts given in C.G. Montifiore and H. Loewe, *A Rabbinic Anthology* (New York: World Publishing Co., 1960), pp. 76, 99, 247–9. For a survey of Moses traditions in ancient Jewish texts, the NT, and rabbinic Judaism, see now Daniel K. Falk, 'Moses', in *The Eerdmans Dictionary of Early Judaism* (ed. John J. Collins and Daniel C. Harlow; Grand Rapids, MI: Eerdmans, 2010), pp. 967–70.

[45] R. Le Déaut, 'Aspects de l'Intercession dans le Judaïsme Ancien', *JSJ* 1 (1970): pp. 35–57.

[46] Paul's reference in Rom. 8:27 to the Spirit interceding (ὑπερεντυχάνει) for believers seems particularly to do with the difficulty believers may face in knowing how to pray, the Spirit assisting or interpreting their inarticulate groanings (στεναγμοῖς ἀλαλήτοις).

[47] See also Hengel, 'Sit at My Right Hand!', pp. 141–3, which includes analysis of the comparative frequency of the two expressions in several bodies of Koine Greek texts.

[48] E.g. ἐκ δεξιῶν used in portraying the Solomon with Bathsheba seated on a throne 'on his right' (3 Kgdms 2:19); and in Ps. 44:10 the queen is standing 'on your right'.

[49] A person on the right of another in the LXX: Gen:13 – 14; Deut 33:2; 2 Kgdms 16:6; 3 Kgdms 2:19; 1 Chron. 12:2; 2 Chron. 18:18; 1 Esd 9:43;

2 Esd 18:4; Pss 15:8; 44:9; 90:7; 108:6,31; 109:1,5; Sir 12:12; Zech. 3:1; 12:6; Ezek. 16:46; 21:16; 1 Macc. 9:12. In addition, there are another twenty instances where ἐκ δεξιῶν describes something as on/to the right of something/someone. The construction ἐν δεξιᾷ is used several times in LXX to refer to something in the right hand of someone, e.g. Ps. 3:16; Ep Jer 13 – 14.

[50] Ibid., 141 n. 52. Hengel surveyed the Greek pseudepigrapha and Apostolic Fathers, and on Greek papyri referred to Edwin Mayser, *Grammatik der griechischen Papyri aus der Ptolemärerzeit*, II/1 (Berlin: de Gruyter, 1926), 23; and Vol. II/2 (1934), 37, 147, 224, 384. I have done my own survey of NT, LXX and Apostolic Fathers and confirm Hengel's findings. More widely, *LSJ* (s.v. δεξιός) gives examples of ἐκ δεξιῶν, ἐπὶ δεξιά, and ἐν τοῖς δεξιοῖς as well as a few other phrasings for 'on the right hand/side'. Per *PGL* (s.v. δεξιός), the usual phrase referring to the position of Christ/the Son in relation to the Father in Patristic texts is ἐκ δεξιῶν. But cf. the Greek form of the Apostles' Creed, which has καθεζόμενον ἐν δεξιᾷ θεοῦ πατρός. In the several creedal statements cited in Athanasius, *De Syn.* 22-25 (Migne, *PG* 26, col. 720) as presented at the Council of Antioch (341 CE), one (Bishop Theophronios) refers to Christ as seated ἐκ δεξιῶν τοῦ πατρός, whereas the others all have him ἐν δεξιᾷ τοῦ πατρός.

[51] Mark 10:37–40/Matt. 20:21–3; Mark 15:27/Luke 23:33; Matt. 25:33–4; 27:38; Luke 1:11.

[52] Matt. 22:44/Mark 12:36; Luke 20:42; Matt. 26:64/Mark 14:62/Luke 22:69; Acts 2:34; 7:55–6; Heb. 1:13; and also Mark 16:19. Likewise, the citation of Psalm 16(LXX 15):8–11 in Acts 2:25 follows the LXX in using ἐκ δεξιῶν.

[53] ἐν δεξιᾷ τοῦ θεοῦ (Rom. 8:34; Eph. 1:20; Col. 3:1; Heb. 10:12; 1 Pet. 3:22); ἐν δεξιᾷ τῆς μεγαλωσύνης (Heb. 1:3); ἐν δεξιᾷ τοῦ θρόνου τῆς μεγαλωσύνης (Heb. 8:1); ἐν δεξιᾷ τε τοῦ θρόνου τοῦ θεοῦ (Heb. 12:2).

[54] Loader, 'Christ at the Right Hand', pp. 212–13; Hengel, 'Sit at My Right Hand!', pp. 141, 173. Similarly, Gorgues, *A la droite de Dieu*, pp. 54–5.

[55] Perhaps there is a similar slight distinction in English between referring to someone as 'to the right (side)' of another and saying that someone is 'at the right side' of another.

[56] Note, e.g. Gen. 48:13, where Joseph takes Ephraim 'in his right hand but on Israel's left' (ἐν τῇ δεξιᾷ ἐξ ἀριστερῶν δὲ Ισραηλ), and takes Manasseh 'in his left hand but on Israel's right' (ἐν τῇ ἀριστερᾷ ἐκ δεξιῶν δὲ Ισραηλ).

[57] Since the influential study by Ernst Lohmeyer, *Kyrios Jesus: Eine Untersuchung zu Phil. 2,5-11* (Heidelberg: C. Winter, 1928; reprinted Darmstadt: Wissenschaftliche Buchgesellschaft, 1961), many (most?) NT scholars have judged Phil. 2:6–11 to derive from an early Christian hymn/ode and have proposed various reconstructions of it. This has been challenged by a number of scholars recently, however, e.g. Gordon Fee ('Philippians 2:5-11: Hymn or Exalted Pauline Prose?', *BBR* 2 [1992]: pp. 29–46; Gordon Fee, *Paul's Letter to the Philippians*. NICNT (Grand Rapids, MI: Eerdmans, 1995), pp. 192–4 n. 4, citing there others as well who share his doubts). The question is not vital to my discussion here. Whether appropriated or composed by Paul, Phil. 2:6–11 reflects and presupposes a profound and boldly innovative reading of Isaiah 45:22–5 that is likely earlier than the date of the epistle.

[58] Ralph P. Martin, *Carmen Christi: Philippians 2:5-11 in Recent Interpretation and in the Setting of Early Christian Worship* (Grand Rapids, MI: Eerdmans, rev. edn, 1983; lst edn, 1967) is wholly given to assessing the vast body of scholarly publications on the passage, and Martin notes the preoccupation with the first few verses. The discussion continues, as reflected, e.g. in the more recent multi-author volume: Ralph Martin and Brian Dodd, eds, *Where Christology Began: Essays on Philippians 2* (Louisville, KY: Westminster/John Knox Press, 1998). I have addressed the passage in two earlier publications: Larry W. Hurtado, 'Jesus as Lordly Example in Philippians 2:5-11', in *From Jesus to Paul: Studies in Honour of Francis Wright Beare* (ed. P. Richardson and J. C. Hurd; Waterloo: Wilfrid Laurier University Press, 1984), pp. 113–26; Larry W. Hurtado, *How on Earth Did Jesus Become a God? Historical Questions About Earliest Devotion to Jesus* (Grand Rapids, MI: Eerdmans, 2005), pp. 83–107. But one of the most important studies has never been published, the PhD thesis by Takeshi Nagata, 'Philippians 2:5-11. A Case Study in the Contextual Shaping of Early Christology' (PhD, Princeton Theological Seminary, 1981).

[59] Perhaps the most well-known advocate of Adam-allusion in Phil. 2:6–11 is J.D.G. Dunn. See e.g. his recent defence of this view: 'Christ, Adam, and Pre-existence', in Martin and Dodds, *Where Christology Began*, pp. 74–83. Cf. my own view in Hurtado, *How on Earth*, pp. 96–102. John R. Levison, *Portraits of Adam in Early Judaism*, JSPSupp 1 (Sheffield: JSOT Press, 1988) dealt a rather serious blow to previously frequent claims about a supposedly cohesive and influential body of 'Adam speculation' in ancient Judaism.

[60] E.g. for the passage McLean, *Citations and Allusions*, lists as citations only Rom. 14:11 and Justin, *1 Apol.* 1:52, and for allusions only Phil. 2:10–11.

[61] On the passage, see David B. Capes, *Old Testament Yahweh Texts in Paul's Christology* (WUNT 2/47; Tübingen: Mohr, 1992), pp. 157–60; and Gordon D. Fee, *Pauline Christology: An Exegetical-Theological Study* (Peabody, MA: Hendrickson, 2007), pp. 393–401.

[62] As indication of this, Paul uses κύριος sometimes in reference to God and at other times in reference to Jesus. See, esp. Capes, *Old Testament Yahweh Texts*, pp. 90–148.

[63] See e.g. Larry W. Hurtado, 'The Binitarian Shape of Early Christian Worship', in *The Jewish Roots of Christological Monotheism* (ed. Carey C. Newman, James R. Davila and Gladys S. Lewis; Leiden: Brill, 1999), pp. 187–213, also published in my book, A*t the Origins of Christian Worship* (Grand Rapids, MI: Eerdmans, 2000), pp. 63–97.

[64] J.B. Lightfoot, *St. Paul's Epistle to the Philippians* (London: Macmillan, 1913; reprint, Grand Rapids, MI: Zondervan, 1953), p. 114, characterized Phil. 2:10–11 as 'modelled on Isaiah xiv.23 . . . the text being modified to suit St Paul's application to the Son'. G.F. Hawthorne, *Philippians. Word Biblical Commentary, Vol. 43* (Waco: Word Books, 1983), p. 92, referred to Isa. 54:23 as 'woven here into the structure of vv 10-11'.

[65] Fee, *Philippians*, p. 222.

[66] A number of important witnesses have ἐξομολογήσεται in v. 11, and opinion is divided over whether the subjunctive or this future form is the earlier reading. The subjunctive form could be an assimilation to the form of κάμψη (v. 10), or the future form may have been introduced influenced by the verb-form in Isa. 45:23. N-A28 prefers the subjunctive form, but cf. Lightfoot, *Philippians*, p. 115. The Alexandrinus text of Isa. 45:23 has ἐξομολογήσεται (supported also by Q ℵ), whereas Vaticanus (also ℵ) has ὀμεῖται. Fee judged the latter 'almost certainly created by Origen in his Hexapla as a "correction" toward the Masoretic text', noting also that in Paul's explicit citation of Isa. 45:23 in Rom. 14:11 he has ἐξομολογήσεται, which suggests that the Alexandrinus reading was the one that he knew, and that he did not create it (*Philippians*, p. 223 n. 28).

[67] Exegetes differ over whether 'every knee / tongue' in vv. 10–11 includes inanimate things as well. Cf. e.g. Lightfoot, *Philippians*, p. 115 and Fee, *Philippians*, p. 224 n. 34. The issue is not important for my purpose here.

68 Fee, *Philippians*, p. 224.

69 Cf. the discussion of Phil. 2:6–11 by Richard Bauckham, *Jesus and the God of Israel: 'God Crucified' and Other Studies on the New Testament's Christology of Divine Identity* (Milton Keynes: Paternoster Press, 2008), pp. 197–210, who urges that the text presents Jesus as participating in 'the unique divine sovereignty over all things' (p. 199), and thereby 'included in the unique identity' of God (p. 209).

70 Cf. Adela Yarbro Collins, 'Psalms, Philippians 2:6-11, and the Origins of Christology', *BibInt* 11 (2003): pp. 361–72, who proposed that the passage is 'a prose hymn or a brief encomium in rhythmic prose' that 'compares Jesus favourably with typical rulers' (p. 371), composed by Paul 'to instruct the Philippians in cultural terms familiar to them' (p. 372). A somewhat similar view is expressed by Samual Vollenweider, 'Der "Raub" der Gottgleichheit: Ein religionsgeschichtlicher Vorschlag zu Phil 2.6(-11)', *NTS* 45 (1999): pp. 413–33. But, although it is obviously true that Philippi was a Roman colony and that ruler-cults were a ubiquitous feature of the religious environment, there is, in fact, no overt reference in Philippians to ruler-cults (Roman or other), and the immediate textual context clearly indicates that the focus of the passage in Philippians is on Jesus as the 'Lordly example' for believers, especially in their relationships with one another (Hurtado, 'Jesus as Lordly Example', pp. 113–26). Whatever the merits of this proposal (and I find it of limited cogency), Yarbro Collins ignores entirely the remarkable rereading of Isa. 45:22–5 reflected (and presupposed) in the Philippians passage. I am also bound to mention that the classic essay by Samuel Sandmel, 'Parallelomania', *JBL* 81 (1962): pp. 1–13, may still be instructive in assessing such proposals about putative analogies. Cf. e.g. Otfried Hofius, *Der Christushymnus Phil.* 2, 6-11, WUNT 17 (Tübingen: Mohr-Siebeck, 1976).

71 Nagata, 'Philippians 2:5-11', 287. And see also his characterization of what he called the early Christian 'midrashic' engagement with the Isaiah text reflected in Phil. 2:9–11: 'It is quite plausible that the peculiar inconsistency between the use of the first person pronoun ἐμοι and the regular νουν τῷ θεῷ (i.e., third person), as the object of homage in one and the same direct speech in Isa 45:23, provides the occasion for a midrashist to distinguish the name YHWH=*kyrios* which is the name of the speaker . . . referred to in v. 23 by ἐμοι and the figure designated by θεός in v. 23. It is this name, YHWH=*kyrios*, that provides the connection between *kyrios*-acclamation and Isa 45:23, whereas τῷ θεῷ

in Isa 45:23 is expanded to εἰς δόξαν θεοῦ πατρός in Phil 2:11.' See also pp. 298–301. I do not find 'midrashic' a particularly appropriate term for the process, however.

72 See esp. Nagata, 'Philippians 2:5-11', pp. 279–80.

73 Nagata, 'Philippians 2:5-11', pp. 298–301.

74 If, as seems entirely likely, Jesus' followers referred to him as 'master' during his ministry, there was certainly a radical and extremely rapid escalation in their sense of his status as 'lord/master' in the 'post-Easter' period. See e.g. Larry W. Hurtado, 'Homage to the Historical Jesus and Early Christian Devotion', *Journal for the Study of the Historical Jesus* 1 (2003): pp. 131–46, republished in Hurtado, *How on Earth*, pp. 134–51.

75 See e.g. Martin Hengel, 'Abba, Maranatha, Hosanna und die Anfänge der Christologie', in *Studien zur Christologie, Kleine Schriften IV* (Tübingen: Mohr Siebeck, 2006), pp. 496–534.

76 As Hengel put it with reference to Psalm 110:1 ('Sit at my Right Hand!', p. 210), and so I think also was the case with Isa. 45:22–5, the biblical text 'must have immediately jumped out and helped [Jewish] Christians not only to interpret and thus to proclaim the phenomenon of the appearances of Jesus, the crucified Messiah, but also *just to understand* it'.

77 See also the analysis in Capes, *Old Testament Yahweh Texts*, pp. 123–30; Fee, *Pauline Christology*, pp. 259–67; and, more briefly, Mark A. Seifrid, 'Romans', in *Commentary on the New Testament Use of the Old Testament* (ed. G.K. Beale and D.A. Carson; Grand Rapids, MI: Baker Academic, 2007), pp. 685–6 (pp. 607–94).

78 Jewett, *Romans*, p. 851. Other instances of the formula include Num. 14:28; Zeph. 2:9; Jer. 22:24; 26:18; and eleven cases in Ezekiel.

79 As observed by Jewett, *Romans*, pp. 851–2.

80 In these verses Jesus is referred to as 'Lord' at least seven times: vv. 4b, 6 (3x), 8 (3x), not counting λέγει κύριος in v. 11. Fee, *Pauline Christology*, p. 260, must have included the *kyrios* in v. 4a in his total of eight, but I am not so sure of this.

81 The variant-reading, θεός, in v. 4 supported by a number of witnesses is probably an assimilation of this statement to v. 3, and κύριος has better witnesses.

82 The variant ἀνέστη, instead of ἔζησεν is probably an assimilation to the more frequent terms used for Jesus' resurrection, esp. perhaps 1 Thess. 4:14, as judged by B.M. Metzger, *A Textual Commentary on the*

Greek New Testament (Stuttgart: United Bible Societies, 2nd edn, 1994), p. 468.

83 Noting the duality throughout Rom. 14:1–10, J. Ross Wagner wrote, 'In this way, Paul boldly places the risen Jesus within the bounds of the identity of the God of Israel' ('Isaiah in Romans and Galatians', in *Isaiah in the New Testament* [ed. Steve Moyise and Maarten J.J. Menken; London: T&T Clark, 2005], p. 127 [pp. 117–32]). Wagner here draws upon Bauckham's emphasis on Jesus being included within 'the divine identity'.

84 So esp. Capes, *Old Testament Yahweh Texts*, pp. 123–30, and the weighing of arguments by Fee, *Pauline Christology*, pp. 263–7, who also comes down in favour of a reference to Jesus.

85 So also e.g. Bauckham, *Jesus and the God of Israel*, p. 209. He contends also that 'Jesus is not added alongside the one God of Israel but included in the unique identity of that God'. I cannot here engage the latter category, and content myself with observing that Paul read a duality in the Isaiah text.

86 In Rom 14:10, the likely reading is 'βήματι τοῦ θεοῦ', but in 2 Cor. 5:10 Paul also refers to a universal accountability 'ἔμπροσθεν τοῦ βήματος τοῦ χριστοῦ', further reflecting this duality.

87 See e.g. John J. Collins, 'Powers in Heaven: God, Gods, and Angels in the Dead Sea Scrolls', in *Religion in the Dead Sea Scrolls* (ed. John J. Collins and Robert A. Kugler; Grand Rapids, MI: Eerdmans, 2000), pp. 9–28. He observes (p. 27) that, although the Qumran texts posit many heavenly beings as part of God's retinue, 'we do not find any figure in the Scrolls who exercises judgment on a throne of glory like the Son of Man in the *Similitudes of Enoch*, still less any one exalted above the angels as Christ is in the New Testament'. See also L.W. Hurtado, 'Monotheism, Principal Angels, and the Background of Christology', in *The Oxford Handbook of the Dead Sea Scrolls* (ed. Timothy H. Lim and John J. Collins; OUP, 2010), pp. 546–64.

88 Cf. Maurice Casey, 'Christology and the Legitimating Use of the Old Testament in the New Testament', in *The Old Testament in the New Testament: Essays in Honour of J.L. North* (ed. Steve Moyise; Sheffield: Sheffield Academic Press, 2000), pp. 42–64, who seems to me to be virtually 'tone-deaf' to the astonishing view of Jesus reflected in the reading of Isa. 45:22–5 in the Pauline texts. That there is no objection to it reflected in Paul's letters tells us nothing about what non-Christian Jews thought of it. As should be obvious, Paul's letters address

issues of belief and practice *within* the churches to which he wrote, and only give a few glimpses of what outsiders thought of Christian beliefs. But such glimpses as we have, e.g. 1 Cor. 1:18–25, indicate that the gospel and its claims were treated with disdain. And Rom. 9:1–5; 10:1–13; 2 Cor. 3:12 – 4:6 rather clearly indicate that the 'blindness' and 'hardness' of Paul's fellow Jews was centred on their refusal/inability to recognize the significance of Jesus.

[89] See my discussion in Hurtado, 'Monotheism, Principal Angels, and Christology', pp. 554–6. Note also the unnamed figure in *4Q491*[c] (*4QSelf-Glorification Hymn*[b]) who claims 'a mighty throne in the congregation of the gods' (1:5) and in related terms a uniquely high status.

[90] See e.g. James R. Davila, 'The Dead Sea Scrolls and Merkavah Mysticism', in *The Dead Sea Scrolls in Their Historical Context* (ed. Timothy H. Lim; Edinburgh: T&T Clark, 2000), pp. 249–64; and James R. Davila, 'Exploring the Mystical Background of the Dead Sea Scrolls', in *The Oxford Handbook of the Dead Sea Scrolls* (ed. Timothy H. Lim and John J. Collins; OUP, 2010), pp. 433–54.

[91] Timothy H. Lim, *Pesharim* (London: Sheffield Academic Press, 2002); Bilhah Nitzan, 'The Continuity of Biblical Interpretation in the Qumran Scrolls and Rabbinic Literature', in *The Oxford Handbook of the Dead Sea Scrolls* (ed. Timothy H. Lim and John J. Collins; OUP, 2010), pp. 337–49, includes a good bibliography on Qumran biblical interpretation.

[92] David E. Aune, 'Charismatic Exegesis in Early Judaism and Early Christianity', in *The Pseudepigrapha and Early Biblical Interpretation* (ed. James H. Charlesworth and Craig A. Evans; Sheffield Academic Press, 1993), pp. 126–50; and the earlier study by Otto Betz, *Offenbarung und Schriftforschung in der Qumransekte*, WUNT 6 (Tübingen: Mohr, 1960).

[93] Larry W. Hurtado, 'Religious Experience and Religious Innovation in the New Testament', *JR* 80 (2000): pp. 183–205, republished in Hurtado, *How on Earth*, pp. 179–204; Larry W. Hurtado, *Lord Jesus Christ: Devotion to Jesus in Earliest Christianity* (Grand Rapids, MI: Eerdmans, 2003), pp. 64–74; Larry W. Hurtado, 'Revelatory Experiences and Religious Innovation in Earliest Christianity', forthcoming in *ExpTim*.

[94] Paul's brief description of actions characteristic of group-worship in 1 Cor. 14:26–33 reflects the type of lively and spiritually fervent situation that I describe.

2. 'He Interpreted to Them the Things About Himself in All the Scriptures'

[1] Maurice Casey argues that 'no version of this view should be regarded as tenable', and sees it as hermeneutically significant that Jesus' usage was not fulfilling any particular expectation. Maurice Casey, *The Solution to the 'Son of Man' Problem* (London: Continuum, 2009), p. 82.

[2] Israel Knohl argues (against consensus) that such a messianic conception did exist prior to Jesus, and sees it as hermeneutically significant that Jesus adopts his particular messianic mission in the context of this interpretative influence: 'It emerges that Jesus of Nazareth identified with the figure of the tortured and slain messiah that he had learned of from traditions in the vein of *The Gabriel Revelation*.' Israel Knohl, *Messiahs and Resurrection in 'The Gabriel Revelation'* (Kogod Library of Judaic Studies 6; London: Continuum, 2009), p. 87.

[3] Gerd Lüdemann finds it decisive that the evangelists were at odds with prior readings of the Scriptures: 'The long and short of it is that New Testament authors have systematically mistaken or distorted the meaning of Old Testament texts in the service of polemical and doctrinal agendas. Matthew's five citations of prophecy in his nativity account are among the best-known examples of the practice, and perhaps the most comically inapposite.' www.bibleinterp.com/oppeds/oldt314159.shtml (accessed 31 May 2013).

[4] Conservative and sceptical scholars alike frequently denounce an overly simplistic conception of 'fulfilment'.

[5] G.K. Beale argues that the 'assumption of Jewish influence on NT exegesis of the Old may be questioned'. G.K. Beale, *Handbook on the New Testament Use of the Old Testament: Exegesis and Interpretation* (Grand Rapids, MI: Baker Academic, 2012), p. 3. In a review of this work, Pheme Perkins finds Beale's approach in this regard questionable: www.bookreviews.org/pdf/8636_9470.pdf (accessed 7 May 2014).

[6] Friedrich Ungerer and Hans-Jorg Schmid, *An Introduction to Cognitive Linguistics* (London: Longman, 1996), p. x.

[7] David Lee, *Cognitive Linguistics: An Introduction* (Melbourne: OUP, 2001), p. 2.

[8] Wallace Chafe, *Discourse, Consciousness and Time: The Flow and Displacement of Conscious Experience in Speaking and Writing* (Chicago: University of Chicago Press, 1994), p. ix.

[9] Gary B. Palmer, *Toward a Theory of Cultural Linguistics* (Austin: University of Texas Press, 1996), p. 2.

[10] Ian G. Malcolm and Farzad Sharifian, 'Aspects of Aboriginal English Oral Discourse: An Application of Cultural Schema Theory', *Discourse Studies*, 4/2 (2002): p. 169–81; p. 170.

[11] Hans-Georg Gadamer reflects on the early Greek recognition that any knowledge is attained by beings who possess preliminary frameworks of understanding. Such a being 'is always already equipped with a knowledge of where it stands with everything, not only in relation to a future manipulation of it for purposes of providing for something but also entirely apart from that, merely to ensure that nothing unknown or unfamiliar is within the horizon of its vision'. Hans-Georg Gadamer, *Plato's Dialectical Ethics: Phenomenological Interpretation Relating to the Philebus* (trans. Robert M. Wallace: New Haven, CT: Yale UP, 1991), p. 22. Gadamer uses the Heideggerian concept of 'Dasein' here as the embodied knower. Interestingly, even the hard sciences are now seeing the need to acknowledge the mediation of interpretative models for human knowledge: 'Until the advent of modern physics it was generally thought that all knowledge of the world could be obtained through direct observation, that things are what they seem, as perceived through our senses. But the spectacular success of modern physics, which is based upon concepts such as Feynman's that clash with everyday experience, has shown that this is not the case. The naive view of reality therefore is not compatible with modern physics. To deal with such paradoxes we shall adopt an approach that we call model-dependent realism. It is based on the idea that our brains interpret the input from our sensory organs by making a model of the world. When such a model is successful at explaining events, we tend to attribute to it, and to the elements and concepts that constitute it, the quality of reality or absolute truth. But there may be different ways in which one could model the same physical situation, with each employing different fundamental elements and concepts.' Stephen Hawking and Leonard Mlodinow, *The Grand Design: New Answers to the Ultimate Questions of Life* (New York: Bantam Books, 2010), p. 7. Hawking and Mlodonow seem oddly unaware of the long pedigree of this perspective, before modern physics.

[12] See further Farzad Sharifian, *Cultural Conceptualizations and Language: Theoretical Framework and Applications* (Amsterdam: John Benjamins, 2011).

[13] Chafe, *Discourse*, p. 33.

[14] Palmer, *Toward a Theory*, p. 47.

[15] Palmer, *Toward a Theory*, p. 113.

[16] Chafe, *Discourse*, p. 27.

[17] Palmer, *Toward a Theory*, p. 116.

[18] Melina Magdalena and Peter Mühlhäusler, 'Lexical Developments in Greenspeaking', in Paul Skandera (ed.) *Phraseology and Culture in English* (Berlin: Mouton de Gruyter, 2007): pp. 275–302; p. 278.

[19] Sharifian, *Cultural Conceptualizations and Language*, p. 37.

[20] Palmer, *Toward a Theory*, p. 6.

[21] Sharifian, *Cultural Conceptualizations and Language*, p. 217.

[22] Palmer, *Toward a Theory*, p. 39.

[23] William Labov, *Principles of Linguistic Change volume 3: Cognitive and Cultural Factors* (Chichester: Wiley-Blackwell, 2010), p. 15.

[24] Farzad Sharifian, Adriano Truscott, Patricia Königsberg, Ian G. Malcolm and Glenys Collard, *'Understanding Stories My Way': Aboriginal-English Speaking Students' (Mis)understanding of School Literacy Materials in Australian English* (Leederville, WA: Institute for Professional Learning, Department of Education, 2012).

[25] Sharifian et al., *'Understanding'*, pp. 30ff.

[26] Hui Leng, *A Study of Intercultural Discourse Between Mainland Chinese Speakers of English and Anglo-Australians* (Dalian: Liaoning Normal UP, 2007).

[27] Francis Conlan, *Searching for the Semantic Boundaries of the Japanese Colour term 'ao'* (Unpublished PhD thesis, Edith Cowan University, 2005).

[28] Farzad Sharifian, 'L1 cultural conceptualisations in L2 learning', in Farzad Sharifian and Gary B. Palmer (eds) *Applied Cultural Linguistics: Implications for Second Language Learning and Intercultural Communication* (Amsterdam: John Benjamins, 2007).

[29] Farzad Sharifian, *Cultural Conceptualizations and Language: Theoretical Framework and Applications* (Amsterdam: John Benjamins, 2011), p. 216.

[30] Ian G. Malcolm and Farzad Sharifian, 'Multiword units in Aboriginal English', in *Phraseology and Culture in English* (ed. Paul Skandera; Berlin: Mouton de Gruyter, 2007): pp. 375–98; p. 380.

[31] Anna Wierzbicka, *What Did Jesus Mean?* (Oxford: OUP, 2001).

[32] Eugene A. Nida, 'The Role of Context in the Understanding of Discourse', in *Discourse Analysis and the New Testament: Approaches and*

Results (ed. Stanley E. Porter and Jeffrey T. Reed; Sheffield Academic Press, 1999): pp. 20–27.

[33] Stanley E. Porter and Jeffrey T. Reed, eds, *Discourse Analysis and the New Testament: Approaches and Results* (Sheffield Academic Press, 1999), p. 140.

[34] Stanley E. Porter and Jason C. Robinson, *Hermeneutics: An Introduction to Interpretive Theory* (Grand Rapids: Eerdmans, 2011), p. 297.

[35] Darrell L. Bock, *A Theology of Luke and Acts: Biblical Theology of the New Testament* (Grand Rapids, MI: Zondervan, 2012), p. 29.

[36] Interestingly, this is strongly evocative of Paul's theology. N.T. Wright comments, 'Paul believes both that the covenant promises were at last fulfilled and that this constituted a massive and dramatic irruption into the processes of world history unlike anything before or since. And at the heart of both parts of this tension stands the cross of the Messiah, at once the long-awaited fulfilment and the slap in the face for all human pride. Unless we hold on to both parts of this truth we are missing something absolutely central to Paul.' N.T. Wright, *Paul in Fresh Perspective* (Minneapolis: Fortress Press, 2005), p. 54.

[37] It would be too simplistic, then, to see here 'a triumphalist "prophecy-fulfilment" arrangement in which the "old" is valuable only insofar as it serves as a signpost pointing to the "new"'. Matthew Myer Boulton, 'Supersession or Subsession? Exodus Typology, the Christian Eucharist and the Jewish Passover Meal', *Scottish Journal of Theology* 66/1 (2013): pp. 18–29; p. 18.

[38] Bock aptly comments, 'Anyone can now see from Luke's account that Jesus' position is proclaimed in the Scriptures as well as being verified by events and his own teaching (Acts 1.1).' Cited in Bock, *Theology*, p. 413; emphasis ours.

[39] In terms of continuity, we would include the prefigurings of typology in the OT itself, and in early Judaism, that are explored in the scholarship of Leonhard Goppelt, Francis Foulkes and, more recently, Darrell Bock. G.K. Beale presents his own estimation of typology as follows: 'OT passages do not receive brand-new or contradictory meanings but undergo an organic expansion or development of meaning, such as the growth of an "acorn to an oak tree, a bud to a flower, or a seed to an apple"' (*Handbook*, p. 27). We would tweak the imagery by pointing out that the seed will not grow 'unless it dies'; and its subsequent growth may be so astonishing as to be almost inexplicable to the initial onlooker, who sees only, perhaps, a mustard seed. Similarly,

NT messianic typology comes from the OT and early Judaism, via the reconfiguring triggering event of the coming of Jesus of Nazareth.

3. Jesus and Scripture: Scripture and the Self-Understanding of Jesus

[1] This chapter developed out of some thoughts I presented for the first time in 'Jesus and the Jewish Traditions of His Time', *Early Christianity* 1 (2010): pp. 344–71, now in *Acts of God in History: Studies Towards Recovering a Theological Historiography* WUNT 317 (ed. Christoph Ochs and Peter Watts; Tübingen: Mohr Siebeck, 2013), pp. 85–120 (pp. 111–18).

[2] See N.T. Wright, *The New Testament and the People of God* (Christian Origins and the Question of God 1; London: SPCK, 1992), pp. 241–3; N.T. Wright, *Jesus and the Victory of God* (Christian Origins and the Question of God 2; London: SPCK, 1996), pp. 137–44 (on 'Worldviews and Mindsets').

[3] I have developed this understanding of Scripture more fully in, 'The Term and Concept of Scripture', in *What is Bible?* (ed. Karin Finsterbusch and Armin Lange; CBET 67; Leuven: Peeters, 2012), pp. 235–81, also in Deines, *Acts of God in History*, p. 263–308; Roland Deines, 'Did Matthew Know He was Writing Scripture? Part 1', *EuroJTh* 22 (2013), pp. 101–9 (the second part will appear in vol. 23 [2014]); Roland Deines, 'Revelatory Experiences as the Beginning of Scripture: Paul's Letters and the Prophets in the Hebrew Bible', to appear in the Festschrift for Zipora Talshir (ed. Cana Werman; Winona Lake: Eisenbrauns, 2014). For the importance of salvation history see Martin Hengel, ' "Salvation History": The Truth of Scripture and Modern Theology', in *Reading Texts, Seeking Wisdom* (ed. D.F. Ford and G. Stanton; London: SCM Press, 2003), pp. 229–44; Roland Deines, 'The Recognition of God's Acts in History in the Gospel of Matthew: An Exercise in Salvation History', *Acts of God in History*, pp. 311–50.

[4] On Jewish names in the second-temple period see the now complete survey in Tal Ilan, *Lexicon of Jewish Names in Late Antiquity: Part I: Palestine 330 BCE – 200 CE* (TSAJ 91; Tübingen: Mohr Siebeck, 2002); *Part II: Palestine 200 – 650* (TSAJ 148; Tübingen: Mohr Siebeck, 2012); *Part III: The Western Diaspora 330 BCE – 650 CE* (TSAJ 126; Tübingen: Mohr Siebeck, 2008); *Part IV: The Eastern Diaspora 330 BCE – 650 CE*

(TSAJ 141; Tübingen: Mohr Siebeck, 2011). For a short summary see Tal Ilan, 'Names', *The Eerdmans Dictionary of Early Judaism* (DEJ) (ed. John J. Collins and Daniel C. Harlow; Grand Rapids, MI: Eerdmans, 2010): pp. 990f.

5 Cf. Matt. 23:29 par. Luke 11:47; the Jewish text *The Lives of the Prophets (Vitae Prophetarum)*, which originated most probably in the time before AD 70, is a collection of twenty-three short biographies of biblical prophets, giving details about their place of origin, their miracles, their death (mostly in violent circumstances), and their burial place. The geographic interest in this small book is clearly evident and some have even assumed that its original purpose was to serve as a kind of guidebook to the places mentioned in the text. For a comprehensive commentary see Anna Maria Schwemer, *Studien zu den frühjüdischen Prophetenlegenden* (2 vols.; TSAJ 49–50; Tübingen: Mohr Siebeck, 1995–6). For the text see D.R.A. Hare, *OTP* 2, pp. 379–99; for a brief introduction see Peter Enns, 'Lives of the Prophets', *DEJ*, pp. 892–4.

6 A similar shortcoming can be observed in some quarters of the current research done with regard to the use of OT texts in NT writings, when the sought after precision in delineating and differentiating allusions and echo-levels is taken to the extreme. For a brief overview see Greg K. Beale, *Handbook on the New Testament Use of the Old Testament* (Grand Rapids, MI: Baker Academic, 2012), pp. 29–35.

7 Steve Moyise, 'Jesus and the Scriptures of Israel', in *Handbook of the Study of the Historical Jesus* (ed. Tom Holmén and Stanley E. Porter; Leiden: Brill, 2011), pp. 1137–67 (p. 1137), see also Steve Moyise, *Jesus and Scripture* (London: SPCK, 2010), pp. 122f. ('Appendix I: Index of Jesus' quotations in the Gospels'); Craig L. Blomberg, 'Matthew' in *Commentary on the New Testament Use of the Old Testament* (ed. Greg K. Beale and Don Carson; Grand Rapids, MI: Baker Academic, 2007), pp. 1–109.

8 The Jewish(–Christian) context of Matthew's Gospel is widely accepted nowadays; see the recent discussion in D.A. Hagner, *The New Testament: A Historical and Theological Introduction* (Grand Rapids, MI: Baker, 2012), pp. 216f. (see also pp. 200f., 206–11).

9 For a discussion see Hagner, *New Testament*, pp. 154–62.

10 The number of such unintended allusions and echoes could be easily multiplied. For a maximalistic approach in this respect see Dale C. Allison, *The Intertextual Jesus: Scripture in Q* (Harrisburg, PA:Trinity Press, 2000).

[11] FQ = fulfilment quotation.

[12] Cf. Blomberg, 'Matthew', p. 37: This is an unmarked quotation, and perhaps best understood not as 'a particular scheme of prophecy and fulfillment' but in the way that 'Jesus simply lapses into biblical language', which is exactly what one expects somebody with a biblical mindset to do.

[13] The preceding reference to Tyre and Sidon (Matt. 11:22) can also be seen as a reference to the prophetic traditions about their destruction, see e.g. Isa. 23; Ezek. 26 – 28; Joel 3:4–8; Amos 1:9f.; Zech. 9:2b–4.

[14] Cf. Craig A. Evans, '"Have You Not Read . . .?" Jesus' Subversive Interpretation of Scripture,' in *Jesus Research: An International Perspective* (ed. J.H. Charlesworth and P. Pokorný; Grand Rapids, MI: Eerdmans, 2009), pp. 182–98.

[15] The introduction to the actual quotation is reminiscent of the formulaic fulfilment quotations and it is open for debate whether the evangelist added this to what Jesus said. But it can also be argued that such use of Scripture by Jesus is the origin of the fulfilment quotations.

[16] For a fourfold, but nevertheless quite similar delineation see John A.T. Robinson's remarkable piece, 'Did Jesus Have a Distinctive Use of Scripture?' in his *Twelve More New Testament Studies* (London: SCM, 1984), pp. 35–43. He distinguishes between: the 'allusive use' (pp. 37f.); the 'confirmatory use', demonstrating 'how the events of the life of Jesus fulfil the Old Testament' (p. 38), which are more often comments of the evangelists and, when they appear as sayings of Jesus, are 'read back on to his lips rather than the other way around' (p. 39); the 'argumentative use' (p. 39); and finally the 'challenging use of Scripture', characterized by such formulas as 'Have you not read?' (p. 40). Robinson sees this fourth use as the distinctive feature of Jesus' teaching (p. 43).

[17] See my 'Not the Law but the Messiah: Law and Righteousness in the Gospel of Matthew – An Ongoing Debate', in *Built Upon a Rock: Studies in the Gospel of Matthew* (ed. Daniel M. Gurtner and John Nolland; Grand Rapids, MI: Eerdmans, 2008), pp. 53–84 (p. 64f.).

[18] For a fuller discussion see my *Die Gerechtigkeit der Tora im Reich des Messias: Mt 5,13–20 als Schlüsseltext der matthäischen Theologie*, WUNT 177 (Tübingen: Mohr Siebeck, 2004), pp. 389–92.

[19] Scribe(s): Matt. 8:19; 22:36; Pharisees: Matt. 9:11; 22:15f.; scribes and Pharisees: Matt. 12:38; Sadducees: Matt. 22:24.

[20] See Rainer Riesner, 'Jesus as Preacher and Teacher', in *Jesus and the Oral Gospel Tradition* (ed. Henry Wansbrough; JSNTSup 64; Sheffield:

Sheffield Academic Press, 1991 = London: T&T Clark, 2004), pp. 185–210 (pp. 186–8); Rainer Riesner, 'From the Messianic Teacher to the Gospels of Jesus Christ', in *Handbook for the Study of the Historical Jesus* (ed. Tom Holmén and S. E. Porter; 4 vols; Leiden: Brill, 2011), pp. 405–46 (pp. 414f.).

21 But cf. Craig A. Evans, 'Jewish Scripture and the Literacy of Jesus', in *From Biblical Criticism to Biblical Faith* (ed. C.A. Evans and W.H. Brackney; Macon, GA: Mercer UP, 2007), pp. 41–54: 'The comments in John 7:15 and Acts 4:13 should not be taken to imply that Jesus and his disciples were illiterate. In fact, the opposite is probably the intended sense . . . That is, despite not having had formal training, Jesus and his disciples evince remarkable skill in the knowledge of Scripture and ability to interpret it and defend their views' (p. 43).

22 Matt. 4:4 quoting Deut. 8:3. The prophet Ezekiel, who in a vision had to eat a scroll written on by God, is a good example of this way of 'eating' God's word so that it really becomes one's own (Ezek. 2:7 – 3:3, see also Rev. 10:9f.).

23 See Hans-Georg Gadamer, *Truth and Method* (trans. Joel Weinsheimer and Donald G. Marshall; London: Sheed & Ward, 2nd edn, 1989), who makes a strong philosophical argument for the necessity of prejudices to form understanding. On the importance of 'memory refraction' for the integration of new experiences see also Anthony Le Donne, *Historical Jesus: What Can We Know and How Can We Know It?* (Grand Rapids, MI: Eerdmans, 2011); on John the Baptist as one of the prophets see pp. 81–92. This book is a more popular spin-off of Le Donne's major publication, *The Historiographical Jesus: Memory, Typology and the Son of David* (Waco, TX: Baylor UP, 2009).

24 For a discussion see Robert H. Gundry, *The Use of the Old Testament in St. Matthew's Gospel*, NovTSup 18 (Leiden: Brill, 1975), pp. 11f.; W.D. Davies and Dale C. Allison, *The Gospel of Matthew*, vol. II: Commentary on Matthew VIII–XVIII, ICC (Edinburgh: T&T Clark, 1991), p. 249f.

25 See Rainer Kessler, *Maleachi* (Herders Theologischer Kommentar zum Alten Testament; Freiburg: Herder, 2011), p. 228f.; for the use in Mark 1:2f., see p. 245.

26 In the LXX, Isa. 26:7 provides the only evidence for a combination of κατασκευάζω with ὁδός. In the MT the way is prepared for the *zaddiq* (sing.), and it is possible to read v. 7 in light of v. 8, namely that YHWH is the *zaddiq* for whom the way must be prepared. The LXX translates

the twice-used singular of *zaddiq* in v. 7 with εὐσεβῶν (gen. plural of εὐσεβής), which means that the translators read v. 7 as a continuation of v. 6.

[27] Discussed by A. Yarbro Collins, *Mark: A Commentary* (Hermeneia; Philadelphia: Fortress, 2007), pp. 135f.; R.T. France, *The Gospel of Mark*, NIGTC (Grand Rapids, MI: Eerdmans, 2002), pp. 63f. A fuller treatment can be found in Rick E. Watts, 'Mark', in *Commentary on the New Testament Use of the Old Testament* (ed. Greg Beale and Don Carson; Grand Rapids, MI: Baker Academic, 2007), pp. 111–249 (pp. 113–20), Rick E. Watts, *Isaiah's New Exodus and Mark*, WUNT 2.88 (Tübingen: Mohr Siebeck, 1997), pp. 60–90.

[28] See e.g. Davies and Allison, *Matthew*, p. 246.

[29] Moyise, 'Jesus and the Scriptures of Israel', p. 1138. See e.g. E.B. Powery, *Jesus Reads Scripture: The Function of Jesus' Use of Scripture in the Synoptic Gospels*, BIS 63 (Leiden/Boston: Brill, 1999).

[30] See my comments in 'Jesus and the Jewish Traditions of His Time', p. 113f. A further notable exception (besides the ones already mentioned in this chapter) is Ben F. Meyer, 'Appointed Deed, Appointed Doer: Jesus and the Scriptures', in *Authenticating the Activities of Jesus* (ed. Bruce Chilton and Craig A. Evans; NTTS 28.2; Leiden: Brill, 1999 = paperback edn, 2002), pp. 155–76.

[31] R.T. France, *Jesus and the Old Testament: His Application of Old Testament Passages to Himself and His Mission* (London: Tyndale, 1971), p. 13.

[32] See above n. 27.

[33] See e.g. Beale and Carson, *Commentary*, pp. 14–18 on Matt. 4:1–11 or pp. 21–9 on Matt 5:21–48.

[34] I found nothing in the general introduction by Beale/Carson, and nothing in the introduction to the chapter on Matthew by Craig L. Blomberg (Beale and Carson, *Commentary*, p. 1f.), who instead discusses from where the tax-collector Levi-Matthew might have gleaned his scriptural knowledge. The introduction to Mark's Gospel (Beale and Carson, *Commentary*, pp. 111–13) reflects the difficulties scholars face when they have to deal with this question: Rick Watts alternates constantly between Jesus as the one who uses Scripture in a certain way and phrases like 'Mark or his Jesus', 'Mark's Jesus', etc. No attempt is made to bring the evangelist's use of Scripture into line with Jesus' own argument, although Watts rightly comments that although 'the conviction of the Scripture's abiding authority' is upheld, this was done 'always through the even greater hermeneutical authority

of Jesus'. This 'greater hermeneutical authority of Jesus' is, however, nowhere explained, and the following sentence again leaves room for some uncertainty as to whether Watts is thinking of the historical Jesus or 'Mark's Jesus' when he says that 'Mark's Jesus . . . magisterially opens up new understandings by means of his own unique combination of previously unrelated texts' (p. 112). This same ambiguity can be found throughout his commentary, see e.g. pp. 154–5 on Isa. 6:9–10 in Mark 4:11. By contrast, David W. Pao and Eckhard Schnabel in their introduction to Luke highlight Jesus' 'prophetic use of Scripture' as the origin for Luke's (Beale and Carson, *Commentary*, pp. 251–3).

[35] Greg Beale, *Handbook on the New Testament Use of the Old Testament* (Grand Rapids, MI: Baker Academic, 2012).

[36] The possibility is discussed by Gustav Wohlenberg, *Das Evangelium des Markus*, Kommentar zum Neuen Testament 2 (Leipzig: A. Deichert, 1910), pp. 16f., 36f. (with references to other exegetes supporting this understanding. See also the discussion of France, *Gospel of Mark*, p. 53, who acknowledges that the genitive may 'be read either as subjective . . . or objective' (similarly also Watts, 'Mark', p. 120), although he allows at the most a certain intended ambiguity on the part of Mark, with a clear preponderance for the genitive objective. He rightly points to Mark 1:14f., which 'will make it clear that the εὐαγγέλιον is in fact *preached by* Jesus as well' (emphasis in the original). For a parallel introduction to a biblical book (or part thereof) see Neh. 1:1 in the LXX = 2 Esd. 11:1 λόγοι Νεεμια υἱοῦ Αχαλια. Also Hos. 1:2a can be adduced to support the reading of 'Jesus Christ' as the actual originator of what follows.

[37] The closest parallel for this kind of interpretation would be Jesus' self-application of Ps. 110:1 (see below). For Jesus' self-understanding of being sent by the Father, the parallels from John's Gospel especially are abundant.

[38] See Evans, 'Jewish Scripture and the Literacy of Jesus', p. 53: 'The sudden emergence of a prolific literary tradition from an illiterate founder is not impossible of course, but it is less difficult to explain if Jesus were in fact literate.'

[39] John D. Crossan, *The Historical Jesus: The Life of a Mediterranean Jewish Peasant* (San Francisco: Harper, 1991), pp. 421f. For a helpful critique of this misleading term see Sharon L. Mattila, 'Jesus and the "Middle Peasants"? Problematizing a Social-Scientific Concept', *CBQ* 72 (2010): pp. 291–313.

[40] C.H. Dodd, *According to the Scriptures* (London: Nisbet, 1952), p. 110. See also Robinson, 'Did Jesus Have a Distinctive Use of Scripture?', pp. 35–43.

[41] See below n. 48.

[42] Beale, *Handbook of the New Testament Use of the Old Testament*, p. 96.

[43] Cf. Paul Foster, 'Prophets and Prophetism in Matthew', in *Prophets and Prophecy in Jewish and Early Christian Literature*, WUNT 2.286 (ed. Joseph Verheyden, Korinna Zamfir and Tobias Nicklas; Tübingen: Mohr Siebeck, 2010), pp. 117–38: Matthew 'presents a radical re-interpretation of those twin pillars [= the law and the prophets] of tradition, which from his perspective are both fulfilled and subsumed under the authority of Jesus' (p. 119), and the way this is done portrays Jesus 'as the authoritative teacher and interpreter of these traditions' (p. 120).

[44] The parallel Luke 13:34 contains the same understanding: 'Jerusalem, Jerusalem, the city that kills the prophets and stones those who are sent to it! How often have I desired to gather your children together as a hen gathers her brood under her wings, and you were not willing!'

[45] Cf. further Matt. 24:35: 'Heaven and earth will pass away, but my words will not pass away.' See those sayings where Jesus connects eschatological fate to one's relation to 'his name' (Matt. 7:22f.; 10:22,41f.; 18:5; 19:29; see also 12:21; 23:39; 24:5; 28:19) and what one might or might not have done 'because of me' (5:10f.; 10:39; 16:25; 19:29).

[46] *Against Apion* 2.175–178, cf. Ant. 4.209–411.

[47] Crossan's (*Historical Jesus*, pp. 370f.) and others' position, according to which Jesus was illiterate, is the result of a fixation on a particular social model in which a member of the '*peasant* class' to which Jesus belongs (see above n. 39) has to be illiterate, see also Crossan, *Jesus: A Revolutionary Biography* (San Francisco: Harper, 1994), pp. 25f.

[48] Jesus' knowledge and learning of Scripture is regularly discussed in connection with his upbringing and education, see John P. Meier, *A Marginal Jew: Rethinking the Historical Jesus*, vol. I: *The Roots of the Problem and the Person* (ABRL; New York: Doubleday, 1991), pp. 268–78 (although narrowed down in focus to the question 'Was Jesus Illiterate?'); R. Riesner, *Jesus als Lehrer*, WUNT II/7 (Tübingen: Mohr Siebeck, 3rd edn, 1993), esp. pp. 224–45; Riesner, 'Messianic Teacher', pp. 409–13; Gerd Theißen and Anette Merz, *The Historical Jesus: A Comprehensive Guide* (Philadelphia: Fortress Press, 1998), pp. 319–21; Alan R. Millard, *Reading and Writing in the Time of Jesus* (New York: New York UP, 2000), pp. 146; 155f.; 188; Craig A. Evans,

'Context, Family and Formation', *The Cambridge Companion to Jesus* (ed. M. Bockmuehl; Cambridge: CUP, 2001), pp. 11–24 (pp. 15–21); Steven M. Bryan, *Jesus and Israel's Traditions of Judgement and Restoration*, SNTSMS 117 (Cambridge: CUP, 2002), pp. 46–87 ('Jesus and the Scriptures of Israel'); Paul Foster, 'Educating Jesus: The Search for a Plausible Context', *JSHJ* 4 (2006): pp. 7–33; James D.G. Dunn, 'The Thought World of Jesus', *Early Christianity* 1 (2010): pp. 321–43 (esp. pp. 330–38), see also James D.G. Dunn, *Jesus Remembered, Christianity in the Making* 1 (Grand Rapids, MI: Eerdmans, 2003), pp. 312–15; a full monograph on this topic is now available with Chris Keith, *Jesus' Literacy: Scribal Culture and the Teacher from Galilee*, LNTS 413/LHJS 8 (London: T&T Clark, 2011), who allows Jesus to have, at best, a 'craftman's literacy' (p. 110), mainly based on Sir. 38:24–34, according to which 'widespread literacy' among those dealing with manual labour could not be presupposed (pp. 84f., 111, 113, 131f.). What Keith ignores in his rich study is that the hellenization of Judaism meant an increased focus on education, and that Sirach stands at the beginning of a development and is about two hundred years earlier than Jesus. He also ignores the evidence of Paul as a near contemporary of Jesus, who was a manual labourer and nevertheless received a formal education. And although he concedes 'that history is littered with exceptions to generalities' (p. 168) he is not willing to consider Jesus and his family as a possible exception. The question of Jesus' familiarity with Scripture is not really addressed in the book, and the long list of 'if ever' Jesus did or said-questions on pp. 177f. seems to indicate that he assumes Jesus actually never did anything like this.

49 Deines, 'Jesus and the Jewish Traditions of His Time', p. 118.

50 The following is a mere sketch which I will present in a fuller referenced form in my book on James, the brother of Jesus (*Jakobus – Jesus älterer Bruder?*), which will appear in 2015 in the series Biblische Gestalten (Leipzig: Evangelische Verlagsanstalt).

51 Cf. further Deines, 'Jesus and the Jewish Traditions of His Time', p. 115 n. 76. Note also how self-evidently Luke 1:63 presupposes writing utensils in the house of Elisabeth and Zacharias; on this see Alan Millard, 'Zechariah Wrote (Luke 1:63)', in *The New Testament in Its First Century Setting* (FS Bruce W. Winter; ed. P. J. Williams et al.; Grand Rapids, MI: Eerdmans, 2004), pp. 48–55. For the wider family clan of Jesus, including the family of John the Baptist, as the nucleus of the earliest church see the challenging contribution of John A.T.

Robinson, 'How Small was the Seed of the Church?', in his *Twelve More New Testament Studies* (London: SCM, 1984), pp. 95–111.

52 Crucial is Richard Bauckham, *Jude and the Relatives of Jesus in the Early Church* (London: T&T Clark, 1990), pp. 171–8 (on authorship of Jude), pp. 225–31 (on Jude and Enoch); see also Richard Bauckham, *Jude, 2 Peter*, WBC 50 (Waco, TX: Word, 1983), pp. 7f., 14–16, Richard Bauckham, *James: Wisdom of James, Disciple of Jesus the Sage, New Testament Readings* (London: Routledge, 1999), p. 57; Roland Deines, 'God or Mammon: The Danger of Wealth in the Jesus Tradition and in the Epistle of James', *Anthropologie und Ethik im Frühjudentum und im Neuen Testament: Wechselseitige Wahrnehmungen* (ed. Matthias Konradt and Esther Schläpfer; WUNT 322; Tübingen: Mohr Siebeck, 2014), pp. 327–85 (p. 363).

53 A position strongly defended recently by David A. deSilva, *The Jewish Teachers of Jesus, James, and Jude: What Earliest Christianity Learned from the Apocrypha and Pseudepigrapha* (Oxford: OUP, 2012), pp. 45–54.

54 Otto Betz, '"Kann denn aus Nazareth etwas Gutes kommen?" Zur Verwendung von Jesaja Kap. 11 in Johannes Kap. 1', *Jesus: Der Messias Israels*, WUNT 42 (Tübingen: Mohr Siebeck, 1987), pp. 387–97. On Isa. 11:1 and Matt. 2:23 see also Deines, Gerechtigkeit der Tora, pp. 473–8.

55 Cf. Justin Taylor, *Where Did Christianity Come From?* (Collegeville, MN: Liturgical Press, 2001), pp. 125–8; Bargil Pixner, *With Jesus Through Galilee: According to the Fifth Gospel* (Rosh Pina: Chorazin, 1992), pp. 13–18; Riesner, 'Messianic Teacher', pp. 413f.; the lengthy discussion of the Nazoreans in Epiphanius (*Panarion* 29) is highly confused but contains some hints to their pre-'Christian' tradition; on the Nazoreans see Ray A. Pritz, *Nazarene Jewish Christianity: From the End of the New Testament Period until Its Disappearance in the Fourth Century* (Jerusalem: Magness, 1992), on their specific interpretation of Isaiah see Pritz, *Nazarene Jewish Christianity*, pp. 57–70; Wolfram Kinzig, *'The Nazoraeans', Jewish Believers in Jesus: The Early Centuries* (ed. O. Skarsaune and R. Hvalvik; Peabody, MA: Hendrickson, 2007), pp. 463–87 (on their interpretation of Isaiah, pp. 474–8, and, in the same volume, Oskar Skarskaune, 'Fragments of Jewish Christian Literature Quoted in Some Greek and Latin Fathers', pp. 325–78 [pp. 373–8]).

56 Josephus, Antiquities 18.116–119, see John P. Meier, *A Marginal Jew: Rethinking the Historical Jesus*, vol. II: *Mentor, Message, and Miracle*, ABRL (New York: Doubleday, 1994), pp. 56–62 (on Josephus); on John the Baptist and Jesus see Meier, *Marginal Jew*, pp. 100–233.

[57] Meier, *Marginal Jew*, p. 176.

[58] To follow up on this see my 'Pre-existence, Incarnation and Messianic Self-understanding of Jesus in the Work of Martin Hengel' in *Acts of God in History*, pp. 407–45 (first published in *Earliest Christian History: Essays from the Tyndale Fellowship in Honor of Martin Hengel* [ed. Michael F. Bird and Jason Maston; WUNT 2.320; Tübingen: Mohr Siebeck 2012], pp. 75–116), and in the same volume 'Can the "Real" Jesus be Identified with the Historical Jesus? Joseph Ratzinger's (Pope Benedict XVI) Challenge to Biblical Scholarship', pp. 351–406.

4. Acts 4:23–31 and a Biblical Theology of Prayer

[1] I think of Augustine's *Confessions*, Calvin's chapter on prayer in the *Institutes* (III.20) and Spurgeon's prayers as examples.

[2] See e.g. Joel B. Green, 'Persevering Together in Prayer: The Significance of Prayer in the Acts of the Apostles', in *Into God's Presence: Prayer in the New Testament* (ed. Richard N. Longenecker; Grand Rapids, MI: Eerdmans, 2001), pp. 183–202; Geir Otto Holmås, *Prayer and Vindication in Luke-Acts: The Theme of Prayer Within the Context of the Legitimizng and Edifying of the Lukan Narrative* LNTS 433 (London: T&T Clark, 2011); Robert J. Karris, *Prayer and the New Testament: Jesus and His Communities at Worship* (New York: Crossroad, 2000), pp. 40–81; Peter T. O'Brien, 'Prayer in Luke-Acts', *TynBul* 24 (1973): pp. 111–27; Allison A. Trites, 'The Prayer Motif in Luke-Acts', in *Perspectives on Luke-Acts* (ed. Charles H. Talbert; Danville: Association of Baptist Professors of Religion, 1978), pp. 168–86.

[3] Rudolf Pesch, *Die Apostelgeschichte* EKKNT 5 (Zürich: Neukirchener, 1986), 1:178.

[4] Thus clueing readers that words are about to become important in the story.

[5] This theme is not separable from Luke's major emphasis on the fulfilment of Scripture (see esp. Luke 24:25–27, 44–49).

[6] Only Luke notes the interchange between Herod and Pilate, inferred in Acts 4:27.

[7] The question marks here and below highlight three allusions to Ps 2 in the Acts 4 prayer beyond the direct quotation. The first allusion is the reference to Jesus as God's ('holy)' 'servant' in the prayer of the church (Acts 4:27, 30), which builds on earlier uses in Acts 3:13, 26 to the

resurrected and glorified Jesus, the Christ. The term 'servant' is dropped once the gospel leaves Jerusalem and other terms are used when Jesus is proclaimed in synagogues as risen from the dead according to the Scriptures, including 'son' (Acts 9:20; 13:33b; cf. 7:56). On one of these occasions Ps 2:7 is quoted in full (Acts 13:33); I am suggesting that text may be assumed in the prayer of Acts 4:24–30. The second allusion to Ps 2 in the church's prayer is its exposition of God's will working through the opponents of Jesus (and the apostles and church), which subverts their 'plotting', demonstrated, again, by the resurrection and exaltation of Jesus. The third allusion to threats is clear.

8 So also Joseph A. Fitzmyer, *The Acts of the Apostles* AB 5 (New York: Doubleday, 1998), p. 306, and others.

9 Hermann Gunkel and Joachim Begrich, *Introduction to Psalms: The Genres of the Religious Lyric of Israel* (trans. James D. Nogalski; Macon, GA: Mercer, 1998), p. 207. On p. 213 Gunkel says that these two forms 'correspond to one another like the two shells of a mussel'. See pp. 199–221 for his exposition of features of thanksgiving songs of the individual.

10 For a more recent application of the form, see Patrick D. Miller, *They Cried to the Lord: The Form and Theology of Biblical Prayer* (Minneapolis: Fortress Press, 1994), pp. 178–232.

11 Cf. Gen. 14:19; Exod. 20:11; Acts 14:15; 17:24.

12 Most commentators separate the two psalm quotes in their structure of the unit but the Greek syntax seems to join them by using two aorist substantive participles (*ho poiēsas . . . ho . . . eipōn*).

13 Linda M. Maloney, *'All that God Had Done with Them': The Narration of the Works of God in the Early Christian Community as Described in the Acts of the Apostles*, AUS VII/91 (New York: Peter Lang, 1991), p. 51.

14 Maloney, *All that God*, pp. 194–5.

15 Maloney, *All that God*, pp. 46–7.

16 See the recent study of Stanley E. Porter, 'Scripture Justifies Mission: The Use of the Old Testament in Luke-Acts', in *Hearing the Old Testament in the New Testament* (ed. Stanley E. Porter; Grand Rapids, MI: Eerdmans, 2006), pp. 104–26. Porter does not treat Acts 4:23–31, presumably because it does not touch on 'mission'.

17 See Peter Doble, 'The Psalms in Luke-Acts', in *The Psalms in the New Testament* (ed. Steve Moyise and Maarten J.J. Menken; London: T&T Clark, 2004), pp. 83–117, for this general tendency in Luke-Acts, and Table 4.4 and n. 8 above for support.

[18] These include: Pss 2; 18; 20; 21; 45; 72; 101; 110; 132; 144:1–11 and possibly 89:47–52.

[19] Gunkel and Begrich, *Introduction*, p. 99. Complaint or lament (requests for help directed to YHWH, e.g. Pss 20; 45; 72; 132; 144:1–11), thanksgivings (responses to the hearing of prayer by YHWH, e.g. Pss 18; 21:2–7) and hymns (which praise God for the king; e.g. Pss 21; 101); see Gunkel and Begrich, *Introduction*, pp. 103, 110, 111. Victory is invariably attributed to the powerful presence of YHWH and/or to the close relationship of the king to YHWH.

[20] The verb to 'seek refuge' (*ḥsh*) in YHWH is frequent in the Psalter (e.g. Pss 5:11; 7:1; 11:1; etc.; see *BDB*, p. 340). Here I take the line to be said by the king about YHWH rather than by a court poet, etc. about the king; so also, John Goldingay, *Psalms* (Grand Rapids, MI: Baker Academic, 2006–8), p. 1:96.

[21] Goldingay, *Psalms*, p. 96.The common view among commentators that the Sitz im Leben of this psalm is a coronation ceremony fails at this point since the rebellion conceived by the poet is against a sitting monarch.

[22] Heb. *'ăspĕrāh* is probably better translated as 'recount'. Maloney, *All that God*, p. 10, lists Pss 9:1; 22:22,30; 26:7; 66:16; 71:15; 75:1; 88:11 as using the piel of *spr* for a report (of thanksgiving); Ps. 2:7 is not included in her count.

[23] In the editing of the Psalter, Ps. 2 possibly 'headlines' the conflicts with enemies found in other royal psalms (e.g., Pss 18; 110; 144) as well providing the theological underpinning for the king's confidence in seeking the help of YHWH in the midst of trials (e.g. Pss 18:3–6; 20:5c; 21:2,4, etc.).

[24] The significance of the royal psalms within the composition of the Psalter is generally recognized by scholars; see the foundational works by Gerald H. Wilson, *The Editing of the Hebrew Psalter* (SBLDS 76; Chico, CA: Chico, 1985); Gerald H. Wilson, 'The Use of Royal Psalms at the "Seams" of the Hebrew Psalter', *JSOT* 35 (1986): pp. 85–94.

[25] The reversal of fortunes theme in Luke–Acts is well-traced by John O. York, *The Last Shall Be First: The Rhetoric of Reversal in Luke*, JSNTSup 46 (Sheffield: JSOT Press, 1991).

5. Becoming Prophets: Acts 19:34–43 and Peter's Appropriation of Prophecies About Jesus

1 Jan Assmann, *Religion and Cultural Memory* (trans. Rodney Livingstone; Stanford, CA: Stanford UP, 2006 [2000: Religion und kulturelles Gedächtnis]), p. 8.

2 Yael Zerubavel, *Recovered Roots: Collective Memory and the Making of Israeli National Tradition* (Chicago, IL: University of Chicago Press, 1995), p. 7.

3 Zerubavel, *Recovered Roots*, pp. 6–7; italics original.

4 'Cultural memory' is the progression to a time distinguished from the present that identifies the past as past, but preserves the memory for the present, thereby establishing 'tradition'. See, Alan Kirk, 'Social and Cultural Memory', in *Memory, Tradition, and Text*, ed. Alan Kirk and Tom Thatcher (Atlanta, GA: Society of Biblical Literature, 2005), p. 6.

5 Jeffrey K. Olick, Vered Vinitzky-Seroussi and Daniel Levy, 'Introduction', in *The Collective Memory Reader* (Oxford: OUP, 2011), p. 37.

6 Merlin Donald, *Origins of the Modern Mind* (Cambridge, MA: Harvard UP, 1991), p. 313.

7 ESS contains, 'singles entries', which Donald calls, 'exograms, after [Karl] Lashley's term engram, which referred to a single entry in the biological memory system. An exogram is simply an external memory record of an idea. In both engrams and exograms there are retrievable traces of past experience that can be used to determine future interpretations of the world. Similarly, exograms and engrams are both interpretable only by the individual mind, which must provide the referential basis for understanding the memory record. Exograms, however, are inherently very different from engrams. Whereas engrams are built-in devices, genetically limited to the format of the central nervous system, exograms are virtually unlimited in both format and capacity. Engrams are impermanent, at best lasting only as long as the life of a single individual; exograms can be made permanent, outlasting individuals and, at times, entire civilizations.' Donald, *Origins*, pp. 314–15, italics added. See also, Karl S. Lashley, 'In Search of the Engram', Society of Experimental Biology, Symposium 4: pp. 454–82.

8 Donald, *Origins*, p. 314, italics original.

9 Cf. Eviatar Zerubavel, *Time Maps: Collective Memory and the Social Shape of the Past* (Chicago, IL: University of Chicago Press, 2003), pp. 5–6.

[10] Chris Keith, Jesus' *Literacy*, LNTS (London: T&T Clark, 2012), p. 56.

[11] Anthony Le Donne, *The Historiographical Jesus: Memory, Typology, and the Son of David* (Waco, TX: Baylor UP, 2009), p. 66.

[12] Le Donne, *Historiographical*, 51.

[13] Cf. studies on 'forgetting': Paul Ricouer, *Memory, History, Forgetting* (trans. Kathleen Blamey and David Pellauer; Chicago, IL: University of Chicago Press, 2006); Elena Esposito, 'Social Forgetting: A Systems-Theory Approach', in *A Companion to Cultural Memory Studies* (ed. Astrid Erll and Ansgar Nünning; Berlin: Walter de Gruyter, 2012), pp. 181–90; Maureen Junker-Kenny, 'Memory and Forgetting in Paul Ricouer's Theory of the Capable Self', in *A Companion to Cultural Memory Studies* (ed. Astrid Erll and Ansgar Nünning; Berlin: Walter de Gruyter, 2012), pp. 203–11; James Fentress and Chris Wickham, *Social Memory: New Perspectives on the Past* (Oxford: Blackwell, 1992), pp. 39–40.

[14] Le Donne, *Historiographical*, p. 54.

[15] Le Donne, *Historiographical*, p. 55, italics original.

[16] The process of Le Donne's conclusion is visually similar to Ricouer, though his conceptual basis is formed from interaction with Heidegger, Schleiermacher, etc. See Le Donne's summary, *Historiographical*, p. 66.

[17] This is Le Donne's Figure 4.2 'The Mnemonic Cycle', taken from Le Donne, *Historiographical*, 66.

[18] It must therefore be kept in mind that certain modes of memory entail a certain understanding from the audience. 'Only when authors and recipients of a mnemonic community share the knowledge of genre conventions (and suspect, for example, that at the end of a detective novel the murder case will be solved) can one speak of the existence of a genre . . . [C]ertain genres, such as biography, comedy or tragedy, are the source of conventionalized, generic schemata for the coding of versions of the past. We draw on such patterns when we tell the stories of our lives as well as in the writing of historiography . . . Genre schemata are, however, not neutral containers to be filled with specific memories. Instead, they are charged with ideological meaning. Genres such as epic poetry, tragedy and romance carry values, norms and worldviews.' Astrid Erll, *Memory in Culture* (New York, NY: Palgrave Macmillan, 2011), p. 74.

[19] Rafael Rodriguez, *Structuring Early Christian Memory*, LNTS (London: T&T Clark, 2010), p. 44. See also, Maurice Halbwachs, *On Collective Memory* (ed. and trans. Lewis A. Coser; Chicago, IL: University of Chicago Press, 1992), p. 22.

[20] Rodriguez, *Structuring*, pp. 64–79.

[21] Kirk, 'Social and Cultural', p. 18.

[22] Rodriguez, *Structuring*, p. 82; italics original. Actualization here is used in the same way as in Erll's model.

[23] Rodriguez, *Structuring*, p. 83.

[24] N.T. Wright, *The New Testament and the People of God* (Minneapolis, MN: Fortress Press, 1992), p. 224.

[25] Lev. 20:24–6; *Jubilees* 22:16. On the complex situation of Jewish distinctions for holiness, etc. see, Eckhard Schnabel, *Acts*, ZECNT (Grand Rapids, MI: Zondervan, 2012), pp. 488–90; and Michael F. Bird, *Crossing over Land and Sea* (Peabody, MA: Hendrickson, 2010), p. 63, regarding the Qumran community.

[26] Markus Bockmuehl, *Simon Peter in Scripture and Memory: The New Testament Apostle in the Early Church* (Grand Rapids, MI: Baker, 2012), pp. 165–76.

[27] Bockmuehl, *Simon Peter*, p. 73 n. 86: 'Galatians 2 and Acts 10 most obviously come to mind, and some of the second-century fathers still maintain a memory of Peter as an observant Jew. (see, e.g., Irenaeus, Haer. 3.12.15; 3.13.1; cf. Tertullian, Marc. 4.11).'

[28] Bird, *Crossing*, p. 5. See also, N.T. Wright, *New Testament and the People of God*, p. 247.

[29] Michael F. Bird, *Jesus and the Origins of the Gentile Mission* (London: T&T Clark, 2003), p.126.

[30] Dunn recognizes the shift beginning earlier: 'not simply could [Peter] now eat "unclean" meat with a good conscience, but he must not call any other person "unclean".' James D.G. Dunn, *Beginning from Jerusalem, Christianity in the Making*, Vol. 2 (Grand Rapids, MI: Eerdmans, 2010), p. 394; italics original. Cf. Schnabel, *Acts*, p. 492.

[31] On this confusion see Craig S. Keener, *The Historical Jesus of the Gospels* (Grand Rapids, MI: Eerdmans, 2009), p. 391; David W. Pao, *Acts and the Isaianic New Exodus* (Grand Rapids, MI: Baker, 2000), pp. 111–46; Wright, *New Testament and the People of God*, p. 268.

[32] Wright, *New Testament and the People of God*, p. 268: 'In terms of the first level of covenantal purpose, the call of Israel has as its fundamental objective the rescue and restoration of the entire creation.'

[33] Bird's summary of texts in *Jesus*, p. 137 n. 66: Isa. 40 – 66; Amos 9:11–12 (LXX); Zech. 1:16, 2:11; *Tobit* 14:5–6; *Sib. Or* 3:290–94, 616–34, 715–20, 772–4; *1 Enoch* 90:33; *T. Naph*. 8:1–5; *T. Benj*. 9:2; 2 Bar. 68:5.

[34] Bird, *Jesus*, pp. 130–31. Cf. Isa. 2:2–3, 45:18–49, 66:1–24; Jonah; Dan. 9.

[35] Keener, *Historical Jesus*, pp. 36, 246.

[36] This is noted to occur throughout Israel's history accompanying messianic declarations tinged with restoration eschatology. See Dale C. Allison, Jr, *Constructing Jesus* (Grand Rapids, MI: Baker, 2010), pp. 74–6. See also, Bird, *Jesus*, p. 132.

[37] Allison, *Constructing*, pp. 113–15.

[38] Pao, *Acts*, p. 112.

[39] Richard Bauckham, 'The Restoration of Israel in Luke-Acts', in *The Jewish World Around the New Testament* (Grand Rapids, MI: Baker, 2010 [Mohr Siebeck: 2008], pp. 357–61.

[40] Bird, *Jesus and the Origins*, pp. 125–72.

6. Scripture and Identity in Galatians

[1] Paul's identification of believers (both Jew and Gentile) as 'the Israel of God' (Gal. 6:16) should not be interpreted as supersessionist, but strictly eschatological as his preceding insistence on the decisiveness of the new creation makes clear (Gal. 6:15). He thus stands apart from Justin Martyr and subsequent Christian writers, who in one way or another identitfied Christians as a new people that constituted a true Israel, and sometimes also as the true Greeks.

[2] 1 Cor. 10:32. That the 'church of God' has an earthly presence and expression does not at all mean for Paul that its identity is thereby defined.

[3] It is not the case, then, that Christ fits into a storyline of Scripture, but that Scripture finds its coherence and meaning in the crucified and risen Christ. He is the meta-narrative of Scripture.

[4] I refer to the influential work of the social anthropologist, Fredrik Barth. See especially F. Barth, ed., *Ethnic Groups and Boundaries* (Bergen/Boston: Universitetsforlaget/Little, Brown & Co., 1969) pp. 9–38. There have been, of course, criticisms of Barth's view. As becomes apparent in the immediately following discussion, his approach can readily absorb the persisting relevance of birth and homeland. Likewise, the correction of Barth's theory to include elements of cultural content 'within' the boundaries, such as the myth of a common ancestry and shared historical memories, does not vitiate his insight that boundary markers play a decisive role in the determining of ethnic identity. On this topic, see especially *Ethnicity* (ed. J. Hutchinson and A.D. Smith;

Oxford: OUP, 1996) pp. 1–14. For a recent example (among many) of the appropriation of the insights of social anthropology, see Christopher D. Stanley, 'The Ethnic Context of Paul's Letters', in *Christian Origins and Hellenistic Judaism: Social and Literary Contexts for the New Testament* (TENTS 2; ed. S.E. Porter and W.J. Porter; Leiden: Brill, 2013), pp. 177–201. With reference to the Christian self-designations in the NT, see Paul R. Trebilco, *Self-Designations and Group Identity in the New Testament* (Cambridge/New York: Cambridge UP, 2011), pp. 1–15.

5 This understanding is corroborated in various ways in antiquity. One thinks immediately of identification as a 'Greek' (as opposed to a Jew or barbarian), which obviously is based on cultural and behavioral norms (including language), and not on descent. Likewise, Christian apologists attempted variously to identify Christians as 'true Greeks' or 'true Hebrews'. On this phenomenon, see A.P. Johnson, *Ethnicity and Argument in Eusebius' Praeparatio Evangelica* (Oxford Early Christian Studies; OUP, 2006).

6 See e.g. Josephus, *Vita* 427. See D.R. Schwartz, '"Judean" or "Jew"? How Should we Translate Ioudaios in Josephus?' *Jewish Identity in the Greco-Roman World = Jüdische Identität in der Griechisch-Römischen Welt* (AGJU 71; ed. J. Frey; Leiden: Brill, 2007), pp. 3–27.

7 The author of *1 Macc.* likely regards Jason's adherents as having abandoned their identity as Jews: they 'made for themselves foreskins' and thus 'withdrew from the holy covenant, yoked themselves with Gentiles, and sold themselves to practice evil' (*1 Macc.* 1:15). Mattathias and his followers are subsequently reported as 'striking down' such persons, who are now characterized as 'sinners and lawless ones' (*1 Macc.* 2:44). In the similar report concerning Jason's program that appears in *2 Macc.*, the expression 'Judaism' appears for the first time (2 *Macc.* 2:21), standing in contrast with 'Hellenism' (2 *Macc.* 4:13). In all probability, the wearing of the Greek hat signalled the embrace of a Greek identity (2 *Macc.* 4:12). The characterization of certain persons as 'sinners' or 'tax-collectors' in the gospels very likely signals that they are regarded as no longer properly Jews. See Matt. 18:17. Jesus' words about being delivered into 'the hands of sinners' are thus profoundly ironic (Mark 14:41 and parallels).

8 This traversing of boundary markers could be understood as 'a new birth'. See *Philo, Virt.* 102–8, 179; *Jos. Asen.* 8:1–11; 15:1–11; 20:7; 27:10;

Josephus, Ant. 13:257–8 (on the Idumeans, who submitted to circumcision and the form of Jewish life under Hyrcanus, so that since that time they have remained Jews; see, however, also *Ant.* 14:403, where Antigonus II calls Herod an 'Idumean', which Josephus interprets as 'a half-Jew': in the context of a claim to kingship, birth counts for something); b. *Yebam.* 47b ('when [a proselyte] comes up from his baptism, he is like an Israelite in every respect'); Epictetus, *Dissertationes* 2.9.21–2. Admittedly, qualifications could be (and, in fact, for legal reasons, had to be) attached to the new ethnic identity that came into being in conversion. On this topic see Shaye J.D. Cohen, *The Beginnings of Jewishness: Boundaries, Varieties, Uncertainties* (Hellenistic Culture and Society; Berkeley, CA: University of California Press, 1999), pp. 140–74; Gary G. Porton, *The Stranger Within Your Gates: Converts and Conversion in Rabbinic Literature* (Chicago: University of Chicago, 1994), pp. 166–76.

9 Conversely, according to Paul, it was not his works, but the naked grace of God that preserved him and others (Rom. 11:6).

10 As is clear from the context in which Paul has already referred to his descent, the expression (Εβραῖος ἐξ Εβραίων) signifies language and culture. The 'practices' that Paul names include both what was performed upon him (περιτομῇ ὀκταήμερος), and that which he himself pursued (κατὰ νόμον Φαρισαῖος).

11 The term appears significantly for the first time in contrast with 'Hellenism' in 2 *Macc.* 2:21, and likewise in 2 *Macc.* 8:1, 14:38 (2x), 4 *Macc.* 4:26. It is equally significant that *1 Macc.* 2:44,48 identifies those who were Jewish by birth as 'sinners', a term which it also uses for Gentiles (*1 Macc.* 1:10,34,44; 2:62).

12 Paul not only exposes Cephas' hypocrisy in his question. He also brings to expression the form of the life of faith that Cephas had adopted prior to his failure, and which becomes the topic of his rebuke in the following argument.

13 Rom. 2:27.

14 See H. Koester, 'φύσις', *TDNT* 9:262.

15 See Gal. 2:7–9. This judgement is not overturned by the Lukan usage of Acts 10:45; 11:2, which expresses a Gentile or Pauline understanding retrospectively.

16 This interpretation of the usage, which parallels the reference to 'a person in Christ' (2 Cor. 12:2), is the only reasonable way to make sense of Paul's statement: 'a person of the works of the Law is not justified, except through the faith of Jesus Christ.' It is impossible for

Paul to think of works of the law as cooperating with faith in justification. Despite the attempts of interpreters to read the expression ἐὰν μη as introducing an adversative, wider usage shows that that it in all probability signals an exception.

[17] In a radical shift away from Paul, later Christian apologists operated with basically the same 'fluid' rather than fixed understanding of ethnicity, and on this basis identified Christians as true Hebrews and the church as the true Israel — or, alternatively, as the true Greeks. On this topic see Denise K. Buell, *Why This New Race? Ethnic Reasoning in Early Christianity* (Gender, theory, and religion; New York: Columbia University Press, 2005); A.P. Johnson, *Ethnicity and Argument in Eusebius' Praeparatio Evangelica* (Oxford early Christian studies; Oxford University Press, 2006).

[18] Caroline Johnson Hodge, *If Sons, Then Heirs: A Study of Kinship and Ethnicity in the Letters of Paul* (Oxford: OUP, 2007), reads Paul as constructing a new, merely social identity, thus missing the essential thrust of his thought.

[19] Matters changed in the next generation of Christians. One is reminded of *Did.* 8:1, 'And let not your fastings be with the hypocrites, for they fast on the second day and the sabbath. But you shall fast on the fourth day and on the day of preparation.'

[20] Paul's argument in the body of Galatians contains three basic movements (3:1–14; 3:15 – 4:20; 4:21–31), all of which are directed to the question of identity as it is determined by the Scriptures. It is governed throughout by the distinction between the promise given to Abraham and the law given at Sinai. For Paul, the identity of believers, whether Jew or Gentile, is determined by this distinction.

[21] With the expression 'works of the Law', Paul signifies outward and visible observance of the requirements of the Law. See Mark A. Seifrid, *Christ, Our Righteousness: Paul's Theology of Justification* (NSBT 9; Downers Grove, IL: Apollos / InterVarsity Press, 2000), pp. 99–105.

[22] On this expression see n. 39 below.

[23] Paul draws the citation from Gen. 12:3 and 22:18, the beginning of God's dealings with Abraham, and the final word of blessing after the call to sacrifice Isaac. We need not make a choice between the two texts. The promise is likewise repeated to Isaac (Gen. 26:4), and Jacob (Gen. 28:14).

[24] As is well known, the situation is comparable to the conversion of King Izates, as it is reported by Josephus, *Ant.* 20, 34–48.

[25] Gal. 1:6–9; 3:1–5; 4:8–20; 5:7–12.

[26] Gal. 2:3,14; 6:12.

[27] See the great confession of Neh. 9:6–37, esp. v. 29 (which recalls Lev. 18:5). So, for example, James M. Scott, '"For as Many as Are of Works of the Law Are Under a Curse" (Gal 3:10)', *Paul and the Scriptures of Israel* (JSNTSup 83; ed. C.A. Evans and J.A. Sanders; Sheffield: JSOT Press, 1993), pp. 183–221.

[28] Since the return from exile, Jews had seen not only the restoration of national sovereignty, but also the extension of the land to near Solomonic dimensions during the period of Hasmonean rule. The zenith was under John Hyrcanus I (135–104 BC). The Megillat Taanit celebrates the victories of this period and beyond. As a theological and literary construct, the interpretive paradigm of a continuing 'exile' of Israel ignored such intervening events. Even if one adopted the identity offered by this pattern, it was not clear what time it was: was the present time the time of 'return' and divine intervention, or was it still the time to 'seek the welfare of the city' where one lived in 'exile', whether that city was in the Diaspora or in the land (Jer. 29:7)?

[29] On this paradigm, see the significant and underestimated work by the late Mark Adam Elliott, *The Survivors of Israel: A Reconsideration of the Theology of Pre-Christian Judaism* (Grand Rapids, MI: Eerdmans, 2000). In the midst of judgement, God preserved a faithful remnant. It was not uncommon for early Jewish sectarian groups to identify themselves as that remnant. This self-understanding is apparent in the Qumran literature. It need not have been limited to the sectarians. Even the Pharisees, who constituted the main stream, had to define themselves over against other Jews. It is hard to imagine that despite their efforts at reform they regarded themselves as equally guilty of idolatry and rebellion as all other Jews of their time or, for that matter, the generation of the exile itself. One of the new realities of postexilic life was the recognition that each one would die for their own sins (esp. Ezek. 18:1–32).

[30] Paul's two statements in Gal. 3:11–12, in which he draws on Hab. 2:4 and Lev. 18:5, are definitional, establishing the twofold claim that faith is the only means of justification according to Scripture, and that the law, with its necessity of the doing of the divine requirements, does not belong to the reality of faith. The appeal to Hab. 2:4 likely recalls Israel's failure and the judgement that came on it. But it also brings a reminder of the promise of deliverance and the faith that works deliverance in

the midst of judgement. As we have noted, Hab. 2:4 does not suggest the pattern of sin, exile and return, but that of the destruction and the preservation of a believing remnant.

[31] This confessional use of the first-person plural, and in Rom. 7:7–25, the first-person singular appear prominently in Paul's letter to Rome. He thereby invites his readers to his theology.

[32] It appears prominently in Rom. 3:19–20 ('we know that whatever the Law says'), and in first-person singular form in Rom. 7:7–25.

[33] So, too, B. Byrne, *'Sons of God' – 'Seed of Abraham': A Study of the Idea of Sonship of God of All Christians in Paul Against the Jewish Background* (Analecta biblica 83; Rome: Pontificio Instituto Biblico, 1979), pp. 155–6.

[34] Paul supports this brief confession with reference to Deut. 21:23, which had come to be interpreted in reference to Roman crucifixion, and thus here refers to Christ's cross. See 4Q169 (Pesher Nahum); 11Q19, 64,6–13 (Temple Scroll).

[35] See below, and likewise Gal. 3:23–9.

[36] Paul here recapitulates what he has said in 3:1–14 in fresh perspective. In the first movement of his argument, Paul insists that sonship to Abraham is based on faith, and the 'gospel' announced to Abraham within the narrative of Scripture is that all the Gentiles would receive blessing in him as a believer. In the second movement of his argument, Paul's attention shifts from faith to the promise(s) of God that underlie faith and from which it proceeds. By means of this expansion and explanation, he defends his preceding assertions concerning faith. The expanded argument contains several discreet units. In the first of these, Paul simultaneously establishes the priority of promise to the law and asserts that its fulfilment now has arrived. Christ is the single 'seed' who is the heir to the promises spoken to Abraham. According to Paul, those promises constituted a 'testament' from God, which the law, which arrived 430 years later (cf. Exod. 12:40), could not annul. As is apparent, Paul has shifted perspective, from the question of the human reception of blessing, to God's initiative in granting blessing. One might, in a sense, describe Paul's thinking as salvation-historical, since the temporal priority of God's promises to the law, and thus their inviolability, is central to his argument. But the sharp distinction that he draws between promise and law runs into an aporia, which he resolves only in the following units. And his apodictic identification of Christ as the promised seed of Abraham implies an eschatological

interruption rather than the unfolding of a narrative. Paul does not bother to explain or defend his dramatic interpretive leap. He simply names Christ as the one in whom the promises to Abraham have come to eschatological fulfilment.

37 For Paul, the promises given to Abraham's seed have been 'figured out', but yet not fulfilled in Isaac, who remains unmentioned in Gal. 3. Likewise, in Rom. 4:13–25, Isaac is only implicitly present and overshadowed by Christ: Isaac's birth ex nihilo anticipates and is fulfilled in the resurrection of Jesus from the dead (Rom. 4:23–5).

38 Within the Genesis narrative itself, Isaac remains an underdeveloped character, in contrast with the other patriarchs.

39 Gal 2:16 (2x),20; 3:22. I am responding here, of course, to the thesis of R.B. Hays, *The Faith of Jesus Christ: An Investigation of the Narrative Substructure of Galatians 3:1–4:11* (Chico, CA: Scholars Press, 1983). See further Mark A. Seifrid, *'The Faith of Christ', The Faith of Jesus Christ: Exegetical, Biblical, and Theological Studies* (ed. M.F. Bird and P.M. Sprinkle; Peabody, MA: Hendrickson, 2010), pp. 129–46.

40 This understanding of Christ, and of the arrival of the eschaton in him appears also in other ways in Galatians. The Galatians once received Paul as 'an angel of God, as Christ Jesus' (Gal. 4:14). Paul here recalls not only the shocking weakness of the cross, but also the glory of the resurrection (Gal. 1:8; 2 Cor. 11:14). His assertion that 'the Jerusalem above, who is free' is the 'mother' of believers likewise signals that he presents Christ here as the crucified and risen Lord, in whom the eschaton has entered the world. His reinterpretation of the inheritance of the land as the gift of the Spirit corresponds to this eschatological identity that he ascribes to believers, and corresponds to his transposition of the promise of the land to the life to come and to the kingdom (Gal. 5:21; 1 Cor. 6:9–10; 15:50; Rom. 4:13–14; 8:17).

41 Provided that χριστοῦ is the original reading in 1:6.

42 Cf. P.T. Forsyth, *The Cruciality of the Cross* (London: Hodder & Stoughton, 1909), p. 27.

43 As others have noted, it is at these two critical points that the interpretation of salvation in terms of Jesus' faithfulness displays its fundamental weakness. One might be faithful to the point of death, but death itself can no longer be a matter of faithfulness. Death comes upon us. Likewise, and even more pointedly, no one can raise themselves from the dead. It must be done for us.

[44] The 'mediator' is clearly Moses. On the tradition that the Law was administered through angels, see Acts 7:53; Heb 2:2; *Midr. Exod* 29,8. It is likely drawn from Deut 33:2, which speaks of the Lord coming with 'a myriad of holy one(s)'. See LXX: ἐκ δεξιῶν αὐτοῦ ἄγγελοι μετ' αὐτοῦ.

[45] See Rom. 3:29–30, where Paul interprets God's unity as requiring that God justify circumcision and uncircumcision, Jews and Gentiles in the same way.

[46] On this theme, see Emmanuel. L. Rehfeld, *Relationale Ontologie bei Paulus: die Ontische Wirksamkeit der Christusbezogenheit im Denken des Heidenapostels* (WUNT 2/326; Tübingen: Mohr Siebeck, 2012). Nevertheless, against Rehfeld's tendency, there is also a place within Paul's thought for an ontology of substance, as is clear from his recognition of the abiding relevance of earthly identities.

[47] We have noted already that within the expression 'faith of Christ' the genitive relation is neither subjective nor objective, but is best understood as presenting the source of faith. This interpretation suggests itself especially in this context, since Paul immediately speaks of the time 'before faith came', and obviously connects the coming of faith with the coming of Christ. Faith is present 'in Christ Jesus' (Gal. 3:23–6). See below.

[48] For Paul, the final, eschatological form of knowledge is not that of knowing something, not even knowing something about Scripture. It is a communication between God and the human being, a communication that takes place in the crucified and risen Christ. The Spirit explores and reveals the very depth of God's being and thoughts, which, as Paul makes clear, are nothing other than unfathomable beneficence and goodness. They are the 'mind of Christ' that has been given to the apostle (1 Cor. 2:10–16). Present, earthly knowledge, the knowledge about 'things', is by all means valuable in Paul's view. But it is fragmentary, and will finally be done away with. It is, furthermore, subject to perversion in self-seeking and boasting, and thus to becoming nothing other than the wisdom of this world, which is opposed to the cross. Eschatological knowledge is the full knowledge and reception of God that is itself enveloped in God's knowledge and acceptance of us in Christ: 'Then I shall know fully, just as I have been fully known' (1 Cor. 13:12). Earthly knowledge shall not survive the eschatological transition, but shall be transcended by the knowledge of God's love and the love that flows back again out of that love

toward God and toward all others (1 Cor. 8:3). This eschatological knowledge of God has been given in Christ and is communicated to the human heart by the apostolic gospel, and thus by the whole of Scripture. As we have observed, it presently remains bound to earthly, partial knowledge, and is communicated in definite words. It cannot be reduced to an 'I–Thou' relation. Nevertheless, Paul's eschatological reserve concerning present human knowledge of 'things' is of fundamental significance to understanding his message. It raises immediate questions concerning any attempt to construct a meta-narrative by which the whole of Scripture and of God might be known. It likewise points to the fundamental significance of the question of identity. For Paul, we rightly know ourselves, corporately and individually, only as we hear God's address to us in Scripture, and thus in Christ.

49 At this point the theology of Galatians touches that of the Corinthian correspondence.

50 The Lukan account in Acts presents the same pattern of Jew-on-Jew violence.

51 Paul appeals to the witness of the law, which for him as Scripture not only presents the divine demands, but also bears witness to the gospel (Gal. 4:21–31): 'Tell me, you who want to be under the Law, do you listen to the Law?' (Gal. 4:21). The 'Law' here obviously refers pars pro toto to the Pentateuch. Paul reads, or more properly 'hears' the law as it bears its witness to the gospel, speaking in the scriptural narratives within which it is embedded. These stories display and define the divine purpose for the law. Yet Paul does not appeal to a storyline. He instead finds figures within the scriptural narrative which manifest in advance the pattern of God's eschatological work in Christ.

52 See the pronouncement of judgement on Babylon, Isa. 47:8–11, and the charge against and promise to Israel, in Isa. 50:1–3 and Isa. 54:4–8, respectively. The image is likewise reminiscent of the book of Hosea (Hos. 2:4–25).

53 Elsewhere he speaks of being snatched up into Paradise (2 Cor. 12:4).

54 See Rom. 9:6–9, where Paul contrasts the word of promise with natural birth. In Galatians, despite his appeal to the births of Ishmael and Isaac, he is obviously concerned with human works: birth 'according to the flesh' (Gal. 4:23,29) does not refer to natural birth, but to a birth brought about by human plans and intentions.

55 Gen. 17:12; 21:4; cf. Phil. 3:5.

[56] Ishmael remains unnamed. Paul's Galatian readers must make the connection between him and Judaism for themselves, and for the ethnic identity they wished to establish.

[57] Paul's allegorizing of the biblical story trades upon the transcending of the earthly reality of Israel by the eschatological purpose of God. While that purpose is not yet visible within the world, it is not a mere 'spiritual' purpose that remains eternally inward and ideational. Nor does Paul's figural interpretation entail supersessionism, at least as the term is usually understood. It is not the church that transcends Israel, not even one of Jews and Gentiles, but an eschatological reality that outstrips all its earthly anticipations. I am responding here to Daniel Boyarin, *A Radical Jew: Paul and the Politics of Identity* (University of California, 1994). For a perceptive discussion of Boyarin, and a comparison of his claims to the approaches of Eric Auerbach and Hans Frei, see J.D. Dawson, *Christian Figural Reading and the Fashioning of Identity* (Berkeley: University of California Press, 2002), pp. 207–18.

[58] In early Christian tradition the age to come was associated with life in a heavenly Jerusalem (e.g. Heb. 11:8–10; 12:22–4, 13:14; Rev. 21:9 – 22:5). Paul himself makes use of the image elsewhere (e.g. Rom. 11:26, in interpretive citation of Isa. 59:20: 'the Redeemer shall come from Zion').

[59] Several observations concerning Paul's language here are critically important. First, he is not pitting a church of Gentiles over against the Jewish synagogue. The 'Jerusalem above' who is the mother of believers, both Jew and Gentile, is 'above' all earthly distinctions, including that of Jew and Gentile, as Paul has made clear already (Gal. 3:28). Paul's closing reference to 'the Israel of God' in Gal. 6:16 is to be understood in the same manner. It is only with Justin Martyr, *Dial.*11 that Israel is reinterpreted as referring to the church. With Paul, it is not a reference to a Gentile church, but to an eschatological reality, in which both believing Jews and Gentiles share. In this regard, it is significant that Paul does not contrast the 'Jerusalem above' with a 'Jerusalem below', but instead with 'the present Jerusalem'. By this description, Paul gives an indication that he goes not regard Israel as forever lost, but as still possessing hope. He does not elaborate that hope here, nor is it directly relevant to his argument with the Galatian churches, but he does so later in his letter to Rome.

[60] D. Bonhoeffer, *Life Together* (trans. J.W. Doberstein; New York: Harper and Brothers, 1954), p. 25.

61 Although it does not become apparent in Galatians, for Paul the law participates in this figural witness as well (see e.g. Rom. 10:6–8).

62 This becomes especially clear in Romans: for Paul the gifts and calling of God given to the patriarchs and thus to Israel remain irrevocable, even if they are to come to fulfilment in an unexpected way (Rom. 11:29).

7. The 'Seed', the 'Many' and the 'One' in Galatians 3:16: Paul's Reading of Genesis 17 and its Significance for Gentiles

1 The exact phrase 'and to your seed' occurs twice in an address to Abraham in the Hebrew text of Genesis: 13:15 and 17:8 (cf. 24:7 LXX). In both cases, the promises of land are in view. The latter is most likely to be the primary source of Paul's quotation, since there are two other terms linking Gal. 3:15–18 to Gen. 17: 'covenant' (Gen. 17:2,4,7,9ff./ Gal. 3:15,17; cf. Martinus C. de Boer, *Galatians: A Commentary* [NTL; Louisville, KY: Westminster John Knox, 2011], p. 222 n. 319) and 'many' (Gen. 17:5/Gal. 3:16; see below). C. John Collins, 'Galatians 3:16: What Kind of Exegete was Paul?', *TynBul* 54/1 (2003), argues that 'the land promise texts (such as Gn. 13:15; 17:8) are not an encouraging line for investigation', since 'the local nature of the promised land would not easily serve Paul's argumentative purpose for the Gentiles' (p. 82). Collins prefers Gen. 22:17–18 as the source of the quotation. However, Gen. 22:17–18 does not contain the term 'and' (kai), which Paul deliberately includes in his quotation (Thomas R. Schreiner, *Galatians* [ZECNT; Grand Rapids, MI: Zondervan, 2010], p. 230). Furthermore, since Paul universalizes the promise of land (Rom. 4:13), there is no reason to think he cannot also here reinterpret the promise of land to refer to the giving of the 'Spirit' (Gal. 3:14) and participation in new creation (cf. Gal. 5:5; 6:15).

2 J. Christiaan Beker, *Paul the Apostle: The Triumph of God in Life and Thought* (Philadelphia: Fortress Press, 1980), pp. 48–51; Hans Dieter Betz, *Galatians: A Commentary on Paul's Letter to the Churches in Galatia* (Hermeneia; Philadelphia: Fortress Press, 1979), p. 157; F.F. Bruce, *The Epistle to the Galatians: A Commentary on the Greek Text* (NIGTC; Exeter: Paternoster, 1982), pp. 171–3; Ermest De Witt Burton, *A Critical and Exegetical Commentary on the Epistle to the Galatians* (ICC; Edinburgh:

T&T Clark, 1921), pp. 181–2; Brendan Byrne, 'Sons of God' – 'Seed of Abraham' (*AnBib* 83; Rome: Biblical Institute Press, 1979), pp. 159–60; De Boer, *Galatians*, pp. 221–3; James D.G. Dunn, *The Epistle to the Galatians* (BNTC; Peabody, MA: Hendrickson, 1993), pp. 183–5; E. Earle Ellis, *Paul's Use of the Old Testament* (Grand Rapids, MI: Eerdmans, 1957), pp. 70–73; G. Walter Hansen, *Galatians* (IVPNTC; Leicester: IVP, 1994), pp. 97–8; Richard B. Hays, *Echoes of Scripture in the Letters of Paul* (New Haven, CT: Yale UP, 1989), pp. 85, 121; Robby J. Kagarise, 'The "Seed" in Galatians 3:16: A Window to Paul's Thinking', *EvJ* 18/2 (2000); Richard N. Longenecker, *Galatians* (WBC 41; Dallas, TX: Word, 1990), pp. 131–2; J. Louis Martyn, *Galatians: A New Translation with Introduction and Commentary* (Anchor; New York: Doubleday, 1997), pp. 338–40; Heinrich Schlier, *Der Brief an die Galater* (MKEKNT 15; Göttingen: Vandenhoeck & Ruprecht, 1989), pp. 144–6; Schreiner, *Galatians*, pp. 228–30; Max Wilcox, 'The Promise of the "Seed" in the New Testament and the Targumim', *JSNT* 5 (1979); Ben Witherington III, *Grace in Galatia: A Commentary on St Paul's Letter to the Galatians* (Edinburgh: T&T Clark, 1998), pp. 244–5.

3 E.g. Deut. 1:8, 34:4; Josh. 24:3; Ps. 105:6; Isa. 41:8; cf. John 8:33; Heb. 2:16. See Longenecker, *Galatians*, p. 131.

4 Cf. C. John Collins, 'A Syntactical Note (Genesis 3:15): Is the Woman's Seed Singular or Plural?', *TynBul* 48/1 (1997): p. 143.

5 E.g. John Barton, *People of the Book?: The Authority of the Bible in Christianity* (London: SPCK, rev. edn. 1988), p. 28; Burton, *Galatians*, pp. 181–2; Martyn, *Galatians*, p. 340.

6 David Daube, *The New Testament and Rabbinic Judaism* (London: University of London Athlone, 1956), pp. 440–41. Daube also points to the rabbinic interpretation of the creation of 'man' in Gen. 1:27; 5:1 in which a generic singular is changed into a specific singular (pp. 441–3).

7 Jason S. DeRouchie and Jason C. Meyer, 'Christ or Family as the "Seed" of Promise? An Evaluation of N.T. Wright on Galatians 3:16', *Southern Baptist Journal of Theology* 14/3 (2010): pp. 38–40.

8 Argued in most detail by Wilcox, 'Promise of the "Seed"': pp. 5–6; cf. James M. Scott, *Adoption as Sons of God: An Exegetical Investigation into the Background of* ΥΙΟΘΕΣΙΑ *in the Pauline Corpus* (WUNT II 48; Tübingen: Mohr Siebeck, 1992), pp. 180–82.

9 Such forms of citation tend to emphasize the distinctive character and significance of the cited text (Francis Watson, *Paul and the Hermeneutics of Faith* [London: T&T Clark, 2004], pp. 44–6).

[10] See below.

[11] N.T. Wright, *The Climax of the Covenant: Christ and the Law in Pauline Theology* (London: T&T Clark, 1991), pp. 162–8; cf. Benjamin Wisner Bacon, 'On Gal. iii.16', *JBL* 16 (1897); Robert L. Brawley, 'Contextuality, Intertextuality, and the Hendiadic Relationship of Promise and Law in Galatians', *ZNW* 93 (2002): p. 104.

[12] Wright, *Climax*, p. 163.

[13] Wright, *Climax*, p. 167.

[14] Pace Wright, *Climax*, p. 163.

[15] Wright may be assuming that, in light of Christ's advent, Paul regards the covenant with Abraham in Gen. 17 as having been suitably modified so that the requirement for circumcision is nullified (cf. Wright, *Climax*, p. 36). The problem with this understanding, of course, is that it contradicts Paul's own assertions here (Gal. 3:15,17): once a covenant is ratified, it cannot be modified!

[16] Wright is reading the ultimate conclusion of his argument (Gal. 3:28–9) back into the details (Gal. 3:16) (cf. A. Andrew Das, *Paul, the Law, and the Covenant* [Peabody, MA: Hendrickson, 2001], p. 73 n. 79; DeRouchie and Meyer, 'Christ or Family?', p. 37). In this respect, Wright is subject to the very criticism he levels at the majority view: 'the point seems to depend on v.29 for its completion, and is therefore not fully comprehensible as it stands' (Wright, *Climax*, p. 159).

[17] Paul R. Williamson, *Abraham, Israel and the Nations: The Patriarchal Promise and its Covenantal Development in Genesis* (JSOTSup 315; Sheffield: Sheffield Academic Press, 2000), pp. 135–40.

[18] Williamson, *Abraham*, pp. 99–113.

[19] A concept that is flagged, but not developed, in Gen. 12:3; cf. Gal. 3:8.

[20] Cf. Beker, *Paul the Apostle*, p. 48; Martyn, *Galatians*, p. 340; Schreiner, *Galatians*, pp. 34–5.

[21] Gordon J. Wenham, *Genesis 16-50* (WBC 2; Dallas: Word, 1994), p. 21.

[22] Williamson, *Abraham*, p. 166.

[23] Cf. Williamson, *Abraham*, pp. 157–66. We may also note that a similar distinction between the plural nations who will be blessed in Abraham and the singular seed of Abraham is made in Gen. 22:17–18. Again, it is Abraham's obedience, not the obedience of the nations, which is directly on view.

[24] Watson, *Hermeneutics*, p. 212. Watson is seeking to demonstrate how Paul exploits this seemingly paradoxical relationship between universal and particular in Rom. 4 (pp. 210–19). We are seeking to

demonstrate that Paul is also exploiting the distinction in Gal. 3, for a slightly different purpose.

[25] The fact that the term 'many' (*polys*) is a reference to Gen. 17 is further supported by the fact that Paul elsewhere directly cites Gen. 17:5 (Rom. 4:17).

[26] Cf. Scott W. Hahn, 'Covenant, Oath and the Aqedah: Διαθήκη in Galatians 3:15-18', *CBQ* 67/1 (2005): pp. 95–7, who sees in the term 'one' (Gal. 3:16) a reference to Isaac, Abraham's 'one'/'only' son (Gen. 22:2,12,16), whose binding in the Aqedah incident (Gen 22:1–16) prefigures Christ's death 'on wood' (Gal. 3:13). Cf. also Watson, *Hermeneutics*, pp. 191–2.

8. Taking with One Hand, and Giving with the Other? The Use of Psalm 68:18 in Ephesians 4:8

[1] All translations in this chapter are the author's own except where otherwise noted.

[2] There are, of course, doubts about Pauline authorship of Ephesians. For ease of expression I will simply speak of the author as Paul as has been traditionally understood.

[3] Joseph A. Fitzmyer, 'The Use Of Explicit Old Testament Quotations in Qumran Literature and in the New Testament', *NTS* 7/4 (1961): p. 325.

[4] Peter Thomas, The Letter to the Ephesians (Grand Rapids, Mich.: W.B. Eerdmans Publishing Co., 1999), p. 293.

[5] Jerome, *Commentariorum in Epistolam as Ephesios* 4:8, *PL* 26:498A-B.

[6] Jerome, *Commentariorum in Epistolam as Ephesios* 4:8, *PL* 26:498B.

[7] Atto, In Epistolam Ad Ephesios 4:8 *PL* 134:566A.

[8] Robert C. Hill, Theodoret of Cyrus: Commentary on The Letters of St Paul. Volume 2. (Holy Cross Orthodox Press, 2007), p. 46.

[9] 'The Prophet says in the Psalm 'He received gifts among people', but he [Paul] says 'he gave gifts to people'. The one [word] us the same as the other', John Chrysostom, *In Epistulum ad Ephesios* XI, *PG* 62:81.

[10] Hugo Grotius, Annotationes in Vetus Testamentum (vol. 1; Groningen: Zuidema, 1875), p. 395.

[11] Johannes Coccejus, *Exercitatio de Principio Epistolae ad Ephesios cum Commentario in Totam Epistolam* 4:8, *Opera* 4:118.

[12] Paul Baynes, *An Commentary upon the Whole Epistle of St Paul to the Ephesians* (Edinburgh: James Nichol, 1866), p.250.

[13] John Owen, *A Discourse on Spiritual Gifts* 1, *Works* 4:421–422; *A Discourse on Spiritual Gifts* 6, 488–489.

[14] Charles Hodge, *A Commentary on the Epistle to the Ephesians* (New York: Robert Carter & Brothers, 1866), p. 215–216.

[15] Coccejus follows him, *Exercitatio de Principio Epistolae ad Ephesios cum Commentario in Totam Epistolam* 4:8, *Opera* 4:118.

[16] John Owen, *A Discourse on Spiritual Gifts* 6, pp. 488–9.

[17] Richard A. Taylor, "The Use of Psalm 68:18 in Ephesians 4:8 in Light of the Ancient Versions," *Bibliotheca Sacra* 148, no. 591 (1991): p. 327.

[18] Thomas Cajetan, *In Omnes F. Pauli et Aliorum Apostolorum Epistolas Commentarii* (vol. 5; Lugduni: Sumptibus Iacobi et Petri Prost., 1639), p. 233.

[19] 'Ebraea quidem hunc sensum habent, sed non haec verba', Martin Bucer, *Epistola D. Pauli Ad Ephesios* (Strassburg, 1527), p. 83.

[20] Wolfgang Musculus, *In Epistolas Apostoli Pauli, Ad Galatias & Ephesios, Commentarii* (Basileae: Ex Officina Heruagiana per Eusebium Episcopium, 1569), p. 103.

[21] 'Quod ergo Paulus pro eo quod in Hebraeo legimus, Accepisti dona ab hominibus, reddidit, Et dedit dona hominibus, ad sensum respexit', *In Omnes Apostolicas Epistolas, Divi Videlicet Pauli XIIII. Et VII. Canonicas, Commentarii Heinrychi Bullingeri* (Tiguri: Christoph Froschauer, 1549), p. 429.

[22] 'the Apostle, citing the place [Ps. 68:18] with some variation of the words, but keeping close to the sense and purpose, doth shew, was now fulfilled by Christ', James Fergusson, *A Brief Exposition of the Epistles of Paul to the Galatians and Ephesians* (London: Stationers, 1659), p. 247.

[23] 'Qui enim spolia accipiunt victores à devictis hominibus, ut in suos homines spargant accipiunt', Bullinger, *In Omnes Apostolicas Epistolas*, p. 429.

[24] John Calvin, *Commentaries on the Epistles of Paul to the Galatians and Ephesians* (trans. William Pringle; Edinburgh: Calvin Translation Society, 1854), p. 273.

[25] Calvin, Commentaries, p. 273.

[26] Cited in Taylor, The Use of Psalm 68, p. 332.

[27] George B. Caird, "The Descent of Christ in Ephesians 4, 7–11," in *SE, Vol. 2: Part 1: The New Testament Scriptures* (ed. Frank L. Cross; Berlin: Akademie-Verlag, 1964), pp. 535–45; G.B. Caird, *Paul's Letters from Prison: Ephesians, Philippians, Colossians, Philemon* (Oxford: OUP, 1976), pp. 73–5.

[28] Markus Barth, *Ephesians 4–6* (vol. 34A; Anchor Bible Commentary; Garden City, N.Y.: Doubleday, 1974), pp. 475–476.

[29] Andrew T Lincoln, *Ephesians* (WBC 42; Waco, TX: Word, 1990), pp. 246–7.

[30] W. Hall Harris, *The Descent of Christ: Ephesians 4:7-11 and Traditional Hebrew Imagery* (Biblical Studies Library; Grand Rapids, MI: Baker, 1998), pp. 171–91.

[31] Rudolf Schnackenburg, *The Epistle to the Ephesians: A Commentary* (Edinburgh: T & T Clark, 1991), p. 177.

[32] Thorsten Moritz, *A Profound Mystery: The Use of the Old Testament in Ephesians* (NovTSup 85; Leiden: E.J. Brill, 1996), pp. 74–5.

[33] Jonathan M. Lunde and John Anthony Dunne,'Paul's Creative and Contextual Use of Psalm 68 in Ephesians 4:8,' *WTJ* 74 (2012): p. 104.

[34] Frank Thielman, Ephesians 4:7–11, in *Commentary on the New Testament Use of the Old Testament* (ed. Gregory K. Beale and Donald A. Carson; Grand Rapids: Baker Academic, 2007), p. 823; Frank Thielman, *Ephesians* (Grand Rapids, Mich.: Baker Academic, 2010), p. 267.

[35] Lunde and Dunne, 'Paul's Creative and Contextual Use' p. 105; Timothy G. Gombis, 'Cosmic Lordship and Divine Gift-Giving: Psalm 68 in Ephesians 4:8,' *NovT* 47, no. 4 (2005): p. 370.

[36] Appearing in 1:9; 3:3,4,9; 5:32; and 6:19.

[37] Thielman, *Ephesians*, pp. 194–5.

[38] Hans-Joachim Kraus, *Psalms 60–150* (Continental Commentaries; Minneapolis: Fortress Press, 1993), p. 628.

[39] Mitchell Dahood, *Psalms II: 51–100* (Anchor Bible Commentary; New York: Doubleday, 1968), p. 133.

[40] Allan Harman, *Psalms Volume 1: Psalms 1–72* (Fearn: Mentor, 2011), p. 491.

[41] Frank-Lothar Hossfeld and Erich Zenger, *Psalms 2: A Commentary on Psalms 51–100* (ed. Klaus Baltzer; trans. Linda M. Maloney; Hermeneia; Fortress Press, 2005), p. 160–1.

[42] Bullinger, *In Omnes Apostolicas Epistolas*, p. 428.

[43] Here I have found especially helpful Harman, *Psalms Volume 1*, pp. 491–503.

[44] Tate is apt: 'This section [vv. 15–18] is as obscure in details as the preceding. In general, the strophe sets forth the selection of a mountain for Yahweh's abode, which is contrasted with the mighty mountain of God in Bashan', Marvin E Tate, *Psalms 51–100* (WBC 20; Nashville, TN: T. Nelson Publishers, 1991), p. 180.

[45] Verse 17 is obscure. Sinai is like a reference to God, 'Sinai is in the sanctuary', so Tate, *Psalms 51–100*, p. 181. Moreover, the sanctuary is more likely Zion than Sinai because the preceding verses speak of the mountain God has chosen to dwell upon, namely Zion (Ps. 132:13–14).

[46] Tate, *Psalms 51–100*, p. 181.

[47] 'Tum certe dona inter homines accepit, populum Israël, quem peculiarem sibi populum fecit', Bucer, *Epistola D. Pauli Ad Ephesios*, p. 83.

[48] Gary V. Smith, "Paul's Use of Psalm 68:18 in Ephesians 4:8," *JETS* 18, no. 3 (1975): p. 187; B. F. Westcott, *Saint Paul's Epistle to the Ephesians: The Greek Text, with Notes and Addenda* (London; New York: Macmillan, 1906), pp. 60–61.

[49] Bullinger speaks of *spolium*, 'spoils' or 'booty', *In Omnes Apostolicas Epistolas*, 428–429. Jerome uses *manubia* or 'spoils', Jerome, *Commentarium in Epistolam ad Ephesios*, 4:8, *PL* 26:498A.

[50] John Goldingay, *Psalms. Volume 2: Psalms 42–89* (Baker Commentary on the Old Testament; Grand Rapids: Baker Academic, 2007), p. 325; Harman, *Psalms Volume 1*, p. 497; Gerald H. Wilson, *Psalms Volume 1* (NIV Application Commentary; Zondervan, 2002), p. 940; C. H. Spurgeon, *The Treasury of David. Volume 1: Psalm 1–89* (Grand Rapids: Baker, 1984), p. 221.

[51] 'In which place of the Psalm, *David* doth look through the ark, a type and shadow, to Christ the substance, and in a prophetical way', Fergusson, *A Brief Exposition*, p. 246.

[52] Calvin, *Commentaries*, p. 273.

9. The Use of the Old Testament in Philippians

[1] M. Silva, 'Old Testament in Paul', in *DPL*, p. 630.

[2] Silva, 'Old Testament', p. 630.

[3] Silva, 'Old Testament', p. 630.

[4] Silva, 'Old Testament', p. 630.

[5] Silva, 'Old Testament', p. 630.

[6] E.E. Ellis, *Paul's Use of the Old Testament* (Edinburgh: Oliver & Boyd, 1957), pp. 150–52; Silva, 'Old Testament', p. 630. See also R.B. Hays, *Echoes of Scripture in the Letters of Paul* (New Haven / London: Yale UP), p. 21.

[7] First and Second Thessalonians have even fewer OT references with no citations and only conceptual intertextuality with things like the

fatherhood of God and *Christos* (1 Thess. 1:1), idolatry (1 Thess. 1:9), Satan (1 Thess. 3:18), holy ones/saints (1 Thess. 4:13), day of the Lord (1 Thess. 5:2), angels (2 Thess. 1:7), and others. There are no direct citations of the OT. Similarly Philemon has no citations but concepts such as *Christos* (Phlm. 1) and holy ones/saints (1:5,7). Although Jewish law is clearly tied up with the problems in Cretan Christianity, again there are no OT citations but conceptual references such as *Christos* (e.g. Titus 1:1), the fatherhood of God (Titus 1:3), circumcision (Titus 1:10), 'Jewish myths' (Titus 1:14), genealogies (Titus 3:9), and quarrels about the law (Titus 3:9).

8 Hays, *Echoes*, p. 24 states that the clause is found only in Job; however, this is incorrect.

9 Translation mine. The NET Translation reads, 'To be sure, I know that he who is about to undo me on earth is everlasting. May my skin, which patiently endures these things, rise up; for these things have been accomplished on me by the Lord'. However, ἐκλύω can be taken as 'release' or 'deliver' as in the Brenton translation (cf. Isa. 46:2). It can also mean 'loosen a yoke' in a positive sense (Gen. 27:40) or 'loosen bonds' (*3 Macc.* 6:27). Otherwise it means to 'release' emotion (*4 Macc.* 15:24), to be exhausted in strength (2 Sam. 21:15), to have muscles loosened, slackened (Gen. 49:24); a heart loosened, set free from fear (Deut. 20:3), and the hands of God to deliver not slackened (Josh. 10:6). It is often used of people who are faint or weakened generally (2 Sam. 16:14; 17:2,29; 21:11; 2 Chron. 15:7; Ezra 4:4; Jdt. 14:6; *1 Macc.* 9:8; Prov. 3:11; 6:3; Sir. 43:10; Isa. 13:7; 29:9; 51:20; Jer. 4:31; 12:5; 30:30; Ezek. 7:17; 31:15), from lack of food (Judg. 8:15; 1 Sam. 14:28; *1 Macc.* 3:17; Lam. 2:19), drink (2 Sam. 16:2), fear (2 Sam. 4:1), or war (*1 Macc.* 10:28; Jer. 45:5; Lam. 2:12). It can mean people afraid to take the land (Josh. 18:3), people released as in left behind (1 Sam. 30:21), or departed, left (*2 Macc.* 12:18; 13:16).

10 Hays, *Echoes*, p. 22.

11 Scholarship is divided over whether Paul is in Caesarea, Ephesus or Rome, with the latter two most popular among contemporary scholars. While I strongly prefer Rome as I will argue in my forthcoming EEC commentary, it doesn't particularly affect this paper, so I will not discuss it here. See M.J. Keown, *Philippians* (EEC; Bellingham, WA: Lexham Press, 2014).

12 For a discussion of the two options with a preference for the 'help given by the Spirit', see P.T. O'Brien, *The Epistle to the Philippians: A*

Commentary on the Greek Text (NIGTC; Grand Rapids, MI: Eerdmans, 1991), pp. 110–12.

13 For example, G.F. Hawthorne and R.P. Martin, *Philippians* (WBC 43; Dallas, TX: Word, rev. edn, 2004), pp. 49–50.

14 For example, O'Brien, *Philippians*, pp. 109–10.

15 Also suggested by M. Silva, *Philippians* (BECNT; Grand Rapids, MI: Baker Academic, 2nd edn, 2005), p. 71.

16 See M. J. Keown, *Congregational Evangelism in Philippians: The Centrality of an Appeal for Gospel Proclamation to the Fabric of Philippians* (Milton Keynes: Paternoster, 2008), p. 126 n. 12; G.D. Fee, *Paul's Letter to the Philippians* (NICNT; Grand Rapids, MI: Eerdmans, 1995), p. 131.

17 For a full discussion of this text see my EEC forthcoming commentary in which I refute the idea that Paul was considering voluntary death, suicide, or was speaking with some doubt. I flag the possibility that Paul considered escape from Roman prison.

18 Similarly, Hays, *Echoes*, p. 22.

19 Job is of course destitute (Job 1:6 – 2:10). Job 13:16 lies in Job's defence in Job 12 – 14 to Zophar who challenges Job's defence telling him that God exacts of him 'less than your guilt deserves', i.e. he deserves worse (Job 11:6).

20 O'Brien, *Philippians*, p. 109 notes that ἀποβαίνω εἰς is found nowhere else and 'is clearly dependent on and explained by the Job passage'.

21 See Hays, *Echoes*, pp. 21–4 who describes it as an echo which Paul has appropriated for his circumstances. He writes, '[b]y echoing Job's words, Paul the prisoner tacitly assumes the role of righteous sufferer, as paradigmatically figured by Job. Awaiting his trial, he speaks with Job's voice to affirm confidence in the favorable outcome of his afflictions; thereby, he implicitly transfers to himself some of the significations that traditionally cluster about the figure of Job'. Similarly, G.W. Hansen, *The Letter to the Philippians* (PNTC; Grand Rapids, MI/ Nottingham, England: Eerdmans, 2009), p. 77.

22 Markus Bockmuehl, *The Epistle to the Philippians* (BNTC; London: Continuum, 1997), pp. 82–3.

23 See J. Gnilka, *Der Philipperbrief* (HTKNT 10.3; Freiburg: Herder, 4th edn, 1987), pp. 65–6; Hawthorne and Martin, *Philippians*, p. 49.

24 E.g. Hansen, *Philippians*, p. 289; Silva, *Philippians*, p. 194.

25 See Keown, *Congregational Evangelism*, pp. 63–4.

[26] Some scholars believe that both the return of Christ and the Lord's presence are in mind, e.g. O'Brien, *Philippians*, pp. 188–9; Hawthorne and Martin, *Philippians*, p. 245.

[27] M.J. Keown, 'How Much Should We Sing?' *Stimulus* 19.3 (Nov. 2012), p. 8 where I note that ψαλμός likely refers to 'Old Testament Psalms drawn from the LXX, the foundational song-book of the early Christian church'.

[28] Although Paul uses πορεύσονται, it translates hā·lăḵ, cf. περιπατέω, Phil. 3:17,18.

[29] See W. Hendriksen and S.J. Kistemaker. *Exposition of Philippians* (NTC 5; Grand Rapids, MI: Baker Book House, 1953–2001), p. 61 who notes Prov. 11:30 (see also Bockmuehl, *Philippians*, p. 69; Hawthorne and Martin, *Philippians*, p. 33). Silva, *Philippians*, p. 52 notes Prov. 11:30, but sees no connection. A number – including Silva, and Hawthorne and Martin – in the same contexts also note Amos 6:12.

[30] See e.g. older works where scholars argued for literary dependence, e.g. L. Cerfaux, 'L'hymne au Christ-Serviteur de Dieu (Phil 2, 6–11 = Is 52, 13–53, 12)' in Recuil Lucien Cerfaux. II. *Études d'exégèse et d'histoire religieuse* (Gembloux: Duculot, 1954), pp. 425–37; J. Jeremias, 'Zur Gedankenführung in den paulinischen Briefen', in *Studia Paulina in Honorem J. de Zwaan* (ed. J.N. Sevenster and W.C. van Unnik; (Haarlem: Hohn, 1953), pp. 146–54. However, it is more likely a conceptual relationship that is in view (see e.g. Hansen, *Philippians*, p. 150; Keown, *Philippians* (EEC), forthcoming.

[31] See my defence of this translation, Keown, *Congregational Evangelism*, pp. 135–44.

[32] See especially Fee, *Philippians*, p. 246. This is questioned by J. Dickson, *Mission-Commitment in Ancient Judaism and in the Pauline Communities: The Shape, Extent and Background of Early Christian Background* (WUNT 2.159; Tübingen: Mohr Siebeck, 2003), pp. 110–13 on the basis that Fee confuses Paul's use of the LXX and MT. In light of Paul's use of both texts and sometimes unclear texts (see above), it is not implausible that Paul is drawing on both.

[33] Silva, *Philippians*, p. 181 describes this as a 'clear allusion', which is overstated.

[34] E.g. Bockmuehl, *Philippians*, pp. 241–2, cf. Dan. 12:3; 1 QM 12.3.

[35] Silva, 'Old Testament', p. 635; Silva, *Philippians*, p. 130.

[36] See especially Lev. 19:5; 22:21,29; Sir. 35:6; Mal. 2:13; Isa. 56:7; Jer. 6:20.

[37] See Gen. 8:21; Exod. 29:18,25,41; Lev. 2:12; 4:31; 6:14; 8:21; 17:4,6; 23:18; Num. 15:3,5,7,10,13,14,24; 18:17; 28:2,6,8,13,24,27; 29:2,6,8,11,13,36; Jdt. 16:16; Sir. 50:15; Ezek. 6:13; 16:19; 20:28.

[38] See for example, O'Brien, *Philippians*, p. 355; Bockmuehl, *Philippians*, p. 187. I am not convinced of this due to the differences in language; see Keown, *Philippians* (EEC), forthcoming.

[39] See Keown, *Philippians* (EEC), forthcoming.

[40] See also J.T. Reed, *A Discourse Analysis of Philippians: Method and Rhetoric in the Debate Over Literary Integrity* (Sheffield: Sheffield Academic Press, 1997), p. 294.

[41] By 'inspired' I do not want to load up the concept with subsequent debates; but they are the primary literature of the Pauline churches and provide types and patterns which reveal the character, will and purpose of God. If 2 Tim. 3:16 is Pauline, the Scriptures are formed from a creational act (cf. Ps. 19) and vital for Christian life.

[42] Such as: 1) Should the Christian use the LXX and/or the MT as the basis for understanding the whole story of Scripture? 2) Should the focus of OT study be the LXX or the MT, or both? 3) Should translations which have sought to be authentic to the text of Scripture be seen as of equal weight to the original languages?

[43] In Isa. 45:14–25 the Hebrew *yhwh* is used eight times (Isa. 45:14,17,18[2x],19,21,24,25); *ʾēl* four times (Isa. 45:14,15,21,22); and *ʾĕlō·hîm* twice (Isa. 45:15,18). In the LXX *kyrios* is used five times (Isa. 45:14,17,18,19,25) and *Theos* nine times of God (Isa. 45:14,15[2x],18,20,21,22,23,25). These interchangeable terms for God are replaced by Jesus in Phil. 2:9–11.

[44] The argument of the likes of C.K. Barrett, *A Critical and Exegetical Commentary on the Acts of the Apostles* (ICC; Edinburgh: T&T Clark, 1998), p. 781 that 'place of prayer' refers subtly to a synagogue is weak in that Luke is quite comfortable to name the Jewish gathering points 'synagogue' on twenty-two other occasions throughout Acts; and, as such, it makes little sense that he would on this one occasion, 'out of the blue', deviate from this.

[45] The Greek ταις̂ συνελθούσαις γυναιξίν gives no hint of male participants.

[46] One cannot rule out that this was only a particular day in the life of the Jews, proselytes and God-fearers of Philippi and that there were male and female Jews in the city. If there were Jewish women, Luke does not indicate that any were converted.

[47] See B. Witherington III, *The Acts of the Apostles: A Socio-Rhetorical Commentary* (Grand Rapids, MI: Eerdmans, 1998), p. 490.

[48] Witherington, *Acts*, p. 490 notes that their position is potentially due to a lack of recognition of Jews in line with concern over foreign cults.

[49] The participle ὑπάρχοντες can be causal, 'because they are Jews', or a participle of attendant circumstances, 'they being Jews'. If causal, then their troublemaking is directly attributed to their Jewishness enhancing the hint of anti-Semitism.

[50] It is unclear from Acts 16:16–19 whether the girl was converted, returned to her owners, discarded or sold because of her economic uselessness, and joined the nascent church, perhaps domiciled with Lydia. It is not implausible that she is one of either Euodia and Syntyche, the latter name making this possible (although speculative) in light of her previous prophetic role.

[51] The Roman jailor is likely a former Roman soldier granted land in Philippi. The slave girl is likely a young Greek and part of a family devoted to Apollos. Lydia is an Asian from Thyatira, but who has a strong interest in Judaism – a God-worshipper.

[52] Although the numbers of Jews may be small, assuming the historicity of Acts, Luke's account indicates that every other city evangelized and to which Paul wrote included at least some Jewish converts (Corinth, Acts 18:8; Ephesus, Acts 19:1–10, cf. Eph 2:11–22; Thessalonica, Acts 17:1–10, cf. 1 Thess 1:9–10). It is clear from the content of Galatians and Colossians that there was a Jewish influence in the churches (e.g. Gal. 2:15 – 5:15; 6:11–16; Acts 13:43; 14:1; Col. 2:6–23).

[53] With a fair degree of mobility among the wealthier people of the empire, this cannot be underestimated. On mobility, see E.J. Schnabel, *Early Christian Mission: Jesus and the Twelve* (Leicester / Downers Grove, IL: IVP / Apollos, 2004), pp. 632–40.

[54] C.C. Kroeger, 'Women in Greco-Roman World and Judaism', in *DNTB*, p. 1276 notes that Palestinian and Diaspora women were 'afforded limited opportunities for education. They were schooled by their mothers in the household arts and in those parts of the law that dealt with purity issues and the responsibilities of women. These lay heavy upon women, for the law threatened with death in childbirth those who transgressed its strictures.'

[55] Attempts to identify Lydia with Euodia and Syntyche are tenuous; see the comments in F.F. Bruce, *Philippians* (NIBC; Peabody, MA: Hendrickson, 1983, 1989), p. 40. We can rule out her changing her

name to Syntyche which blends σύν with τύχη and has clear pagan associations. It is not implausible, however, that she changed her name to 'Euodia' which blends εὖ and ὁδός indicating 'good journey' or 'good way' and perhaps recalling the Christians being labelled 'the way'. It also sounds like εὐωδία which speaks of 'fragrant' and, as such, the name would be appropriate (Phil. 4:18). However, all such speculations are, at best, perilous.

[56] See Keown, *Congregational Evangelism*, pp. 42–6; Fee, *Philippians*, pp. 34–7.

[57] In Keown, *Philippians* (EEC), forthcoming, I defend a date in AD 63 when Paul's imprisonment has deteriorated perhaps due to the influence of Tigellinus and Poppaea Sabina but preceding the Neronian persecution.

[58] As Fee, *Philippians*, p. 18 notes, 'as in all the Pauline churches these early Gentile believers were thoroughly acquainted with their bibles'. He also notes that this should be understood in an oral framework suggesting that 'early Gentile believers knew the OT infinitely better than most Christians do today'.

[59] This rules out the idea that they are Gentiles, as argues J.J. Gunther, *St. Paul's Opponents and Their Background* (NovTSup 35; Leiden: Brill, 1973); K. Grayston, 'The Opponents in Philippians 3', *ExpTim* 97 (1986), pp. 170–72; or Cynics, see M.D. Nanos, 'Paul's Reversal of Jews Calling Gentiles "Dogs" (Philippians 3:2): 1600 Years of an Ideological Tale Wagging an Exegetical Dog?' *BibInt* 17 (2009), pp. 448–82. We can also rule out their being Gnostics in anything but a proto-Gnostic sense, e.g. Koester, 'The Purpose of the Polemic of a Pauline Fragment (Philippians III)', *NTS* 8 (1961–2), pp. 317–32; C.R. Holladay, 'Paul's Opponents in Phil. 3', *ResQ* 3 (1969), pp. 77–90; W. Schmithals, *Paul and the Gnostics* (trans. J.E. Steely; Nashville, TN: Abingdon, 1972), p. 120.

[60] E.g. G.F. Hawthorne, *Philippians* (WBC 43; Waco: Word, 1st edn, 1983), pp. xliv–xlvii; W. Schenk, *Die Philipperbriefe des Paulus* (Stuttgart: Kohlhammer, 1984), pp. 250–91. Some take them as Jews who are cautionary examples rather than an actual threat to the Philippians, e.g. G.D. Kilpatrick, 'BLEPETE, Philippians 3:2,' in *In Memoriam Paul Kahle* (ed. M. Black and G. Fohrer; Berlin: Töpelmann, 1968), pp. 146–8.

[61] E.g. A.J. Klijn, 'Paul's Opponents in Phil III', *NovT* 7 (1964–65), 278–84; B.D. Rahtjen, 'The Three Letters of Paul to the Philippians', *NTS* 6 (1959–60), pp. 167–73; e.g. J.-F. Collange, *The Epistle of Saint Paul to the*

Philippians (trans. A.W. Heathcote; London: Epworth Press, 1979), pp. 123–39.

62 E.g. G.D. Fee, *Philippians*, p. 295; O'Brien, *Philippians*, pp. 26–34, 354–57; Hansen, *Philippians*, p. 217; Bockmuehl, *Philippians*, p. 182; Silva, Philippians, p. 147; R. Jewett, 'Conflicting Movements in the Early Church as Reflected in Philippians', *NovT* 12 (1970), pp. 362–90, and many others.

63 Some take τὰ αὐτά as referring to what precedes, such as the joy imperative (e.g. Hawthorne and Martin, *Philippians*, p. 173; Hansen, *Philippians*, pp. 213–15; Bockmuehl, *Philippians*, p. 180). This is unconvincing. For critique see Fee, *Philippians*, p. 292 n. 30.

64 F.F. Bruce, 'St. Paul in Macedonia: 3. The Philippian Correspondence', *BJRL* 63 (1981), p. 273 suggests that Polycarp's reference to plural letters may indicate earlier letters to Philippi in which Paul may have warned them (see also I.–J. Loh and E.A. Nida, *A Handbook on Paul's Letter to the Philippians* (UBSHS; New York: UBS, 1995), p. 89). Otherwise, the warnings were from Paul's three visits (Acts 16:11–40; 20:1–2,3) or through co-workers (cf. O'Brien, *Philippians*, p. 350).

65 The Greek scrolls of the OT books could be included in Paul's reference to his books or parchments or scrolls (βιβλίον, μεμβράνα in 2 Tim. 4:13); particularly, the former, cf. Luke 4:17,20; Gal. 3:10. G.W. Knight, *The Pastoral Epistles: A Commentary on the Greek Text* (NIGTC; Grand Rapids, MI/Carlisle, England: Eerdmans/Paternoster Press, 1992), p. 467 notes 'it is possible that Paul refers to the OT writings with plural τὰ βιβλία'.

66 See also S.R. Llewelyn, 'Sending Letters in the Ancient World: Paul and the Philippians', *TynBul* 46 (1995), pp. 337–56; I.H. Marshall, *The Epistle to the Philippians* (London: Epworth, 1992), p. 67; Fee, *Philippians*, p. 261; O'Brien, *Philippians*, p. 130).

67 J. Murphy-O'Connor, *Paul the Letter-Writer: His World, His Options, His Skills* (GNS 41; Collegeville, MN: Liturgical Press, 1995), pp. 39–40 notes that the bearer of the letter 'of course, could supplement the contents of the letter by verbal information or by answering questions'. He cites PLond 42 and PColZen 1.6.

68 Timothy (e.g. Collange, *Philippians*, p. 143), a female (as held by older scholars, e.g. Lydia), or Christ (Wieseler), is implausible unless you argue against integrity and ignore that it is masculine; as is the idea that this is a circumlocution for the whole congregation (e.g. Hawthorne and Martin, *Philippians*, p. 242). It could be Epaphroditus

(e.g. B. Witherington III, *Paul's Letters to the Philippians: A Socio-Rhetorical Commentary*. Grand Rapids, MI: Eerdmans, 2011), p. 239); Luke (Fee, *Philippians*, p. 394), another unknown co-worker, or an unnamed Philippian.

69 Some scholars, e.g. U.B. Müller, *Der Brief des Paulus an die Philipper* (THKNT 11.1; Leipzig: Evangelische Verlaganstalt, 1993), p. 195, believe this is a name. However, it is not found in any sources in the masculine. Some note however, that other similar σύν names are found such as Σύνδρομος, 'Syndromos' (SIJ. 3.1143.3), Σύμμαχος, 'Symmachos' (Pausanius, 4.1.3), and the rare Σύμφωνος, 'Symphonos'. If it is a name, then γνήσιε σύζυγε is a word play similar to Phlm. 11. Alternatively, and more likely, it is a reference to a loyal companion of Paul in Philippi.

70 See also Bruce, *Philippians*, p. 25; Fee, *Philippians*, p. 61; Hansen, *Philippians*, p. 37.

71 See Keown, *Philippians* (EEC), forthcoming, in which I argue Paul emphatically knew he was coming to Philippians based on the Greek αἱρέομαι, 'choose' and καὶ τοῦτο πεποιθὼς οἶδα, 'convinced of this, I know that' (Phil. 1:23,25).

10. The Appropriation of Scripture in 1 Peter

1 Martin Hengel, *Between Jesus and Paul: Studies in the Earliest History of Christianity* (London: SCM, 1983), pp. 48–64 (at p. 64).

2 See, for example, 1 Cor. 9:5, with its reference to the travels of 'the other apostles and the Lord's brothers and Cephas'.

3 Lutz Doering, 'First Peter as Early Christian Diaspora Letter', in *The Catholic Epistles and Apostolic Tradition* (ed. Karl-Wilhelm Niebuhr and Robert W. Wall; Waco, TX: Baylor University, 2009), pp. 215–36, 441–57 ('a letter from the Diaspora [qualified in terms of the Babylonian exile] to the Diaspora', p. 233); cf. Reinhard Feldmeier, *The First Letter of Peter: A Commentary on the Greek Text* (Waco, TX: Baylor University, 2008), p. 32; J. Ramsey Michaels, *1 Peter*, WBC (Waco, TX: Word, 1988), pp. xlvi–xlvii.

4 Although 1 Peter is widely regarded as pseudonymous, a good case can be made for Petrine authorship: see William J. Dalton, *SJ, Christ's Proclamation to the Spirits: A Study of 1 Peter 3:18-4:6*, Analecta Biblica 23 (Rome: Pontificio Istituto Biblico, 2nd edn, 1989), pp. 77–91; Joel B.

Green, *1 Peter, Two Horizons New Testament Commentary* (Grand Rapids, MI: Eerdmans, 2007), pp. 6–8; Karen H. Jobes, *1 Peter*, BECNT (Grand Rapids, MI: Baker Academic, 2005), pp. 14–19; Donald G. Miller, *On This Rock: A Commentary on First Peter*, Princeton Theological Monograph Series 34 (Allison Park, PA: Pickwick, 1993), pp. 57–75; Ben Witherington III, *Letters and Homilies for Hellenized Christians, Volume II: A Socio-Rhetorical Commentary on 1-2 Peter* (Downers Grove, IL: IVP Academic, 2007), pp. 37–51.

5 On which see R. Bauckham, 'James, 1 and 2 Peter, Jude', in *It Is Written: Scripture Citing Scripture: Essays in Honour of Barnabas Lindars* (ed. D.A. Carson and H.G.M. Williamson; Cambridge: CUP, 1988), pp. 303–17 (at pp. 309–13); D.A. Carson, '1 Peter', in *Commentary on the New Testament Use of the Old Testament* (ed. G.K. Beale and D.A. Carson; Grand Rapids, MI: Baker Academic, 2007), pp. 1015–45; Steve Moyise, *The Later New Testament Writings and Scripture: The Old Testament in Acts, Hebrews, the Catholic Epistles and Revelation* (Grand Rapids, MI: Baker Academic, 2012), pp. 42–61; T.P. Osborne, 'L'utilisation des citations de l'Ancien Testament dans la première épître de Pierre', *RTL* 12 (1981), pp. 64–77; William L. Schutter, *Hermeneutic and Composition in 1 Peter*, WUNT 2.30 (Tübingen: Mohr Siebeck, 1989); S. Voorwinde, 'Old Testament Quotations in Peter's Epistles', *Vox Reformata* 49 (1987), pp. 3–16; Susan Ann Woan, *The Use of the Old Testament in 1 Peter, with Especial Focus on the Role of Psalm 34* (unpublished doctoral thesis, University of Exeter, 2008).

6 See Martin Hengel, *Saint Peter: The Underestimated Apostle* (Grand Rapids, MI / Cambridge: Eerdmans, 2010).

7 J. de Waal Dryden, *Theology and Ethics in 1 Peter: Paraenetic Strategies for Christian Character Formation*, WUNT 2.209 (Tübingen: Mohr Siebeck, 2006), pp. 1–53; John H. Elliott, *1 Peter: A New Translation with Introduction and Commentary*, AB (New York: Doubleday, 2000), pp. 11, 37, 67–8, 105; Stephen Ayodeji A. Fagbemi, *Who are the Elect in 1 Peter? A Study in Biblical Exegesis and its Application to the Anglican Church of Nigeria*, Studies in Biblical Literature 104 (New York: Peter Lang, 2007), pp. 54–9; Marie-Louise Lamau, *Des Chrétiens dans le Monde: Communautés Pétriniennes au Premier Siècle, Lectio Divina* 134 (Paris: Cerf, 1988), pp. 36–9; Eduard Lohse, 'Parenesis and Kerygma in 1 Peter' in Charles H. Talbert (ed), *Perspectives on First Peter* (Eugene, OR: Wipf & Stock, 2010 [1986]), pp. 37–59; Troy W. Martin, *Metaphor and Composition in 1 Peter*, SBLDS 131 (Atlanta, GA: Scholars, 1992), pp. 85–134;

Ceslas Spicq, O.P., *Les Épîtres de Saint Pierre,* Sources bibliques (Paris: Gabalda, 1966), pp. 11–12; Lauri Thurén, *Argument and Theology in 1 Peter: The Origins of Christian Paraenesis,* JSNTSup 114 (Sheffield: Sheffield Academic, 1995). Although it has been suggested that 1 Peter can be seen as a 'letter of consolation' (Paul A. Holloway, '*Nihil inopinati accidisse* – "Nothing Unexpected Has Happened": A Cyrenaic Consolatory *Topos* in 1 Pet 4.12ff', NTS 48.3 [2002], pp. 433–48 [at p. 448 n. 75]), we do more justice to more of its contents by seeing it as a paraenetic letter.

8 The letter uses χάρις ten times (1:2,10,13; 2:19,20; 3:7; 4:10; 5:5,10,12).

9 The letter uses πάσχω twelve times (2:19,20,21,23; 3:14,17,18; 4:1(x2),15,19; 5:10) and πάθημα four times (1:11; 4:13; 5:1,9), along with λυπέω (1:6) and λύπη (2:19), πειρασμός (1:6; 4:12) and πύρωσις (4:12), which makes suffering one of its fundamental themes. For a useful survey of studies of this subject, see Travis B. Williams, 'Suffering from a Critical Oversight: The Persecutions of 1 Peter within Modern Scholarship', *CBR* 10.2 (2012), pp. 275–92, and for recent treatments of what 1 Pet. has to say about the suffering of its readers, see Paul A. Holloway, *Coping with Prejudice: 1 Peter in Social-Psychological Perspective,* WUNT 244 (Tübingen: Mohr Siebeck, 2009), esp. pp. 137–232; Travis B. Williams, *Persecution in 1 Peter: Differentiating and Contextualizing Early Christian Suffering,* NovTSup 145 (Leiden/Boston: Brill, 2012), esp. pp. 237–326.

10 'It is precisely in breaking with their own cultural norms in the act of conversion that these Christians became social outsiders: πάροικοι and παρεπίδημοι' (Dryden, *Theology,* p. 129 [his italics]). This is directed against Elliott's view of this terminology, which he takes to be a literal statement of the readers' social position (John H. Elliott, *A Home for the Homeless: A Social-Scientific Criticism of 1 Peter, Its Situation and Strategy, with a New Introduction* (Philadelphia: Fortress Press, 2nd edn, 1990), pp. 21–73, 88–95). For other critical discussions of this view, see Paul J. Achtemeier, 'Newborn Babes and Living Stones: Literal and Figurative in 1 Peter', in *To Touch the Text: Biblical and Related Studies in Honor of Joseph A. Fitzmyer,* S.J. (ed. Maurya P. Horgan and Paul J. Kobelski; New York: Crossroad, 1989), pp. 207–36 (at pp. 216–18, 228); Steven Richard Bechtler, *Following In His Steps: Suffering, Community, and Christology in 1 Peter,* SBLDS 162 (Atlanta, GA: Scholars, 1998), pp. 64–83; Moses Chin, 'A Heavenly Home for the Homeless: Aliens and Strangers in 1 Peter', *TynBul* 42.1 (1991), pp. 96–112; Dryden, *Theology,*

pp. 127–30; Reinhard Feldmeier, *Die Christen als Fremde: Die Metapher der Fremde in der antiken Welt, im Urchristentum und in 1.Petrusbrief*, WUNT 64 (Tübingen: Mohr Siebeck, 1992), pp. 203–10; David G. Horrell, 'Aliens and Strangers? The Socioeconomic Location of the Addressees of 1 Peter', in *Engaging Economics: New Testament Scenarios and Early Christian Reception* (ed. Bruce W. Longenecker and Kelly D. Liebengood; Grand Rapids, MI/Cambridge: Eerdmans, 2009), pp. 176–202; Jason Lim, 'The Use of the Designations "Visiting Strangers and Resident Aliens" in 1 Peter within the Greco-Roman Context', *Jian Dao* 34 (2010), pp. 217–39; Troy W. Martin, *Metaphor and Composition in 1 Peter*, SBLDS 131 (Atlanta, GA: Scholars, 1992), pp. 188–92; Torrey Seland, *Strangers in the Light: Philonic Perspectives on Christian Identity in 1 Peter*, BIS 76 (Leiden: Brill, 2005), pp. 39–78; Williams, *Persecution*, pp. 97–104.

11 Udo Schnelle, *Theology of the New Testament* (trans. M. Eugene Boring; Grand Rapids, MI: Baker Academic, 2009), p. 604.

12 '[A]n important aim of 1 Peter [is] to present the addressees with a self-identity by which to legitimate and understand their existence as minority communities amid a hostile society' (Bechtler, *Following*, p. 136). Cf. Green, *1 Peter*, pp. 14, 15, 46, 201; Nijay K. Gupta, 'A Spiritual House of Royal Priests, Chosen and Honored: The Presence and Function of Cultic Imagery in 1 Peter', *PRSt* 36.1 (2009), pp. 61–76 (at p. 65); David G. Horrell, *1 Peter*, New Testament Guides (London: T&T Clark, 2008), pp. 52, 58, 70–73, 112–13; David G. Horrell, '"Race," "Nation," "People": Ethnic Identity-Construction in 1 Peter 2.9', *NTS* 58.1 (2012), pp. 123–43 (at p. 142); Edgar Krentz, 'Creating a Past: 1 Peter and Christian Identity', *BR* 53 (2008), pp. 41–57 (at pp. 48–9); Ralph P. Martin, '1 Peter', in *The Theology of the Letters of James, Peter, and Jude* (Andrew Chester and Ralph P. Martin; Cambridge: CUP, 1994), pp. 90, 100.

13 '[T]he author is telling a single story that is made up of two interconnected stories, one is the grand narrative of God's saving work (with a particular emphasis on the death and resurrection of Jesus) and the other is the story of the readers (with a particular emphasis on their conversion and present sufferings)' (Dryden, *Theology*, p. 69.) On the role of embedded narrative in 1 Peter, see M. Eugene Boring, *1 Peter*, ANTC (Nashville, TN: Abingdon, 1999), pp. 183–201; M. Eugene Boring, 'Narrative Dynamics in First Peter: The Function of Narrative World', in *Reading First Peter with New*

Eyes: Methodological Reassessments of the Letter of First Peter, LNTS 364 (ed. Robert L. Webb and Betsy Bauman-Martin; London: T&T Clark, 2007), pp. 7–40; Dryden, *Theology*, pp. 55–89; Joel B. Green, 'Narrating the Gospel in 1 and 2 Peter', *Int* 60.3 (2006), pp. 262–77; Abson Prédestin Joseph, *A Narratological Reading of 1 Peter*, LNTS 440 (London: T&T Clark, 2012), pp. 33–62, 172–82.

14 Schutter, *Hermeneutic*, p. 43; Green, *1 Peter*, p. 233 ('teems'); Bauckham, 'James, 1 and 2 Peter, Jude', p. 309 ('lavish'); Carson, '1 Peter', p. 1015 ('rich profusion'); Horrell, *1 Peter*, p. 31 ('saturated'); Elliott, *1 Peter*, p. 16 ('abundant use'); Paul J. Achtemeier, *1 Peter*, Hermeneia (Minneapolis: Fortress, 1996), p. 12 ('abounds').

15 Edward Gordon Selwyn, *The First Epistle of St. Peter: The Greek Text with Introduction, Notes and Essays* (London: Macmillan, 1952), p. 24 ('deeply steeped'); Fika J. van Rensburg, 'The Old Testament in the Salvific Metaphors in 1 Peter' in *The Catholic Epistles and the Tradition*, BETL 176 (ed. J. Schlosser; Leuven: Leuven University, 2004), pp. 381–96 (at p. 390 ['soaked in the scriptural heritage of Israel']). Cf. Boring, *1 Peter*, p. 95 ('obviously saturated with the biblical text'); James D.G. Dunn, *Beginning from Jerusalem, Christianity in the Making*, Volume 2 (Grand Rapids, MI: Eerdmans, 2009), p. 1155 ('its immersion in Scripture').

16 Leonhard Goppelt, *A Commentary on 1 Peter* (ed. Ferdinand Hahn; trans. and augmented by John E. Alsup; Grand Rapids, MI: Eerdmans, 1993), p. 35.

17 Ernest Best, *1 Peter*, NCB (London: Oliphants, 1971), p. 29; Feldmeier, *Peter*, p. 26; Martin, *1 Peter*, p. 88; Steve Moyise, 'Isaiah in 1 Peter', *Isaiah in the New Testament* (ed. Steve Moyise and Maarten J.J. Menken; London: T&T Clark, 2005), pp. 175–88 (at p. 175, where he notes that 'the average number of verses per quotation is: Romans, 7.2; Hebrews, 8.1; 1 Peter, 8.7' [n. 1]).

18 Osborne, 'L'utilisation', p. 65 (nine); Schutter, *Hermeneutic*, pp. 36–7 (nine); Peter H. Davids, 'The Use of Second Temple Traditions in 1 and 2 Peter and Jude', in *The Catholic Epistles and the Tradition*, BETL 176 (ed. J. Schlosser; Leuven: Leuven University, 2004), pp. 409–31 (ten [p. 411]); Jacques Schlosser, 'Ancien Testament et Christologie dans la Prima Petri' in *Études sur la première Lettre de Pierre*, Congrès de l'ACFEB, Paris 1979, Lectio Divina 102 (ed. Charles Perrot; Paris: Cerf, 1980), pp. 65–96 (thirteen [p. 67 n. 17]); Voorwinde, 'Quotations', pp. 4–5 (sixteen); Elliott, p. 13 (eighteen); Steve Moyise, *The Old Testament in the New: An*

Introduction (London: Continuum, 2001), p. 109 (eighteen); Carson, '1 Peter', p. 1015 (about twenty).

[19] Davids finds twenty allusions (Peter H. Davids, *The First Epistle of Peter*, NICNT (Grand Rapids, MI: Eerdmans, 1990), p. 24); Osborne finds twenty-two ('L'utilisation', p. 65); and Schutter finds fifteen 'explicit allusions' and twenty 'implicit allusions' (*Hermeneutic*, pp. 37–8). The most detailed listing finds six 'strong' allusions, thirteen 'significant' allusions, fifteen 'weak' allusions, and seventeen 'echoes' (Woan, *Use*, pp. 269–70). For discussions of what constitutes an 'allusion', see Richard B. Hays, *Echoes of Scripture in the Letters of Paul* (New Haven, CT: Yale University, 1989), pp. 25–32; Steve Moyise, *Evoking Scripture: Seeing the Old Testament in the New* (London: T&T Clark, 2008), pp. 129–30; Stanley E. Porter, 'Allusions and Echoes', in *As It Is Written: Studying Paul's Use of Scripture*, SBL Symposium Series 50 (ed. Stanley E. Porter and Christopher D. Stanley; Atlanta: SBL, 2008), 29–40; Sue Woan, 'The Psalms in 1 Peter' in *The Psalms in the New Testament* (ed. Steve Moyise and Maarten J.J. Menken; London: T&T Clark, 2004), pp. 213–29 (at pp. 213–15); Woan, *Use*, pp. 115–30.

[20] See the discussions in G.K. Beale, *Handbook on the New Testament Use of the Old Testament: Exegesis and Interpretation* (Grand Rapids, MI: Baker Academic, 2012), pp. 31–5 ('echoes'); Elliott, p. 15 ('biblicisms'); Hays, *Echoes*, p. 29 ('echoes'); Jon Paulien, 'Elusive Allusions in the Apocalypse: Two Decades of Research into John's Use of the Old Testament', in *The Intertextuality of the Epistles: Explorations of Theory and Practice, New Testament Monographs* 16 (ed. Thomas L. Brodie, Dennis R. MacDonald and Stanley E. Porter; Sheffield: Sheffield Phoenix, 2006), pp. 61–8 ('echoes'); Porter, 'Allusions and Echoes', pp. 36–9 ('echoes'); Schutter, *Hermeneutic*, pp. 36, 41–3 ('biblicisms').

[21] Carson, '1 Peter', p. 1015. The letter is 'a virtual mosaic of biblical citations and allusions' (Feldmeier, *Peter*, p. 142).

[22] In addition to the commentaries, studies of this passage can be found in Samuel Bénétreau, 'Évangile et Prophétie: Un texte original (1 P 1,10-12) peut-il éclairer un texte difficile (2 P 1,16-21)?', *Bib* 86.2 (2005), pp.174–91; Jean Calloud, 'Ce que parler veut dire', in *Études sur la première Lettre de Pierre*, Congrès de l'ACFEB, Paris 1979, *Lectio Divina* 102 (ed. Charles Perrot; Paris: Cerf, 1980), pp. 175–206; Steve Moyise, *Evoking Scripture: Seeing the Old Testament in the New* (London: T&T Clark, 2008), pp. 78–95; Schutter, *Hermeneutic*, pp. 100–123.

[23] The πνεῦμα χριστοῦ (1:11) is best seen as a reference to the Holy Spirit as Christ-centred in his ministry (Davids, *Peter*, 62; Wayne A. Grudem, *The First Epistle of Peter: An Introduction and Commentary*, TNTC [Grand Rapids, MI: Eerdmans, 1988], p. 69), not to the activity of the pre-existent Christ (*pace* Achtemeier, *1 Peter*, p. 109f; Charles Bigg, *A Critical and Exegetical Commentary on the Epistles of St. Peter and St. Jude*, ICC (Edinburgh: T&T Clark, 2nd edn, 1902], pp. 108–10; Boring, *1 Peter*, p. 66f; Norbert Brox, *Der erste Petrusbrief*, EKKNT (Zurich: Benziger/ Neukirchen-Vluyn: Neukirchener, 1979], p. 70; Goppelt, *1 Peter*, p. 99 n. 84; J.N.D. Kelly, *A Commentary on the Epistles of Peter and Jude*, BNTC (London: Adam & Charles Black, 1969], pp. 60–61; Frank J. Matera, *New Testament Christology* (Louisville, KY: WJK, 1999], p. 176; Miller, *Peter*, p, 144–5; Karl Hermann Schelkle, *Die Petrusbriefe, Die Judasbrief*, HTKNT (Freiburg: Herder, 2nd edn, 1964], p. 41; Schlosser, 'Ancien Testament', pp. 94–5; Jacques Schlosser, *La première Épître de Pierre*, Commentaire biblique: Nouveau Testament 21 (Paris: Cerf, 2011], p. 79; Donald P. Senior, C.P., *1 Peter*, Sacra Pagina (Collegeville, MN: Liturgical, 2003], pp. 34, 38). Peter's point is that 'the Spirit who was the agent of revelation to the prophets of old is the same Spirit of Christ known to the first-century church' (Jobes, p. 101).

[24] Given the way he uses the OT, by προφῆται Peter is probably referring to all of the biblical authors and not just to the prophets as such (Achtemeier, *1 Peter*, p. 108 n. 42; Bauckham, 'James, 1 and 2 Peter, Jude', p. 310; Samuel Bénétreau , *La Première Épître de Pierre* (Vaux-sur-Seine: Edifac, 2nd edn, 1992), p. 93; Miller, *Peter*, p. 143; Schutter, *Hermeneutic*, p. 178; Senior, *1 Peter*, p. 38). Although some have argued that Peter is referring to Christian prophets (James D.G. Dunn, *Christology in the Making: A New Testament Inquiry into the Origins of the Doctrine of the Incarnation* [Philadelphia: Westminster, 1980], p. 159; Selwyn, *St. Peter*, pp. 134, 262–7; Duane Warden, 'The Prophets of 1 Peter 1:10-12', *ResQ* 31 [1989], pp. 1–12), the νῦν of v. 12 serves to locate these prophets in the past, before the era of the gospel. For a critique of this 'Christian prophets' view, see Best, *1 Peter*, pp.83–4; Mark Dubis, *Messianic Woes in First Peter: Suffering and Eschatology in 1 Peter 4:12-19*, Studies in Biblical Literature 33 (New York: Peter Lang, 2002), pp. 108–10; Paul A. Himes, 'Peter and the Prophetic Word: The Theology of Prophecy Traced Through Peter's Sermons and Epistles', *BBR* 21.2 (2011), pp. 227–44 (at pp. 235–7); Thomas R. Schreiner, *1, 2 Peter, Jude*, NAC (Nashville, TN: Broadman & Holman, 2003), pp. 72–3.

[25] That the Spirit was sent from heaven (ἀποσταλέντι ἀπ' οὐρανου) 'reinforces the divine origin and warrant of the message the Christians have received' (Senior, *1 Peter*, p. 4; cf. Bénétreau, *Pierre*, p. 95; Spicq, *Pierre*, p. 57).

[26] Peter's τὰ ἐις Χριστὸν παθήματα has been understood in several ways. For some, it includes the sufferings of Christians along with those of Christ (Bénétreau, *Pierre*, p. 54; Best, *1 Peter*, pp. 83f.; John Calvin, *The Epistle of Paul the Apostle to the Hebrews and the First and Second Epistles of Saint Peter*, Calvin's New Testament Commentaries, Volume 12 [Grand Rapids, MI: Eerdmans, 1963 {1551}]), p. 240; Lewis R. Donelson, *I & II Peter and Jude: A Commentary*, New Testament Library [Louisville, KY: WJK, 2010], p. 37; Dubis, *Woes*, pp. 113–17; Jobes, *1 Peter*, p. 105; Miller, *Peter*, p. 145–7). Others have taken it to mean 'the sufferings of the Christward road' (Selwyn, *St. Peter*, pp. 136, 263; cf. also Boring, *1 Peter*, pp. 67–8 ['sufferings endured for Christ']; Dunn, *Christology*, p. 159). Still others have understood the ἐις temporally: 'the sufferings until Messiah' (Kelly D. Liebengood, Zechariah 9–14 as the Substructure of 1 Peter's Eschatological Program [unpublished Ph.D. thesis, St Andrews University, 2010], p. 171 [taking it to refer to Jesus' return]; Robert L. Webb, 'Intertexture and Rhetorical Strategy in First Peter's Apocalyptic Discourse: A Study in Sociorhetorical Interpretation', in *Reading First Peter with New Eyes: Methodological Reassessments of the Letter of First Peter*, LNTS 364 [ed. Robert L. Webb and Betsy Bauman-Martin; London: T&T Clark, 2007], pp. 72–110 [at pp. 92–3]). Some of those who think that the expression involves believers' sufferings see them as part of the 'messianic woes' (see Dubis, *Woes*, pp. 110–3, referring to earlier studies; Webb, 'Intertexture', pp. 92–93). There are two significant problems with this understanding of τὰ ἐις Χριστὸν παθήματα. First, v. 12 makes it clear that these sufferings (and the subsequent glories) are the subject of the gospel – and the gospel concerns the redemptive sufferings of Jesus, not the sufferings of his people (Achtemeier, *1 Peter*, p. 110). Second, it is difficult to see why the ἐις Χριστόν of v. 11 should be understood any differently from the εἰς ὑμᾶς of v. 10: it thus indicates that these sufferings were 'destined for' Christ (F.J.A. Hort, *The First Epistle of Peter, I.1 – II.17: The Greek Text with Introductory Lecture, Commentary, and Additional Notes* [London: Macmillan, 1898], p. 54; cf. Achtemeier, *1 Peter*, p. 110; Francis Wright Beare, *The First Epistle of Peter: The Greek Text with Introduction and Notes* [Oxford: Basil Blackwell, 3rd edn, 1970], p. 91; Best, *1 Peter*, p. 81; Dubis, *Woes*, pp. 112f.; J.E. Huther, *Critical and Exegetical*

Handbook to the General Epistles of Peter and Jude [Edinburgh: T&T Clark, 1881], p. 73; Jobes, *1 Peter*, pp. 99–100; Kelly, *Peter*, p. 61; Michaels, *1 Peter*, p. 44; Spicq, *Pierre*, p. 56).

27 Note Luke 24:26, and also 1 Cor. 15:3–4 (Jesus' death and resurrection are κατὰ τὰς γραφάς).

28 Bigg, *Peter*, p. 110; Grudem, *Peter*, p. 69; Selwyn, *St. Peter*, p. 137; Witherington, *Peter*, p. 84.

29 Davids, *Peter*, p. 61.

30 Brox, *Petrusbrief*, p. 72; Barth L. Campbell, *Honor, Shame, and the Rhetoric of 1 Peter*, SBLDS 160 (Atlanta, GA: Scholars, 1998), pp. 55–7; Dryden, *Theology*, p. 80; Feldmeier, *Peter*, p. 93.

31 Deut. 4:37; 7:7; 10:15; 14:2; LXX Pss 32:12; 104:5–6,43; 105:4–5; 134:4. This reads ἐκλεκτοί in 1 Pet. 1:1 as substantival rather than adjectival, agreeing with Achtemeier, *1 Peter*, p. 81; Brox, *Petrusbrief*, p. 56; Green, *1 Peter*, p. 14 n.5; Jobes, *1 Peter*, pp. 67, 75; Michaels, *1 Peter*, p. 7; Schlosser, *Pierre*, p. 50.

32 See Deut. 28:25; 30:4; Ps. 146:2 LXX; Isa. 49:6; Jer. 15:7; 41:17 LXX; Dan. 12:2.

33 Achtemeier, *1 Peter*, p. 72.

34 Francis Agnew argues that, like the blood, the obedience concerned is that of Jesus Christ, displayed supremely in his death ('1 Peter 1:2: An Alternative Translation', *CBQ* 45 [1983], pp. 68–73). Although some commentators have endorsed this approach (Elliott, *1 Peter*, p. 319; Green, *1 Peter*, p. 20; Green, 'Faithful Witness', pp. 290–91; Abson Prédestin Joseph, *A Narratological Reading of 1 Peter*, LNTS 440 (London: T&T Clark, 2012), p. 60 n.133; Liebengood, *Zechariah*, pp. 152f.; Earl J. Richard, *Reading 1 Peter, Jude, and 2 Peter: A Literary and Theological Commentary* [Macon, GA: Smith & Helwys, 2000], p. 32), the case against it is strong (see esp. Sydney H.T. Page, 'Obedience and Blood-Sprinkling in 1 Peter 1:2', *WTJ* 72.2 [2010], pp. 291–8; note also the arguments of Schreiner, *Peter*, p. 54–6).

35 His is the view taken in most commentaries. See also Carson, '1 Peter', pp. 1016–17; Paul E. Deterding, 'Exodus Motifs in First Peter', *ConcJ* 7 (1981), p. 60; Victor P. Furnish, 'Elect Sojourners in Christ: An Approach to the Theology of I Peter', *PSTJ* 28 (1975), pp. 1–11 (at p. 6); Page, 'Obedience', pp. 295–7; J.W. Pryor, 'First Peter and the New Covenant (I)', *RTR* 45.1 (1986), pp. 1–4 (at pp. 2–3).

36 Joel B. Green, 'Faithful Witness in the Diaspora: The Holy Spirit and the Exiled People of God According to 1 Peter', in *The Holy Spirit and*

Christian Origins: Essays in Honour of James D.G. Dunn (ed. Graham N. Stanton, Bruce W. Longenecker and Stephen C. Barton; Grand Rapids, MI: Eerdmans, 2004), pp. 282–95 (at p. 288 [his italics]).

[37] For discussions of NT typology, see David L. Baker, *Two Testaments, One Bible: The Theological Relationship between the Old and New Testaments* (Downers Grove: IVP, 3rd edn, 2010), pp. 169–89; E. Earle Ellis, *The Old Testament in Early Christianity: Canon and Interpretation in the Light of Modern Research* (Grand Rapids, MI: Baker, 1992), pp. 61–63, 105–9, 141–57; Leonhard Goppelt, *Typos: The Typological Interpretation of the Old Testament in the New* (trans. Donald H. Madvig; Grand Rapids, MI: Eerdmans, 1982).

[38] J. Ross Wagner, 'Faithfulness and Fear, Stumbling and Salvation: Receptions of LXX Isaiah 8:11-18 in the New Testament', in *The Word Leaps the Gap: Essays in Scripture and Theology in Honor of Richard B. Hays* (ed. J. Ross Wagner, C. Kavin Rowe and A. Katherine Grieb; Grand Rapids, MI: Eerdmans, 2008), pp. 76–106 (at p. 94).

[39] Schutter, *Hermeneutic*, p. 43 (the numbers given refer to the total of quotations and allusions combined).

[40] E. Earle Ellis finds ninety-three quotations (*Paul's Use of the Old Testament* [Edinburgh: Oliver & Boyd, 1957], p. 11), while Moises Silva finds one hundred and seven ('Old Testament in Paul', DPL, p. 631).

[41] See the table in Steve Moyise, *Paul and Scripture* (Grand Rapids, MI: Baker Academic, 2010), pp. 131–2.

[42] W. Bornemann, 'Der erste Petrusbrief – eine Taufrede des Silvanus?', *ZNW* 19 (1919–20), pp. 143–65 (at pp. 147–50). Several more recent studies also regard Psalm 34 as playing a significant role in this letter: Bénétreau, *Pierre*, pp. 49–50; Michael J. Gilmour, 'Crass Casualty or Purposeful Pain? Psalm 34's Influence on Peter's First Letter', *WW* 24.4 (2004), pp. 404–11; Eric James Gréaux, 'The Lord Delivers Us: An Examination of the Function of Psalm 34 in 1 Peter', *RevExp* 106.4 (2009), pp. 603–13; Gene L. Green, 'The Use of the Old Testament for Christian Ethics in 1 Peter', *TynBul* 41.2 (1990), pp. 276–89 (at pp. 280–82); Karen H. Jobes, 'Got Milk? Septuagint Psalm 33 and the Interpretation of 1 Peter 2:1-3', *WTJ* 64.1 (2002), pp. 1–14; Klyne R. Snodgrass, 'I Peter II. 1-10: Its Formation and Literary Affinities', *NTS* 24 (1978), pp. 97–106 (at pp. 102–3).

[43] Schutter, *Hermeneutic*, p. 48. An 'iterative allusion resumes or anticipates part of an OT text cited elsewhere by the author' (p. 36). The explicit allusion he mentions is to Ps. 33:9 LXX in 1 Pet. 2:3, and the

very weak implicit allusion is to Ps. 33:6 in 2:4. He thus insists that Bornemann's conclusions 'outrun the evidence' (*Hermeneutic*, p. 46).

44 Woan, *Use*.

45 Woan, *Use*, pp. 212f. These consist of two quotations (Ps. 34:8 in 1 Pet. 2:3, and 34:13–17 in 3:10–12), one significant allusion (Ps. 34:13 in 2:1), and five weak allusions (Ps. 34:11 in 1:14; 34:4,7,9 in 1:17c; 34:7,9 in 2:17b; 34:4,7,9,19–21 in 3:6b; and 34:17 in 5:7) (Woan, Use, pp. 269–70).

46 Both words (κακός, δόλος) are also found together in Ps. 9:27–8 LXX.

47 It is arguable that the other psalm Peter cites (Ps. 117:22 LXX in 2:7) has had at least as much influence as Ps. 33 LXX.

48 Liebengood, *Zechariah*, esp. pp. 166–202.

49 See chs 3 and 4 respectively.

50 See chs 5 and 6 respectively.

51 See the evaluative comments of Karen H. Jobes, 'The Minor Prophets in James, 1 & 2 Peter and Jude', in *The Minor Prophets in the New Testament* (ed. Maarten J.J. Menken and Steve Moyise; London: T&T Clark, 2009), pp. 135–53 (at pp. 144–5).

52 Frederick W. Danker, 'I Peter 1.24–2.17 – A Consolatory Pericope', ZNW 58 (1967), pp. 93–102 (at pp. 98–9). Dubis (*Woes*, pp. 153f.) is another who sees several allusions to Malachi in 1 Peter. On a more limited scale, Dennis E. Johnson sees the influence of Mal. 3:1–5 in 1 Pet. 4:12–19 ('Fire in God's House: Imagery from Malachi 3 in Peter's Theology of Suffering [1 Pet 4:12–19]', *JETS* 29.3 (1986), pp. 285–94). Since the parallels he finds are conceptual rather than verbal, it is difficult to see how the reader is meant to recognize a link with Malachi in particular. For a critique of Johnson's approach, see Liebengood, *Zechariah*, pp. 121–2.

53 These are in 1:6 [this should probably be 1:7] (Mal. 3:3); 1:17 (Mal. 1:6); 2:17 (Mal. 2:10); 3:9 (Mal. 2:2); and 4:17 (Mal. 3:1). It has to be said that none of these proposed links is particularly close or obvious.

54 These concern God's glory among the nations (2:11–12 [Mal. 1:11–14]); God's judgment (2:12 [Mal. 3:13–18]); respect for authority (2:13–17 [Mal. 1]); slaves of God (2:16 [Mal. 3:17,18,24]); and fear of God (2:17 [Mal. 1:6; 2:5; 3:16–17]).

55 Noted by Bénétreau, *Pierre*, p. 129; Goppelt, *1 Peter*, p. 149 n.64; Grudem, *Peter*, p. 111; Jobes, 'Minor Prophets', p. 143 (this is the only allusion to Malachi that she finds in 1 Peter); Marc E. Kohler, 'La Communauté des Chrétiens selon la première Épître de Pierre', *RTP* 114 (1982), pp. 1–21 (at p. 17 n.53); Schelkle, *Petrusbriefe*, p. 65; Schreiner, *Peter*, p. 115; Selwyn, *St. Peter*, p. 167; Spicq, *Pierre*, p. 92.

[56] Sharon Clark Pearson, *The Christological and Rhetorical Properties of 1 Peter*, Studies in Bible and Early Christianity 45 (Lewiston, NY: Edwin Mellen, 2001), p. 224. This approach is developed in some detail in pp. 231–68.

[57] *Properties*, 221. In his 1981 study, John H. Elliott had drawn attention to the abundance of thematic similarities between Isaiah 40-55 and 1 Peter (*Home*, 125, 155 (n.66)).

[58] 'His indebtedness to Isaiah is clear' (Moyise, 'Isaiah', p. 188); cf. Osborne, 'L'utilisation', pp. 73, 76; Woan, *Use*, p. 213.

[59] Schutter, *Hermeneutic*, p. 43.

[60] Dubis, *Woes*, p. 3; cf. p. 46.

[61] Dubis, *Woes*, p. 187; cf. pp. 46, 59.

[62] Dubis, *Woes*, p. 48.

[63] Dubis' work is examined and critiqued in Markus Theron Klausli, *The Question of the Messianic Woes in 1 Peter* (unpublished PhD dissertation, Dallas Theological Seminary, 2007).

[64] See especially Andrew M. Mbuvi, *Temple, Exile and Identity in 1 Peter*, LNTS 345 (London: T&T Clark, 2007), pp. 28–46. Note, too, Martin's argument that the 'controlling metaphor of 1 Peter is the Diaspora' (*Metaphor*, p. 144).

[65] This is noted by Dubis (*Woes*, p. 62 n. 30), but he seems not to recognize that this undermines the suggested parallel between Peter's readers and Israel-in-exile. Elsewhere he claims that God 'uses their opponents' unjust persecution in order to justly judge them as sinners' (*Woes*, 157). It is difficult to find this view in 1 Peter, however. God is protecting the readers during their sufferings (1:5), not punishing them by means of those sufferings. And the judgement that begins with God's 'house' (4:17) is not punitive but purifying (1:6–7).

[66] Liebengood, *Zechariah*, p. 130 (his italics). There are two strands in Dubis' exposition of this point. On the one hand he asserts that the letter 'has an answer for those who wonder when restoration will occur: restoration from exile has happened in Christ.' (*Woes*, 48; cf. 187). But on the other hand, he says that 'although the exile has not yet ended . . . the restoration is already underway.' (*Woes*, 123). He finds a resolution of this apparent contradiction in the 'already but not yet' character of 'inaugurated eschatology' (*Woes*, 55, 123). However, it is difficult to see how Peter's readers can be still in exile while they are also enjoying restoration from exile. At this point we must surely

conclude that the exile/restoration model has broken down. Cf. Klausli, *Question*, 126.

[67] Dubis, *Woes*, pp. 48, 59, 116, 129, 188.

[68] Mbuvi, *Temple*, pp. 30–33. On this point, see Dubis, *Woes*, pp. 49, 51.

[69] Mbuvi, *Temple*, p. 43. He makes a similar claim in the following: 'The exile motif as used in 1 Peter also incorporates the exodus motif so that the quotations from Exodus have to be understood in light of their reinterpretation within the Second Temple Jewish exile matrix' (*Temple*, p. 30). But again, this seems to have things back-to-front, for the exodus provides the framework within which the exile/restoration pattern is understood.

[70] Mbuvi appears to recognize this when he says that '1 Peter is able to use the Exodus "echoes" to explain the work of Christ as the final liberation from bondage (1.1–4,5–7,18–25) for the Christian believers.' (*Temple*, p. 42).

[71] Achtemeier, *1 Peter*, p. 139; Beare, *Peter*, p. 111; Bénétreau, *Pierre*, pp. 112f.; Brox, *Petrusbrief*, p. 87; Carson, '1 Peter', p. 1019; Elliott, *1 Peter*, pp. 391, 393; Goppelt, *1 Peter*, p. 127; Green, *1 Peter*, p. 54; Grudem, *Peter*, p. 92; Douglas Harink, *1 & 2 Peter*, Brazos Theological Commentary on the Bible (Grand Rapids, MI: Brazos, 2009), pp. 62–3; Hort, *Peter*, p. 93; Jobes, *1 Peter*, pp. 124–5; Kelly, *Peter*, p. 81; Michaels, *1 Peter*, p. 80; Richard, *Peter*, pp. 72, 73; Schelkle, *Petrusbriefe*, p. 53; Spicq, *Pierre*, p. 76.

[72] See especially Jobes, *1 Peter*, pp. 126–30.

[73] For studies of this passage, see Ernest Best, 'I Peter II 4-10 – A Reconsideration', *NovT* 11 (1969), pp. 270–93; John H. Elliott, *The Elect and the Holy: An Exegetical Examination of I Peter 2:4-10 and the Phrase* βασίλειον ἱεράτευμα, NovTSup XII (Leiden: Brill, 1966); Snodgrass, 'I Peter', pp. 97–106.

[74] Paul combines and quotes these texts in Rom. 9:33 (on which see Douglas A. Oss, 'The Interpretation of the "Stone" Passages by Peter and Paul: A Comparative Study', *JETS* 32.2 [1989], pp. 181–200). Their use both there and here suggests that they played a significant role in the early church's evangelistic and catechetical use of the OT. On Peter's use of Isa. 8 in this passage, see (in addition to the commentaries) Wagner, 'Faithfulness', pp. 91–4. On the background to this stone-image, see Norman Hillyer, ' "Rock-Stone" Imagery in 1 Peter', *TynBul* 22 (1971), pp. 58–81.

[75] This is implied by the present tense of the participles: προσερχόμενοι (2:4); πιστεύων (2:6); πιστεύουσιν (2:7): Beare, *Peter*, p. 119; Bénétreau,

Pierre, p. 122; Elliott, *1 Peter*, p. 409; Grudem, *Peter*, p. 98; Hort, *Peter*, p. 105; Miller, *Peter*, pp. 185, 194; Spicq, *Pierre*, p. 82.

76 On the translation and interpretation of 2:7a, see Bechtler, *Following*, pp. 187–8; Bigg, *Peter*, p. 131; Campbell, *Honor*, pp. 85–7; Grudem, *Peter*, pp. 104–5; Huther, *Peter*, p. 114; Jobes, *1 Peter*, pp. 152f.; Michaels, *1 Peter*, p. 104; Schutter, *Hermeneutic*, pp. 133–5.

77 Elliott, *Elect*, p. 143; cf. Kohler, 'Communauté', pp. 15, 17.

78 John H. Elliott, 'The Rehabilitation of an Exegetical Step-Child: 1 Peter in Recent Research', in *Perspectives on First Peter* (ed. Charles H. Talbert; Eugene, OR: Wipf & Stock, 2010 [1986]), pp. 3–16 (at p. 11) (formerly in *JBL* 95.2 (1976), pp. 243–54).

79 In addition to the quotation of Isa. 53:9 in 2:22, Peter refers to Isa. 53:7 in 2:23, to 53:4,12 in 2:24a, to 53:5 in 2:24b, and to 53:6 in 2:25. See the diagram in Schutter, *Hermeneutic*, p. 139. On this passage, see John H. Elliott, 'Backward and Forward "In His Steps": Following Jesus from Rome to Raymond and Beyond. The Tradition, Redaction, and Reception of 1 Peter 2:18-25', in *Discipleship in the New Testament* (ed. Fernando F. Segovia; Philadelphia: Fortress Press, 1985), pp. 184–209; Thomas P. Osborne, 'Guide Lines for Christian Suffering: A Source-Critical and Theological Study of 1 Peter 2,21-25', *Bib* 64 (1983), pp. 381–408; Schlosser, 'Ancien Testament', pp. 83–93.

80 Achtemeier, *1 Peter*, p. 192; Bechtler, *Following*, pp. 152–3; Boring, *1 Peter*, p. 117; Brox, *Petrusbrief*, p. 128; Elliott, 'Backward', pp. 187–9; Goppelt, *1 Peter*, p. 191; Green, *1 Peter*, pp. 77–8, 82; Grudem, *Peter*, p. 128; Jobes, *1 Peter*, pp. 180, 187; Michaels, *1 Peter*, pp. 135, 152; Richard, *1 Peter*, pp. 116–7; Schreiner, *Peter*, p. 134; Senior, *1 Peter*, p. 75.

81 Elliott, 'Backward', p. 187; cf. his 'Jesus Christ the model is Jesus Christ the means' ('Backward', p. 202). Cf. also Achtemeier, *1 Peter*, p. 203; Bechtler, *Following*, p. 193; Bénétreau, *Pierre*, p. 161; Goppelt, *1 Peter*, p. 206; Green, *1 Peter*, p. 83; Miller, *Peter*, pp. 225f.; Schlosser, *Pierre*, p. 172; Schlosser, 'Ancien Testament', pp. 91f., 93; Spicq, *Pierre*, pp. 112f.

82 Green, *1 Peter*, p. 83. Cf. Matera, *Christology*, p. 179.

83 Bechtler, *Following*, p. 194; Elliott, *1 Peter*, pp. 412, 448; Elliott, 'Backward', p. 199.

84 On which see Wagner, 'Faithfulness', pp. 94–6.

85 Wagner, 'Faithfulness', p. 96 (footnote omitted).

86 There is, for example, an important allusion to Isa. 11:2 in 4:14 (on which see Dubis, *Woes*, pp. 119–21, 123; Moyise, 'Isaiah', pp. 185–6).

[87] See Bénétreau, *Pierre*, pp. 66–8; M.-E. Boismard, 'Une liturgie baptismale dans la Prima Petri', *RB* 63 (1956), pp. 182–208 (at pp.190–6); Raymond E. Brown, S.S. and John P. Meier, *Antioch and Rome: New Testament Cradles of Catholic Christianity* (New York: Paulist, 1983), pp. 133–4; Deterding, 'Motifs', pp. 58–67; Joseph, *Reading*, pp. 59–61, 70–71, 73; J.W. Pryor, 'First Peter and the New Covenant (I)', *RTR* 45.1 (1986), pp. 1–4; J.W. Pryor, 'First Peter and the New Covenant (II)', *RTR* 45.2 (1986), pp. 44–51; Schlosser, 'Ancien Testament', p. 66.

[88] The quotation is from Lev. 19:2. The same call is given in Lev. 11:44–5; 20:26.

[89] See e.g. Num. 36:2; Deut. 2:12; 12:9–10; Josh. 11:23; Pss 135:10–12; 136:17–22; Jer. 3:18–19.

[90] See Exod. 6:6; 15:13; Deut. 7:8; 9:26; 13:5; 15:15; 21:8; 24:18; 2 Sam. 7:23; 1 Chron. 17:21; Neh. 1:10; Pss 74:2; 77:15; 78:42; 106:10; 111:9; Isa. 63:8; Mic. 6:4.

[91] See e.g. Exod. 29:38; Lev. 1:10; 4:32; 12:6; 23:12,18; Num. 6:14; 28:3,9,11,19,27; 29:2,8,13. It has been claimed that 1:19 points to Christ as the 'new Passover Lamb' (so Deterding, 'Motifs', p. 58; see also Beare, *Peter*, p. 106; Best, *1 Peter*, p. 90; Boismard, 'Liturgie', p. 193; Boring, *1 Peter*, p. 83; Campbell, *Honor*, pp. 73–4; F.L. Cross, I. *Peter: A Paschal Liturgy* (London: Mowbray, 1954), pp. 24f.; Davids, *Peter*, p. 72f.; Donelson, *Peter*, p. 48; Dubis, *Woes*, p. 50 n.8; Goppelt, *1 Peter*, p. 116; Green, *1 Peter*, p. 41; Gupta, 'Spiritual House', p. 69; Hort, *Peter*, p. 77; Joseph, *Reading*, p. 88; Kelly, *Peter*, p. 75; Lamau, *Chrétiens*, p. 115; Liebengood, *Zechariah*, pp. 153, 173; Martin, '1 Peter', p. 109; Mbuvi, *Temple*, pp. 32–3, 72, 84–5, 132–3; Pearson, *Properties*, p. 106f.; Wolfgang Schrage, 'Der erste Petrusbrief' in Horst Balz and Wolfgang Schrage, *Die "Katholischen" Briefe: Die Briefe des Jakobus, Petrus, Johannes und Judas*, NTD 10 (Göttingen: Vandenhoeck & Ruprecht, 1973), pp. 59–117 (at p. 77); Selwyn, *St. Peter*, p. 146; Senior, *1 Peter*, pp. 44, 46; J.W.C. Wand, *The General Epistles of St. Peter and St. Jude*, Westminster Commentaries (London: Methuen, 1934), p. 56). The major problem with this view is that Exod. 12 speaks only of a πρόβατον τέλειον (v. 5) and does not use either of the key terms ἀμνός or ἄμωμος. (The third term ἄσπιλος does not occur at all in the LXX.)

[92] Exod. 14:13; 15:2; Deut. 32:15; 33:29; LXX Ps. 105:4,8,10,21; Isa. 63:8–9.

[93] See esp. LXX Pss 9:14; 12:5; 13:7; 19:5; 20:1; 34:9; 39:16; 50:12; 52:6; 69:4; 70:23; 94:1; 117:15.

[94] Exod. 15:25; 16:4; 20:20; Deut. 4:34; 8:2; 13:3; 33:8.

95 Deut. 26:5 (Israel παρῴκησεν in Egypt); also Ps. 104:23 LXX. Lev. 25:23 refers to Israel as πάροικοι in Canaan (cf. also Deut. 23:7).

96 Num 6:2, 5, 21; 8:7, 21; 11:18; 19:9, 11–12,17; 31:19–24.

97 Not all proposals regarding the exodus-theme are convincing, however – such as the claim that 2:2 alludes to Exod. 1:7 (Danker, 'Consolatory', p. 95).

98 Exod. 16:9; Lev. 9:5; 21:17,18,21,23; Num. 16:40; 18:22; Deut. 4:11; 5:23; 21:5.

99 We find ἀναφέρειν twenty-five times in Leviticus, for example.

100 Exod. 19:5; 23:22; Deut. 7:6; 26:18. The use of this expression is one of several ways in which this passage (Isa. 43:16–21) deliberately recalls the exodus.

101 Gen. 15:13; Lev. 25:23; Deut. 23:7; 26:5; Ps. 104:12,23 LXX. This language is also used of the exile (1 Esd. 5:7; 2 Esd. 8:35) and of this mortal life (1 Chron. 29:15; Ps. 38:12 LXX).

102 Gen. 50:24–5; Exod. 4:31; 13:19.

103 Deut. 32:36; Ps. 104:25 LXX.

104 Num. 27:17; LXX Pss 76:21; 77:52; Is. 63:11.

105 Exod. 23:25; Deut. 11:26–7,29; 28:2,8; 30:1,19; Josh. 8:34.

106 It is found forty-four times in Leviticus and twenty-one times in Numbers.

107 Exod. 16:7–9,12; Num. 17:20,25.

108 Num. 27:7; 32:19; 33:53; 34:14,15; 35:2; 36:3,9; Deut. 3:18; 4:21; 5:31; 11:31; 12:1; 15:4; 19:10,14; 21:23; 24:4; 25:19; 26:1; 29:8; Josh. 12:6–7; 13:6; 14:3,9,14; 17:4–6; 19:1–2,8–9,49; 23:4; 24:30.

109 This is part of the 'creed' Israelites were to recite when offering their firstfruits to YHWH (Deut. 26:6).

110 Lev. 16:29,31; 23:27,29,32.

111 Exod. 3:19; 6:1; 13:3,9,14,16; Deut. 4:34; 5:15; 6:21; 7:8,19; 9:26; 11:2; 26:8; 2 Esd. 11:10; Ps. 135:11–12 LXX; Dan. 9:15.

112 'Peter views the church as being on the march, like Israel in the wilderness' (Goppelt, *Typos*, p. 152). Cf. Max-Alain Chevallier, 'Condition et Vocation des Chrétiens en Diaspora: Remarques exégétiques sur la première épître de Pierre', *RSR* 48 (1974), pp. 387–98 (at p. 391); Kohler, 'Communauté', pp. 7, 18; Lamau, *Chrétiens*, p. 115; Liebengood, *Zechariah*, pp. 124, 126, 128f., 129, 147, 150, 151, 173, 176.

113 'L'Exode d'Israël fournit tous les moyens d'exprimer la condition unique, paradoxale du peuple de Dieu' (Bénétreau, *Pierre*, p. 67 [my translation]).

[114] Bauckham, 'James, 1 and 2 Peter, Jude', p. 313.

[115] Because Peter does not use ἐκκλησία, but refers to his readers as God's λαός (2:9–10), 'laocentric' is a more appropriate term than 'ecclesiocentric'.

[116] Wagner, 'Faithfulness', p. 97.

[117] Goppelt, *Typos*, p. 155.

[118] Green, 1 *Peter*, p. 227.

[119] Bénétreau speaks of this continuity as involving 'one divine plan, one God who speaks, one single salvation, one single, active Spirit . . . one self-same Word' ('Évangile', p. 176: my translation of '*un plan divin, un Dieu qui parle, un seul salut, un seul Esprit agissant . . . une même Parole*').

11. God Has Spoken: The Renegotiation of Scripture in Hebrews

[1] www.internationalstandardbible.com/C/cedar.html (accessed 7 May 2014).

[2] It may be useful to clarify how 'renegotiation' relates to the term used in a previous chapter, 'reschematization': reschematization refers specifically to the adoption of new or altered mental templates in processing data, perhaps in response to a triggering event; renegotiation is a broader term, which may refer to this alteration of mental imagery, or may refer to its impacts on language and interpretation. In this chapter I prefer to use the broader term.

[3] Farzad Sharifian, 'Cultural Linguistics', p. 4: www.academia.edu/606529/Cultural_Linguistics_Farzad_Sharifians_Inaugural_Professorial_Lecture

[4] Sharifian, 'Cultural Linguistics', p. 5 (accessed 7 May 2014).

[5] For an investigation of the varied overlapping factors at work in linguistic change – including the sudden impact of extra-linguistic factors – see *Language Change: The Interplay of Internal, External, and Extra-Linguistic Factors* (ed. Mari C. Jones and Edith Esch; Contributions to the Sociology of Language, 86; Berlin: Walter de Gruyter, 2002). One contributor notes, 'Linguistic influence cannot be studied in isolation from its setting . . . [I]ndividual linguistic features must be viewed more explicitly in terms of their social embedding and evaluation.' Lars Johanson, 'Contact-Induced Changed in a Code-Copying Framework', *Language Change*, pp. 285–313; 306. William Labov

notes that in some instances of linguistic change, the 'triggering event' might be 'an external event impinging on the linguistic process, like the Norman Invasion or World War II – an event outside of the realm of autonomous linguistic explanation'. William Labov, *Principles of Linguistic Change: Cognitive and Cultural Factors* (Oxford: Wiley-Blackwell, 2010), p. 91.

6 One such follower illustrates this transfiguration: '[Augustine] discovered in the Psalms a vast field of biblical prophecy whose fulfilment in Christ brilliantly illumined the contours of Christianity and invited every Christian reader to apprentice themselves to its wisdom . . . Once Augustine read the Psalms in terms of Paul's insights about Christ's crucified human humility, they yielded an unexpectedly rich trove of insights that permanently altered Augustine's Christian faith and reading of Scripture.' Michael Cameron, *Christ Meets Me Everywhere: Augustine's Figurative Exegesis*, Oxford Studies in Historical Theology (Oxford: OUP, 2012), pp. 166, 167.

7 www.bibleinterp.com/opeds/mad357927.shtml (accessed 4 March 2014).

8 Lee Strobel, *Inside the Mind of Unchurched Harry and Mary: How to Reach Friends and Family Who Avoid God and the Church* (Grand Rapids, MI: Zondervan, 2010), pageless e-book edition.

9 This point has, of course, been made before. Bock usefully points out that 'history was read by both [Christian and Jewish] groups in a way that looked for divine patterns of activity that signalled the re-emergence of divine design in salvific events. This feature of pattern is why prophecy is not limited to directly prophetic prediction. Prophecy also includes the noting of a divine pattern or the typological-prophetic reading of the Bible.' Darrell L. Bock, *A Theology of Luke and Acts: Biblical Theology of the New Testament* (Grand Rapids, MI: Zondervan, 2012), p. 412.

10 Utterers, as slightly distinct to mediators. Ken Schenck rightly notes, 'In Hebrews, God primarily speaks his words through various other media.' Ken Schenck, 'God Has Spoken: Hebrews' Theology of the Scriptures' in Richard Bauckham, Daniel R. Driver, Trevor A. Hart and Nathan MacDonald (eds.), *The Epistle to the Hebrews and Christian Theology* (Grand Rapids, Mich.: Eerdmans, 2009), 321–336; 322.

11 This is a slight adjustment of the translation in Robert B. Wright, *The Psalms of Solomon: A Critical Edition of the Greek Text, Jewish and Christian Texts in Contexts and Related Studies*, 1 (London: T&T Clark, 2007),

p. 179; emphasis mine. I have utilized the word 'gloriously' to capture the play on words in the original.

[12] Sam Janse, *'You are My Son': The Reception History of Psalm 2 in Early Judaism and the Early Church, Contributions to Biblical Exegesis & Theology*, 51 (Leuven: Peeters, 2009), p. 54.

[13] Max Turner, *The Holy Spirit and Spiritual Gifts in the New Testament Church and Today* (Peabody, MA: Hendrickson, rev edn, 1996), p. 5.

[14] Turner, *Holy Spirit*, p. 4.

[15] Turner, *Holy Spirit*, p. 3.

[16] Maurice Casey, *Jesus of Nazareth: An Independent Historian's Account of His Life and Teaching* (London: T&T Clark, 2010), p. 177.

[17] The focus on renegotiated conceptualization is what distinguishes the focus of my interest here from that of Fee, who focuses on the 'triadic experience of God as savior', Gordon D. Fee, 'Paul and the Trinity: The Experience of Christ and the Spirit for Paul's Understanding of God (1999)' in *To What End Exegesis? Essays Textual, Exegetical, and Theological* (Grand Rapids, MI: Eerdmans, 2001), pp. 330–50; p. 333; emphasis mine.

[18] Larry Hurtado makes a similar point about the NT more broadly: 'the NT writings vigorously affirm the "one God" stance inherited from the Jewish matrix of earliest Christian faith but also (and with at least equal vigor) affirm especially the nonnegotiable significance of Jesus in belief and devotional practice, and further, frequently refer to the divine Spirit as the mode or agency by which "God" and Jesus are made present and real to believers.' Larry W. Hurtado, *God in New Testament Theology, Library of Biblical Theology* (Nashville, TN: Abingdon, 2010), p. 100.

[19] Schenck, 'God Has Spoken', p. 334.

[20] These include the following: Otto Michel: 1:1 – 4:13; 4:14 – 10:18; 10:19 – 13:25; Wolfgang Nauck: 1:1 – 4:13; 4:14 – 10:31; 10:32 – 13:25; Louis Dussaut: 1:1 – 5:10; 5:11 – 10:39; 11:1 – 13:21/25; Linda Neely: 1:1 – 4:13; 4:14 – 10:18; 10:19 – 13:21; James W. Thompson: 1:1 – 4:13; 4:14 – 10:31; 10:32 – 13:25; Gareth Cockerill: 1:1 – 4:13; 4:14 – 10:18; 10:19 – 12:29.

[21] The overlapping portions (4:14–16 and 10:19–25) serve as transitional dividers, and represent what Guthrie sees as 'the most prominent use of parallelism in the whole book'. George H. Guthrie, *The Structure of Hebrews: A Text-Linguistic Analysis, Biblical Studies Library* (Grand Rapids, MI: Baker, 1998 [original 1994]), p. 35.

[22] Schenck rightly comments, 'with the introduction "someone, somewhere", he distances the human author from the utterance. The text becomes the logos of God even though God is not the literal speaker'. Schenck, 'God Has Spoken', p. 327.

[23] Sharifian, 'Cultural Linguistics', emphasis mine.

12. Reading the New Testament from the Outside

[1] Donald W.B. Robinson, 'Origins and Unresolved Tensions' in *Interpreting God's Plan: Biblical Theology and the Pastor* (ed. R.J. Gibson; Carlisle: Paternoster, 1998), pp. 1–17; 7.

[2] For example, the Australian Fellowship of Evangelical Students, Matthias Media and the catechetical programmes of many key conservative evangelical churches in Australia, the UK, USA and South Africa.

[3] Graeme Goldsworthy, *Gospel and Kingdom* (Rydalmere: Crossroads, 1994) and Vaughan Roberts, *God's Big Picture: Tracing the Story-Line of the Bible* (IL: IVP, 2006).

[4] Graeme Goldsworthy, 'Is Biblical Theology Viable?' in *Interpreting God's Plan*, pp. 18–46; 29. Goldsworthy identifies the work of John Bright, Geerhardus Vos, Edmund Clowney and Willem VanGemeren as representative of this movement.

[5] D.W.B. Robinson. '"The Church" Revisited: An Autobiographical Fragment', in *Donald Robinson: Selected Works, Volume 1: Assembling God's People* (ed. P.G. Bolt and Mark Thompson; Sydney: Moore College, 2008), pp. 257–71; 260.

[6] J.I. Packer, *'Fundamentalism' and the Word of God* (Leicester: IVP, 1958).

[7] Donald Robinson, 'The Gospel and the Kingdom of God' in *Selected Works*, Volume 1, pp. 387–408; 394.

[8] Gabriel Hebert, *Christ the Fulfiller: Three Studies of the Biblical Types, as They Are Presented in the Old and New Testaments* (Sydney: Anglican Truth Society, 1957).

[9] Donald Robinson, 'Jew and Gentile in the New Testament' in *Selected Works*, Volume 1, pp. 409–29; 409.

[10] Donald Robinson, 'Jew and Greek: Unity and Division in the Early Church', in *Selected Works*, Volume 1, pp. 79–109; 81.

[11] Graeme Goldsworthy, *Christ-Centred Biblical Theology: Hermeneutical Foundations and Principles* (Nottingham: Apollos, 2012).

[12] Robinson, 'Origins and Unresolved Tensions', p. 15.

[13] Robinson, 'Origins and Unresolved Tensions', p. 15.

[14] N.T. Wright has made a similar case recently in *The Case for the Psalms: Why They Are Essential* (New York: HarperOne, 2013).

[15] Goldsworthy, *Christ-Centred Biblical Theology*, p. 203.

[16] So, for example, Goldsworthy now no longer holds that the 144,000 of Rev. 7:4 are a picture of the 'great multitude' of 7:9 precisely because this would involve bestowing on Gentiles the identity of Israel. See *Christ-Centred Biblical Theology*, p. 164.

[17] Robinson, 'Origins and Unresolved Tensions', p. 15.

[18] Robinson, 'Origins and Unresolved Tensions', p. 16.

[19] G.B. Caird, *New Testament Theology* (compiled and ed. L.D. Hurst; Oxford: Clarendon Press, 1994).

[20] N.T. Wright, *The New Testament and the People of God* (London: SPCK, 1992).

[21] See for example, N.T. Wright, *Jesus and the Victory of God* (Minneapolis: Fortress Press, 1996), pp. 322–68.

[22] Wright, *New Testament and the People of God*, pp. 139–44.

[23] See, for example, N.T. Wright, 'Romans 9-11 and the "New Perspective"' in *Pauline Perspective: Essays on Paul, 1978-2013* (London: SPCK, 2013), pp. 392–406.

[24] Alister McGrath, *C.S. Lewis: A Life* (Carol Stream, IL: Tyndale House), pp. 272–4.

Multi-Voiced Church

Stuart & Sian Murray Williams

Multi-Voiced Church argues strongly and persuasively for churches in which everyone is important for the well-being and growth of the community. A multi-voiced church is necessary for genuine mission in today's complex world.

'Those who take the book to heart may find they have a share in making a significant contribution to helping local churches enjoy significant and lasting renewal.' – **Stephen Finamore, Principal of Bristol Baptist College.**

'*Multi-Voiced Church* is an important book that addresses the centuries-old abuse that stifles congregations and exhausts clergy – the silencing of the laity. It is bold, original and practical. Together they have written a multi-voiced book on multi-voiced church life. The medium and the message work together. Wonderful.' – **Alan and Eleanor Kreider, Associated Mennonite Biblical Seminary, Elkhart, Indiana (retired); authors of *Worship and Mission After Christendom* (2009)**

978-1-84227-766-9

Through My Enemy's Eyes

Envisioning Reconciliation in Israel–Palestine

Salim Munayer and Lisa Loden

This unique book addresses reconciliation in the context of the Israeli Messianic Jewish and Palestinian Christian divide. This remarkable work, written in collaboration by a local Palestinian Christian and an Israeli Messianic Jew addresses head-on divisive theological issues (and their political implications); land, covenant, prophecy, eschatology. The struggle for reconciliation is painful and often extremely difficult for all of us. This work seeks to show a way forward.

'This is a unique conversation in which each partner gives full expression to all that they are and think and feel about themelves and the conflict in their land. Above all we come to share the hope and courage that shines through the pain and struggle.' *Christopher Wright, Langham Paternership.*

'Given the divides between their communities, this book is a remarkable achievement, a cry of hope from the land where Jesus walked.' *Chris Rice Duke Divinity School, US.*

Salim Munayer is on the faculty of Bethlehem Bible College, Bethlehem, Palestine and director of Musalaha Ministry of Reconciliation, Jerusalem, Israel. Lisa Loden is on the faculty of Nazareth Evangelical Theological Seminary, Nazareth, Israel, and Director of Advancing Professional Excellence, Israel.

978-1-84227-748-5 (e-book 978-1-84227-859-8)